# VEGETARIAN COOKBOOK FOR BEGINNERS



Effortless Vegetarian Recipes
For Everyday

600 RECIPES

Ashley Colman

ISBN: 979-8407133285

# CONTENTS

# INTRODUCTION

Living a healthier lifestyle can sometimes seem like a huge effort but it's absolutely critical if you want to live a long, healthy life.

Whether you need to re-focus to improve your health, because you just want to feel better about yourself, or because you're concerned about the environmental impact of global food production, there's no denying that making changes can be hard – but in the case of a vegetarian lifestyle, the changes are definitely worth it. Once you're on it, you'll wish that you had started much sooner.

The term "vegetarian" is commonly referred to describe a diet that excludes meat and poultry, and it's based on eating as many vegetables as possible along with some dairy products and sometimes fish. This practice has been proven in numerous studies to be extremely healthy both short-term and long-term. So, if longevity is on your list, read further. Many of the blue zones in the world eat a diet very close to the vegetarian lifestyle, especially the Mediterranean, where eating mostly a plant-based menu in combination with healthy fats, has proved to be a serious candidate for a long, youthful and healthy life. It also virtually eradicates the risk of chronic heart conditions and cancers, and for that reason alone, I would go for it.

## So, how does it work?

There are some different understandings of the term vegetarian. For some, it means excluding all animal products entirely, whereas others might only eat some fish and dairy products, mainly because of their protein content. Either way, going vegetarian is a much healthier option than making meat or dairy products a central part of your diet.

People on the vegetarian lifestyle will eat mostly vegetables, whole grains, fruit, plenty of beans, nuts and seeds. Wherever possible, the focus is on healthy, whole foods – processed food is consumed in only extremely limited quantities, if ever.

## But why would I want to start with the Vegetarian lifestyle?

Do you have a history of cancer or chronic diseases running in your family? Eliminating meat contributes to a vastly reduced risk of cancer. It's also a great choice for anyone who wants to lower their body mass index (BMI) or to reduce their risk from health conditions such as obesity, diabetes and heart disease.

If that wasn't enough, it's a great way of helping the environment as a vegetarian menu can help to reduce greenhouse gases, preserving water and land.

## A VEGETARIAN LIFESTYLE

Adopting a non-meat-based lifestyle is a crucial step in adopting a healthier lifestyle – it can be such a difference it's more helpful to think of it in terms of introducing a gradual lifestyle change, instead of as "starting a diet". In doing so, you will be naturally encouraged to introduce changes in manageable steps. This will help you fully embed the change into your lifestyle in a sustainable way. Very many people fail on traditional "diets" because they are just too difficult to sustain on a day-to-day basis, but a vegetarian lifestyle is so easy to maintain every single day that there isn't a single reason why you shouldn't be making a start today!

### The Basics

Just like a conventional diet, the vegetarian diet has different food groups. Being aware of them can make the initial experience of the diet feel far less overwhelming, and far tastier! All groups are super-healthy, and eating more of any one of the groups will give you that healthy glow almost instantly.

1. **Fruits**

Including any type of fruit is great when you're starting a vegetarian diet. Whilst most people find that they are fine eating any combination of fruits in fairly large quantities, for those who are unused to eating fruit it is advisable to start by eating s maller quantities of familiar fruits and to build up the amount and variety gradually. A super easy way is to think about eating a rainbow – make sure there are a variety of colors on your plate every mealtime.

2. **Vegetables**

Any type of vegetable is welcome on this diet. The beauty of the vegetarian diet is that you will find yourself eating a much wider variety of vegetables than you might otherwise have done on a conventional diet, just to keep things interesting!

3. **Tubers**

The word "tuber" is the family name for root vegetables, so any vegetable that grows beneath the soil's surface is counted as a root vegetable – potatoes, sweet potatoes, carrots, parsnips, beetroot, and even leeks all count as root vegetables. Vegetables from the tuber family are often the most reasonably priced and the addition of just two or three store cupboard ingredients such as a good quality salad oil, herbs and giant couscous, they make the perfect meal.

4. **Whole grains**

Whole grains are the superfoods of grains. They are packed with nutrients, including proteins, fibre, B vitamins, antioxidants and trace minerals such as iron, zinc, copper and magnesium. While trace minerals are only needed in very tiny amounts, they are crucial in maintaining a healthy and strong body that looks great.

5. **Legumes**

You're probably eating legumes without even realising it, and if you're not then you will soon find that it's really easy, enjoyable and delicious to include legumes in your new meal plan.

6. **Dairy**

Dairy is on the menu of almost all people who go vegetarian. The main reason is the high amount of protein, but some people report feeling fuller after consuming cheese or yogurt. Also, those berry smoothies taste amazing with a little bit of cheese.

The great thing about the foods mentioned above is that many of them are not too calorie-dense, which means you can eat them in fairly large quantities without contributing to weight gain. However, you should take care with certain foods such as potatoes as they are very calorie-dense.

These food groups will form the basis of a vegetarian meal plan, but you can easily add variety by including foods such as nuts, seeds and avocados, as well as breads and (plant-based) milks. While these foods are delicious, they are also very calories dense. It's best to only eat them in small amounts and very occasionally if you want to lose weight.

## Is there anything I should be avoiding?

When you adopt a vegetarian diet, you adopt a lifestyle approach that will benefit your health and the environment. You can still enjoy a glass of wine or a delicious dessert every now and then, so it's a great choice for those who don't want anything to be completely excluded!

Always being mindful of what you are reading is important so that you are only eating foods which are as close to their natural states as possible. Ideally, if you are following the diet out of environmental concerns, it's a good choice to eat foods which originate locally to you so you can reduce the environmental footprint of the foods being eaten. Remember to fill up your plate with as many foods from the five food groups as possible, so that you're less tempted to snack later on dense-calorie foods with little nutritional value.

**Foods to eat as little of as possible include:**

- Desserts (unless they are predominantly fruit-based with no added sugar);
- Refined grains (any processed, white carbohydrates such as white bread or pasta);
- Packaged foods such as biscuits or crisps;
- Fish or lean meat products.

## Is seafood off the menu?

Absolutely not! Vegetarian does not mean vegan and neither does monk mode, so if you're a seafood lover then you are absolutely fine to carry on enjoying it as part of your vegetarian meal plan. Seafood is a highly nutritious food and a fabulous source of nutrients including proteins, omega-3 fatty acids, vitamin B12 and, iodine and selenium. There is a growing body of evidence suggesting that vitamin B12 helps to support hormone balance within the body, so it's a great idea to include seafood on your meal plan.

Whether it's to lose weight, to generally feel healthier and fitter, or because of concerns about the environment, everyone has started a new diet. There are so many diets out there which promise success in exchange for often significant sums of money. Still, many people find that they just don't work – the diet might be too restrictive, or just too difficult to follow given the realities of daily life, but that is simply not the case with the vegetarian lifestyle.

What makes the vegetarian diet perfect for everyone is that it takes a holistic approach to food. Nothing except meat is completely off the menu. There is a great variety, that encourages seasonal eating, it is easily adaptable to any meal-time situation, and you can actually learn so much about the food you are eating. In sourcing new foods and researching how to use them in different ways, you are learning something new every day, becoming much fitter and healthier. Start today and you'll be looking, and feeling, better straight away. Let's begin!

# BREAKFAST

## Maple-Cinnamon Cereal Bowls

**Ingredients** for 2 servings

1 cup coconut flakes
2 tbsp butter
1 tbsp ground cinnamon
1 tsp pure maple sugar
2 tbsp cacao nibs
½ cup milk

**Directions** and Total Time: 15 minutes

Preheat the oven to 325°F. Pour the coconut flakes into a bowl and set to the side. Put the butter, cinnamon, and pure maple sugar into a skillet and heat over medium heat. All the mix to melt and stir well. Add the mix to the coconut, stir well, then pour the flakes onto a cookie sheet in a single layer. Cook for 5-7 minutes, making sure to stir 2-3 times to avoid burning. When time is up, allow the flakes to chill on the counter. Spoon equal amounts into two bowls, add the cacao nibs, and pour milk. Serve and enjoy!

## Avocado-Ginger Smoothie

**Ingredients** for 1 serving

½ avocado, pitted and peeled
½ cup milk
½ tsp ground ginger
1 tsp lime juice
1 tbsp date sugar
½ cup ice

**Directions** and Total Time: 5 minutes

Put the avocado, milk, ginger, lime juice, and date sugar in a blender, then choose high and blend for 30-60 seconds. Put ice in last, blend, and serve.

## Feta French Toast

**Ingredients** for 4 servings

½ cup milk
¼ cup feta cheese, crumbled
1 ½ tsp vanilla extract
A pinch of sea salt
½ cup organic cane sugar
1 tbsp ground cinnamon
¼ tsp lemon zest
4 tbsp butter
8 bread pieces
Maple syrup, for serving
1 cup blueberries

**Directions** and Total Time: 25 minutes

In a shallow bowl or pie plate, whisk the milk, feta, vanilla, and salt until the mixture is smooth. In another shallow bowl, whisk sugar, lemon zest, and cinnamon until combined. In a large skillet, melt 1 tablespoon of butter over medium heat. Dip 2 pieces of bread in the milk mixture on both sides. Do not soak. Place the bread in the skillet and cook for about 2 minutes per side. Dip the cooked bread in the cinnamon and sugar mixture on both sides. Shake off any excess. Repeat the process for the rest of the bread. Top with blueberries and syrup.

## Vanilla-Coconut Latte

**Ingredients** for 1 serving

½ cup milk
2 tsp coconut oil
1 ½ cups hot coffee
1 tbsp butter
½ tsp ground cinnamon
¼ tsp vanilla extract
1 scoop collagen powder

**Directions** and Total Time: 10 minutes

Pour the milk and coconut oil into a pan over medium heat. Put the hot coffee, hot milk mix, butter, cinnamon, and vanilla in a blender and hit blend and high for 15-30 seconds. Put the collagen and blend on the lowest setting. Serve and enjoy!

## Coconut Breakfast

**Ingredients** for 2 servings

½ cup slivered almonds
1 tbsp coconut flakes
2 tbsp chia seeds
2 tbsp cacao nibs
2 tbsp sunflower seeds
½ cup milk

**Directions** and Total Time: 5 minutes

Mix the almonds, coconut, chia seeds, cacao nibs, and sunflower seeds, then put equal amounts of the mix into two bowls. Add the milk and serve.

## Almond Bars

**Ingredients** for 4 servings

2 tbsp butter, melted
¼ cup almonds nuts
¼ cup peanut butter
1 tsp pure maple sugar
2 tbsp shredded coconut

**Directions** and Total Time: 10 minutes + chilling time

Put the almonds into your food processor and process until they are tiny grains. Mix the crushed nuts, peanut butter, pure maple sugar, and butter in a bowl and stir, then toss in the shredded coconut. Stir to combine. Lay parchment paper in a loaf pan, making sure to press it inside, then add the mix. Put in the fridge for an hour, then cut the mix into bars. Serve and enjoy!

## Cheddar Grits

**Ingredients** for 4 servings

2 cups milk
Salt and black pepper to taste
1 cup stone-ground cornmeal
¼ tsp garlic powder
¼ cup butter
1 cup grated cheddar cheese

**Directions** and Total Time: 30 minutes

Heat milk, 2 cups water, and salt in a large pot over medium heat. Stir in cornmeal and whisk continuously. Reduce the heat to low and cover the pot. Simmer for 20 to 25 minutes while whisking every 3 to 4 minutes to prevent lumps. When the grits are creamy, remove from the heat and whisk in butter, garlic, and pepper. Next, slowly whisk in the cheddar cheese. Serve hot and enjoy!

## Sunrise Smoothie

**Ingredients** for 2 servings

1 peeled grapefruit, segmented
1 banana
1 cup chopped mango
1 cup chopped peach
1 cup strawberries
1 peeled carrot, chopped
1 cup grapefruit juice

**Directions** and Total Time: 15 minutes + chilling time

Put all the ingredients into your blender and blitz until smooth, adding water if needed. Serve chilled.

## Crunchy Granola

**Ingredients** for 6 servings

3 cups uncooked rolled oats
½ cup butter, melted
¼ cup chopped raw cashews
¼ cup agave syrup
4 tbsp cane sugar
3 tsp ground cinnamon
½ tsp vanilla extract
½ tsp sea salt

**Directions** and Total Time: 20 minutes + cooling time

Preheat the oven to 375°F. Combine oats, butter, cashews, agave syrup, 2 tbsp sugar, 2 tsp cinnamon, vanilla, and salt in a bowl. When well mixed, spread it out on a parchment-lined baking sheet. Bake for 10 minutes. Toss the mixture with a spatula and bake for another 5 minutes until golden. While the granola is cooking, mix the remaining sugar and cinnamon in a small bowl. Remove the baking sheet from the oven and sprinkle the cinnamon sugar over the granola. Let cool completely.

## Morning Sunshine Muffins

**Ingredients** for 6 servings

2 tbsp butter
¼ cup milk
1 tangerine, peeled
1 carrot, coarsely chopped
2 tbsp chopped dried apricots
3 tbsp molasses
2 tbsp ground flaxseed
1 tsp apple cider vinegar
1 tsp pure vanilla extract
½ tsp ground cinnamon
½ tsp ground ginger
¼ tsp ground nutmeg
¾ cup rolled oats
1 tsp baking powder
2 tbsp raisins
2 tbsp sunflower seeds

**Directions** and Total Time: 45 minutes

Preheat the oven to 350°F. Lightly spray a 12-cup muffin tin with cooking oil. Add butter, milk, tangerine, carrot, apricots, molasses, flaxseed, vinegar, vanilla, cinnamon, ginger, and nutmeg to a food processor blender. Puree until mostly smooth. Process the oats in a clean blender jar or food processor until it resembles flour. Pour into a large bowl along with baking powder. Stir in wet ingredients until just comes together. Fold in raisins and sunflower seeds. Divide the batter among the muffin cups. Bake for 30 minutes or until a toothpick in the middle of the muffin comes out clean. Extra time may be needed depending on the weight of your tin.

## Vegetarian Quinoa Cups

**Ingredients** for 6 servings

1 carrot, chopped
1 zucchini, chopped
4 asparagus, chopped
¾ cup quinoa flour
2 tbsp lemon juice
¼ cup nutritional yeast
¼ tsp garlic powder
Salt and black pepper to taste

**Directions** and Total Time: 25 minutes

Preheat air fryer to 340°F. Combine the vegetables, quinoa flour, water, lemon juice, nutritional yeast, garlic powder, salt, and pepper in a medium bowl, and mix well. Divide the mixture between 6 cupcake molds. Place the filled molds into the air fryer and Bake for 20 minutes, or until the tops are lightly browned, and a toothpick inserted into the center comes out clean. Serve cooled.

## Chocolate-Rice Pudding

**Ingredients** for 2 servings

1 cup brown rice
1 tsp ground cinnamon
1 cup milk
1 banana, mashed
2 tbsp cocoa powder
1 tbsp butter
1 tbsp hemp seeds
2 tbsp walnuts
¼ cup strawberries

**Directions** and Total Time: 45 minutes

Add brown rice, cinnamon, milk, and 1 cup water to a medium pot over high heat. Once it comes to a boil, reduce the heat to low and simmer. Cover the pot and cook for 25-30 minutes. As the rice is cooking, combine banana, cocoa powder, butter, and hemp seeds in a medium bowl. When the rice is done, add 1 cup of the rice to a bowl. Next, add half of the pudding. Finally, top with half of the walnuts and berries. Serve warm.

## Mushroom & Chickpea Scramble

**Ingredients** for 1 serving

1 tsp olive oil
½ cup mushrooms, sliced
Salt and black pepper to taste
½ cup green peas
½ cup cooked chickpeas
1 tsp paprika
1 tsp turmeric
1 tbsp nutritional yeast
½ cup grape tomatoes, diced
¼ cup fresh cilantro, chopped

**Directions** and Total Time: 20 minutes

Preheat the oven to 350°F. Add oil to a large skillet over medium heat. Saute mushrooms and salt for 7-8 minutes, stirring occasionally. Stir in green peas. In a separate bowl, mash chickpeas with a fork, then transfer it to the skillet. Cook for a few minutes until they are heated through. Next, stir in paprika, turmeric, nutritional yeast, and black pepper. Add tomatoes and most of the cilantro and cook until just warm. Garnish with the rest of the cilantro. Serve warm and enjoy.

## Energy Matcha

**Ingredients** for 1 serving

1 tsp matcha powder
½ cup boiling water
¼ cup milk
1 tsp coconut oil
1 tsp date sugar
½ tsp ground cinnamon

**Directions** and Total Time: 5 minutes

Pour the boiling water and the matcha in a bowl and stir until well-mixed. Use a frother if you have one. Pour the mix into a blender and add milk, coconut oil, and date sugar in with it. Mix for 15-30 seconds. Add some cinnamon on top and serve.

## Chocolate Pancakes with Coconut Cream

**Ingredients** for 4 servings

1 (15-oz) can coconut milk, refrigerated overnight
½ cup confectioners' sugar
1 cup all-purpose flour
1 tbsp baking powder
1 tbsp sucanat
¼ tsp ground cinnamon
1 tsp orange zest
1 cup rice milk
4 tbsp chocolate sprinkles
2 tbsp canola oil

**Directions** and Total Time: 25 minutes

In a small bowl, scoop out the coconut milk from the can. Use a fork to mash the milk while stirring in confectioners' sugar. Whisk flour, baking powder, sucanat, orange zest, and cinnamon in a large bowl. Fold in rice milk mixture until just combined without overmixing. Fold in 3 tablespoons of chocolate sprinkles. In a large skillet, heat oil over medium heat. Make one pancake at a time with ¼ cup of batter. Cook for 2 minutes until bubbles form in the middle, then flip the pancake. Cook for another 2 minutes until golden and cooked in the middle. Repeat the process with the rest of the batter. Top each serving with chilled coconut whipped cream and chocolate sprinkles. Serve warm.

## Root Veggies with Avocado Dip

**Ingredients** for 2 servings

1 peeled and pitted avocado
1 tbsp apple cider vinegar
1 tsp dried dill
Salt and black pepper to taste
1 peeled sweet potato, cubed
1 beet, peeled and cubed
1 daikon, peeled and cubed
2 baby carrots, cubed
1 tsp dried thyme
¼ tsp cayenne pepper

**Directions** and Total Time: 40 minutes

Preheat the oven to 350°F. Puree avocado, vinegar, dill, salt, and 2-3 tablespoons of water in a blender until smooth. Set to the side. Add sweet potato, beet, daikon, carrots, and enough water to cover them in a large pot. Bring the water to a boil and continue boiling for 15 minutes. When the vegetables are just soft, drain the water. Season with salt, thyme, cayenne, and black pepper. Arrange the vegetables in a single layer on a large baking sheet. Roast for 10-15 minutes or until browned on the edges. Serve with avocado dip and enjoy.

## Peppermint Hot Chocolate

**Ingredients** for 1 serving

1 cup milk
1 ½ tbsp cacao powder
¼ tsp ground cinnamon
1 tbsp date sugar
¼ tsp peppermint extract
1 tbsp heavy cream

**Directions** and Total Time: 10 minutes

Pour the milk into a pan and warm it over low heat, allowing it to bubble. As it heats, put the cacao, cinnamon, date sugar, and peppermint extract in a blender. Pour in the hot milk and blend for 30-60 seconds. Add some whipped heavy cream to the top.

## Coconut Breakfast with Berry & Pecans

**Ingredients** for 2 servings

1 (14-oz) can coconut milk, refrigerated overnight
1 cup granola
½ cup pecans, chopped
1 cup sliced strawberries

**Directions** and Total Time: 15 minutes

Drain the coconut milk liquid. Layer the coconut milk solids, granola, and strawberries in small glasses. Top with chopped pecans and serve right away.

## Cherry-Apple Oatmeal Cups

**Ingredients** for 2 servings

2/3 cup rolled oats
1 cored apple, diced
4 pitted cherries, diced
½ tsp ground cinnamon
¾ cup milk

**Directions** and Total Time: 20 minutes

Preheat oven to 350°F. Mix the oats, apple, cherries, and cinnamon in a baking dish. Add in milk and bake in the oven for 6 minutes, stir well and bake for 6 more minutes until the fruit are soft. Serve cooled.

## Energy Smoothie Bowl

**Ingredients** for 1 serving

¼ avocado
1 apple
1 cup roughly chopped kale
2 peeled kiwis, sliced
1 cup apple juice
¼ cup fresh blackberries
1 tbsp chia seeds

**Directions** and Total Time: 10 minutes

Place the avocado, apple, kale, 1 kiwi, and apple juice in your food processor and pulse until smooth. Pour the mixture into a bowl and top with the remaining kiwi and blackberries. Scatter with chia seeds and serve.

## Easy Oatmeal Bars with Blueberries

**Ingredients** for 6 servings

2 cups uncooked rolled oats
2 cups all-purpose flour
1 ½ cups dark-brown sugar
1 ½ tsp baking soda
Salt to taste
½ tsp ground cinnamon
1 cup coconut oil, melted
4 cups blueberries
¼ cup sucanat
2 tbsp potato starch

**Directions** and Total Time: 50 minutes

Preheat the oven to 425°F. Mix oats, flour, sugar, baking soda, salt, and cinnamon in a large bowl. Pour in oil and stir until combined and crumbly. Add blueberries in another large bowl along with sucanat and potato starch. Stir gently until evenly coated. Place 3 cups of the oat mixture into a greased baking pan and press to form the bottom layer. Top with the blueberry mixture. Sprinkle the rest of the crumble mixture over the blueberries. Bake for 40 minutes. Cool completely. Cut into 6 bars.

## Vegan French Toast

**Ingredients** for 4 servings

1 ripe banana, mashed
¼ cup protein powder
½ cup almond milk
2 tbsp ground flaxseed
4 bread slices
2 tbsp agave syrup

**Directions** and Total Time: 15 minutes

Preheat air fryer to 370°F. Combine the banana, protein powder, almond milk, and flaxseed in a shallow bowl and mix well. Dip bread slices into the mixture. Place the slices on a lightly greased pan in a single layer and pour any of the remaining mixture evenly over the bread. Air Fry for 10 minutes, or until golden brown and crispy, flipping once. Serve warm topped with agave syrup.

## Mashed Potato Taquitos with Hot Sauce

**Ingredients** for 4 servings

1 potato, peeled and cubed
2 tbsp milk
2 garlic cloves, minced
Salt and black pepper to taste
½ tsp ground cumin
2 tbsp minced scallions
4 corn tortillas
1 cup red chili sauce
1 avocado, sliced
2 tbsp cilantro, chopped

**Directions** and Total Time: 30 minutes

In a pot fitted with a steamer basket, cook the potato cubes for 15 minutes on the stovetop. Pour the potato cubes into a bowl and mash with a potato masher. Add the milk, garlic, salt, pepper, and cumin and stir. Add the scallions and cilantro and stir them into the mixture. Set aside. Preheat air fryer to 390°F. Run the tortillas under water for a second, then place them in the greased frying basket. Air Fry for 1 minute. Lay the tortillas on a flat surface. Place an equal amount of the potato filling in the center of each. Roll the tortilla sides over the filling and place seam-side down in the frying basket. Fry for 7 minutes or until the tortillas are golden and slightly crisp. Serve with chili sauce and avocado slices. Enjoy!

## Banana-Blackberry Muffins

**Ingredients** for 6 servings

1 ripe banana, mashed
½ cup milk
1 tsp apple cider vinegar
1 tsp vanilla extract
2 tbsp ground flaxseed
2 tbsp coconut sugar
¾ cup flour
1 tsp baking powder
½ tsp baking soda
¾ cup blackberries

**Directions** and Total Time: 20 minutes

Preheat air fryer to 350°F. Place the banana in a medium bowl. Stir in milk, apple vinegar, vanilla extract, flaxseed, and coconut sugar until combined. In another bowl, combine flour, baking powder, and baking soda. Pour it into the banana mixture and toss to combine. Divide the batter between 6 muffin molds. Top each with blackberries, pressing slightly. Bake for 16 minutes until golden brown and a toothpick comes out clean. Serve cooled.

## Zucchini Vegetarian Tacos

**Ingredients** for 3 servings

1 small zucchini, sliced
1 yellow onion, sliced
¼ tsp garlic powder
Salt and black pepper to taste
1 (15-oz) can refried beans
6 corn tortillas, warm
1 cup guacamole
1 tbsp cilantro, chopped

**Directions** and Total Time: 20 minutes

Preheat air fryer to 390°F. Place the zucchini and onion in the greased frying basket. Spray with more oil and sprinkle with garlic, salt, and pepper to taste. Roast for 6 minutes. Remove, shake, or stir, then cook for another 6 minutes, until the veggies are golden and tender. In a small pan, heat the refried beans over low heat. Stir often. When warm enough, remove and set aside. Place a corn tortilla on a plate and fill it with beans, roasted vegetables, and guacamole. Top with cilantro and enjoy!

## Maple Oat Bread

**Ingredients** for 4 servings

4 cups whole-wheat flour
¼ tsp salt
½ cup rolled oats
1 tsp baking soda
1 ¾ cups milk
2 tbsp pure maple syrup

**Directions** and Total Time: 50 minutes

Preheat the oven to 400°F. In a bowl, mix flour, salt, oats, and baking soda. Add in milk and maple syrup and whisk until dough forms. Dust your hands with some flour and knead the dough into a ball. Shape the dough into a circle and place on a baking sheet. Cut a deep cross on the dough and bake in the oven for 15 minutes at 450°F. Reduce the temperature to 400°F and bake further for 20-25 minutes or until a hollow sound is made when the bottom of the bread is tapped.

## Apple Pancakes

**Ingredients** for 4 servings

1 tbsp olive oil
2 cups milk
1 tsp apple cider vinegar
2 ½ cups whole-wheat flour
2 tbsp baking powder
½ tsp baking soda
1 tsp sea salt
½ tsp ground cinnamon
¼ tsp grated nutmeg
¼ tsp ground allspice
½ cup applesauce
1 cup water

**Directions** and Total Time: 30 minutes

Whisk the milk and apple cider vinegar in a bowl and set aside. In another bowl, combine the flour, baking powder, baking soda, salt, cinnamon, nutmeg, and allspice. Transfer the almond mixture to another bowl and beat with the applesauce and water. Pour in the dry ingredients and stir. Melt some olive oil in a skillet over medium heat. Pour a ladle of the batter and cook for 5 minutes, flipping once until golden. Repeat the process until the batter is exhausted. Serve warm.

## Black Bean & Quinoa Bowl with Avocado

**Ingredients** for 4 servings

1 cup brown quinoa, rinsed
3 tbsp Greek yogurt
½ lime, juiced
2 tbsp chopped fresh cilantro
1 (5 oz) can black beans
3 tbsp tomato salsa
¼ avocado, sliced
2 radishes, shredded
1 tbsp pepitas

**Directions** and Total Time: 25 minutes

Cook the quinoa with 2 cups of slightly salted water in a medium pot over medium heat or until the liquid absorbs, 15 minutes. Spoon the quinoa into serving bowls and fluff with a fork. In a small bowl, mix the yogurt, lime juice, cilantro, and salt. Divide this mixture on the quinoa and top with beans, salsa, avocado, radishes, and pepitas.

## Maple-Walnut Waffles

**Ingredients** for 4 servings

3 tbsp butter, melted
1 ¾ cups whole-wheat flour
1/3 cup ground walnuts
1 tbsp baking powder
1 ½p cups milk
3 tbsp pure maple syrup

**Directions** and Total Time: 15 minutes

Preheat the waffle iron and grease with some butter. Combine the flour, walnuts, and baking powder in a bowl. Set aside. In another bowl, mix the milk and the remaining butter. Pour into the walnut mixture and whisk until well combined. Spoon a ladleful of the batter onto the waffle iron. Cook for 3-5 minutes, until golden brown. Repeat the process until no batter is left. Top with maple syrup to serve.

## Maple Nut & Raisin Granola

**Ingredients** for 6 servings

5 ½ cups old-fashioned oats
1 ½ cups chopped walnuts
½ cup shelled sunflower seeds
1 cup golden raisins
1 cup shaved almonds
1 cup pure maple syrup
½ tsp ground cinnamon
¼ tsp ground allspice
A pinch of salt

**Directions** and Total Time: 20 minutes

Preheat oven to 325°F. In a baking dish, place the oats, walnuts, and sunflower seeds. Bake for 10 minutes. Lower the heat from the oven to 300°F. Stir in the raisins, almonds, maple syrup, cinnamon, allspice, and salt. Bake for an additional 15 minutes. Serve cooled.

## Morning Muesli with Chocolate & Blueberries

**Ingredients** for 5 servings

¼ cup chocolate chips
2 cups spelt flakes
2 cups puffed cereals
¼ cup sunflower seeds
¼ cup almonds
¼ cup raisins
¼ cup dried cranberries
¼ cup chopped dried figs
¼ cup shredded coconut
3 tsp ground cinnamon
½ cup milk
½ cup blueberries

**Directions** and Total Time: 10 minutes

In a bowl, combine spelt flakes, cereals, sunflower seeds, almonds, raisins, cranberries, figs, coconut, chocolate chips, and cinnamon. Toss to mix well. Pour in the milk. Let sit for 1 hour and serve topped with blueberries.

## Almond Muffins with Blueberries

**Ingredients** for 12 servings

1 tbsp coconut oil, melted
1 cup quick-cooking oats
1 cup boiling water
½ cup milk
¼ cup ground flaxseed
1 tsp almond extract
1 tsp apple cider vinegar
1 ½ cups whole-wheat flour
½ cup sugar
2 tsp baking soda
A pinch of salt
1 cup blueberries

**Directions** and Total Time: 30 minutes

Preheat oven to 400°F. In a bowl, stir in the oats with boiling water until they are softened. Pour in the coconut oil, milk, flaxseed, almond extract, and vinegar. Add in the flour, sugar, baking soda, and salt. Gently stir in blueberries. Divide the batter between greased muffin tins. Bake for 20 minutes until lightly brown. Allow cooling for 10 minutes. Using a spatula, run the sides of the muffins to take out. Serve chilled.

## Mango-Almond Quinoa with Raspberries

**Ingredients** for 2 servings

2 tbsp butter
1 cup quinoa
1 tsp ground cinnamon
1 cup milk
1 large mango, chopped
3 tbsp cocoa powder
1 tbsp hemp seeds
1 tbsp walnuts
¼ cup raspberries

**Directions** and Total Time: 35 minutes

In a pot, combine the quinoa, cinnamon, milk, and 1 cup of water over medium heat. Bring to a boil, low heat, and simmer covered for 25-30 minutes. In a bowl, mash the mango and mix cocoa powder, butter, and hemp seeds. In a serving bowl, place cooked quinoa and mango mixture. Top with walnuts and raspberries. Serve.

## Oat Jars with Pecans & Pumpkin Seeds

**Ingredients** for 5 servings

2 ½ cups old-fashioned rolled oats
5 tbsp pumpkin seeds
5 tbsp chopped pecans
5 cups milk
2 ½ tsp agave syrup
Salt to taste
1 tsp ground cardamom
1 tsp ground ginger

**Directions** and Total Time: 10 minutes + chilling time

In a bowl, put oats, pumpkin seeds, pecans, milk, agave syrup, salt, cardamom, and ginger and toss to combine. Divide the mixture between mason jars. Seal the lids and transfer to the fridge to soak for 10-12 hours.

## Sweet Lemon & Quinoa Muffins

**Ingredients** for 5 servings

2 tbsp olive oil
2 eggs
2 cups lemon curd
½ cup brown sugar
1 tsp apple cider vinegar
2 ½ cups whole-wheat flour
1 ½ cups cooked quinoa
2 tsp baking soda
A pinch of salt
½ cup raisins

**Directions** and Total Time: 25 minutes

Preheat oven to 400°F. In a bowl, whisk the eggs. Stir in the lemon curd, sugar, olive oil, and vinegar. Add in flour, quinoa, baking soda, and salt. Put in the raisins, be careful not to be too fluffy. Divide the batter between a greased muffin tin and bake for 20 minutes until golden and set. Allow cooling slightly before removing it from the tin. Serve.

## Banana Oats with Pumpkin Seeds

**Ingredients** for 4 servings

3 cups water
1 cup steel-cut oats
2 bananas, mashed
¼ cup pumpkin seeds
2 tbsp maple syrup
A pinch of salt

**Directions** and Total Time: 35 minutes

Bring water to a boil in a pot, add in oats, and lower the heat. Cook for 20-30 minutes. Put in the mashed bananas, cook for 3-5 minutes more. Stir in maple syrup, pumpkin seeds, and salt. Serve.

### Kale & Pumpkin Stir-Fry

**Ingredients** for 2 servings

1 tbsp olive oil
1 cup pumpkin, shredded
½ onion, chopped
1 carrot, peeled and chopped
2 garlic cloves, minced
½ tsp dried thyme
1 cup chopped kale
Salt and black pepper to taste

**Directions** and Total Time: 25 minutes

Heat the oil in a skillet over medium heat. Sauté onion and carrot for 5 minutes. Add in garlic and thyme and cook for 30 seconds. Place in the pumpkin and cook for 10 minutes until tender. Stir in kale, cook for 4 minutes until the kale wilts. Season with salt and pepper. Serve.

### Lemon-Blackberry Waffles

**Ingredients** for 4 servings

¼ cup butter, melted
1 ½ cups whole-heat flour
½ cup old-fashioned oats
¼ cup sugar
3 tsp baking powder
½ tsp salt
1 tsp ground cinnamon
2 cups milk
1 tbsp fresh lemon juice
1 tsp lemon zest
½ cup fresh blackberries

**Directions** and Total Time: 15 minutes

Preheat the waffle iron. In a bowl, mix flour, oats, sugar, baking powder, salt, and cinnamon. Set aside. In another bowl, combine milk, lemon juice, lemon zest, and butter. Pour into the wet ingredients and whisk to combine. Add the batter to the hot greased waffle iron, using approximately a ladleful for each waffle. Cook for 3-5 minutes, until golden brown. Repeat the process until no batter is left. Serve topped with blackberries.

### Breakfast Couscous with Dates & Nuts

**Ingredients** for 4 servings

½ cup chopped macadamia nuts
3 cups apple juice
1 ½ cups couscous
1 tsp ground cinnamon
¼ tsp ground cloves
½ cup dried dates

**Directions** and Total Time: 20 minutes

Pour the apple juice into a pot over medium heat and bring to a boil. Stir in couscous, cinnamon, and cloves. Turn the heat off and cover. Let sit for 5 minutes until the liquid is absorbed. Using a fork, fluff the couscous and add the dates and macadamia nuts, stir to combine.

### Wake-Up Smoothie

**Ingredients** for 4 servings

1 banana
¼ cup protein powder
1 tbsp flaxseed
1 tbsp cocoa powder
1 tbsp butter
1 tbsp agave nectar
1 cup spinach, chopped
½ cup milk
1 cup water
1 tsp maca powder
1 tsp cocoa nibs

**Directions** and Total Time: 15 minutes

Add all the ingredients to your blender and pureé until smooth. Divide the smoothie between glasses and serve.

### Date-Orange Cups

**Ingredients** for 6 servings

1 tsp vegetable oil
3 cups bran flakes cereal
1 ½ cups whole-wheat flour
½ cup dates, chopped
3 tsp baking powder
½ tsp ground cinnamon
½ tsp salt
1/3 cup brown sugar
¾ cup fresh orange juice

**Directions** and Total Time: 30 minutes

Preheat oven to 400°F. Grease a 12-cup muffin tin with oil. Mix the bran flakes, flour, dates, baking powder, cinnamon, and salt in a bowl. In another bowl, combine the sugar and orange juice until blended. Pour into the dry mixture and whisk. Divide the mixture between the cups of the muffin tin. Bake for 20 minutes or until golden brown and set. Cool for a few minutes before removing from the tin and serve. Enjoy!

### Barley & Oat Porridge with Almonds

**Ingredients** for 4 servings

2 ½ cups vegetable broth
2 ½ cups milk
½ cup steel-cut oats
1 tbsp pearl barley
½ cup slivered almonds
¼ cup nutritional yeast
2 cups old-fashioned rolled oats

**Directions** and Total Time: 25 minutes

Pour the broth and milk in a pot over medium heat and bring to a boil. Stir in oats, pearl barley, almond slivers, and nutritional yeast. Reduce the heat and simmer for 20 minutes. Add in the rolled oats, cook for an additional 5 minutes, until creamy. Serve chilled.

### Chili Swiss Chard & Cheese Scramble

**Ingredients** for 5 servings

2 tsp olive oil
1 cup goat cheese, crumbled
1 onion, chopped
3 cloves minced garlic
1 celery stalk, chopped
2 large carrots, chopped
1 tsp chili powder
½ tsp ground cumin
½ tsp ground turmeric
Salt and black pepper to taste
5 cups Swiss chard

**Directions** and Total Time: 35 minutes

Heat the oil in a skillet over medium heat. Add in the onion, garlic, celery, and carrots. Sauté for 5 minutes. Stir in goat cheese, chili powder, cumin, turmeric, salt, and pepper, cook for 7-8 minutes. Mix in the Swiss chard and cook until wilted, 3 minutes. Allow cooling and seal.

### Tropical Matcha Smoothie

**Ingredients** for 2 servings

1 cup chopped pineapple
1 cup chopped mango
1 cup chopped kale
½ avocado
3 picked mint leaves
½ cup milk
½ cup orange juice
1 tsp matcha tea powder

**Directions** and Total Time: 15 minutes

Place all ingredients in your blender and purée until totally smooth. Serve in glasses and enjoy!

## Walnut & Berry Topped Yogurt

**Ingredients** for 4 servings

4 cups Greek yogurt, cold
2 tbsp honey
2 cups mixed berries, chopped
¼ cup chopped walnuts

**Directions** and Total Time: 10 minutes

In a medium bowl, mix the yogurt and honey until well-combined. Divide the mixture into 4 breakfast bowls. Top with the berries and walnuts. Enjoy immediately.

## Mango-Pumpkin Rice Pudding with Walnuts

**Ingredients** for 4 servings

1cup brown rice
1 ½ cups milk
3 tbsp pure date sugar
2 tsp pumpkin pie spice
1 mango, chopped
2 tbsp chopped walnuts

**Directions** and Total Time: 30 minutes

In a pot over medium heat, add the rice, 2 cups water, milk, sugar, and pumpkin pie spice. Bring to a boil, lower the heat and simmer for 18-20 minutes until the rice is soft and the liquid is absorbed. Put in the mango and stir to combine. Top with walnuts to serve.

## Cheesy Granola

**Ingredients** for 6 servings

2 cups uncooked rolled oats
1 cup chopped walnuts
1 cup chopped raw almonds
6 tbsp olive oil
¼ cup grated Parmesan
2 tsp dried thyme
1 tsp garlic powder
¼ tsp chili powder
Salt and black pepper to taste

**Directions** and Total Time: 25 minutes

Preheat the oven to 375°F. Combine all of the ingredients in a large bowl. When well mixed, spread out onto a parchment-lined baking sheet and bake for 10 minutes. Toss the mixture with a spatula and bake for another 5 minutes until golden. Let cool. Serve and enjoy!

## Kiddo French Toasts with Blueberry Syrup

**Ingredients** for 6 servings

1 banana, mashed
1 cup milk
1 tsp pure vanilla extract
¼ tsp lemon zest
½ tsp ground cinnamon
1 ½ tsp arrowroot powder
A pinch of salt
6 slices whole-grain bread
1 cup blueberries
2 tbsp orange juice
1 tbsp maple syrup

**Directions** and Total Time: 60 minutes

Preheat oven to 350°F. Beat banana, milk, vanilla, lemon zest, cinnamon, arrowroot, and salt in a shallow bowl. Dip the bread in the mixture and arrange in a single layer on a baking dish. Pour excess banana mixture over the bread. Bake for 30 minutes until the bread is just brown. While the toast is baking, add blueberries, orange juice, and maple syrup to a small saucepan over medium heat. Use a spoon to break up the berries and let simmer for 15-20 minutes. Stir occasionally until the syrup has reduced. Plate the toast and drizzle with blueberry syrup.

## Mung Bean Tart

**Ingredients** for 2 servings

2 tsp soy sauce
1 tsp lime juice
1 garlic clove, minced
½ tsp red chili flakes
½ cup mung beans, soaked
Salt and black pepper to taste
½ minced shallot
1 green onion, chopped

**Directions** and Total Time: 20 minutes

Add the soy sauce, lime juice, garlic, and chili flakes to a bowl and stir. Set aside.

Preheat the air fryer to 390°F. Place the drained beans in a blender along with ½ cup of water, salt, and pepper. Blend until smooth. Stir in shallot and green onion, but do not blend. Pour the batter into a greased baking pan. Bake for 15 minutes in the air fryer or until golden. A knife inserted in the center should come out clean. Once cooked through, cut the "quiche" into quarters. Drizzle with sauce and serve. Enjoy!

## Green Hash Browns

**Ingredients** for 4 servings

1 head broccoli, cut into florets
5 tbsp butter
3 eggs, beaten
½ white onion, grated
Salt and black pepper to taste

**Directions** and Total Time: 35 minutes

Pour the broccoli into a food processor and pulse a few times until smoothly grated. Transfer the broccoli into a bowl, add the eggs, white onion, salt, and black pepper. Use a spoon to mix the ingredients evenly and set aside 5 to 10 minutes to firm up a bit. Place a large non-stick skillet over medium heat and drop 1/3 of the butter to melt until no longer shimmering.

Ladle scoops of the broccoli mixture into the skillet (about 3 to 4 hash browns per batch). Flatten the pancakes to measure 3 to 4 inches in diameter, and fry until golden brown on one side, 4 minutes. Turn the pancakes with a spatula and cook the other side to brown too, another 5 minutes. Transfer the hash browns to a serving plate and repeat the frying process for the remaining broccoli mixture. Serve the hash browns warm with green salad.

## Caribbean Granola

**Ingredients** for 5 servings

2 cups rolled oats
¾ cup whole-wheat flour
1 tbsp ground cinnamon
1 tsp ground ginger
½ cup sunflower seeds
½ cup hazelnuts, chopped
½ cup pumpkin seeds
½ cup shredded coconut
1 ¼ cups orange juice
½ cup dried cherries
½ cup goji berries

**Directions** and Total Time: 50 minutes

Preheat oven to 350°F. In a bowl, combine oats, flour, cinnamon, ginger, sunflower seeds, hazelnuts, pumpkin seeds, and coconut. Pour in the orange juice, toss to mix. Bake for 15 minutes. Turn the granola and continue baking until it is crunchy, about 30 minutes. Stir in the cherries and goji berries. Store in the fridge for up to 14 days.

## Fruity Couscous Bowl

**Ingredients** for 1 serving

1 tangerine, zested and juiced
¼ cup whole-wheat couscous
1 cup mixed berries
½ cup cubed cantaloupe
1 tbsp agave nectar
1 tbsp fresh mint, minced
1 tbsp coconut flakes

**Directions** and Total Time: 15 minutes

Preheat the oven to 350°F. Bring tangerine juice and half of the zest to a boil in a small pot. Add dry couscous to a small bowl and pour the tangerine juice over it. Place a plate or plastic wrap over the bowl to trap the steam for 5 minutes. Combine berries, cantaloupe, agave nectar, and the rest of the zest in another bowl. Remove the cover from the couscous and fluff the soft couscous with a fork. Add the fruit, mint, and coconut to the couscous.

## Chia Seed Banana Bread

**Ingredients** for 6 servings

2 bananas, mashed
2 tbsp sunflower oil
2 tbsp maple syrup
½ tsp vanilla
½ tbsp chia seeds
½ tbsp ground flaxseeds
1 cup pastry flour
¼ cup sugar
½ tsp cinnamon
1 orange, zested
¼ tsp salt
¼ tsp ground nutmeg
½ tsp baking powder

**Directions** and Total Time: 35 minutes

Preheat air fryer to 350°F. Place the bananas, oil, maple syrup, vanilla, chia, and flaxseeds in a bowl and stir to combine. Add the flour, sugar, cinnamon, salt, nutmeg, baking powder, and orange zest. Stir to combine. Pour the batter into a greased baking pan. Smooth the top with a rubber spatula and Bake for 25 minutes or until a knife inserted in the center comes out clean. Remove and let cool for a minute. Then cut into wedges and serve.

## Morning Berry Quinoa Bowl

**Ingredients** for 4 servings

3 cups cooked quinoa
1 1/3 cups milk
2 bananas, sliced
1 cup raspberries
1 cup blueberries
½ cup chopped raw walnuts
¼ cup honey

**Directions** and Total Time: 10 minutes

To prepare the bowls, layer the ingredients per bowl as follows. Start with ¾ cup quinoa and drizzle over 1/3 cup milk. Top with ½ banana, ¼ cup raspberries, ¼ cup blueberries, and 2 tablespoons walnuts. Add 1 tablespoon honey over the top of each quinoa bowl. Serve.

## Morning Potato Cakes

**Ingredients** for 6 servings

4 Yukon Gold potatoes
2 cups kale, chopped
1 cup rice flour
¼ cup cornstarch
¾ cup milk
2 tbsp lemon juice
2 tsp dried rosemary
2 tsp shallot powder
Salt and black pepper to taste
½ tsp turmeric powder

**Directions** and Total Time: 50 minutes

Preheat air fryer to 390°F. Scrub the potatoes and put them in the air fryer. Bake for 30 minutes or until soft. When cool, chop them into small pieces and place them in a bowl. Mash with a potato masher or fork. Add kale, rice flour, cornstarch, milk, lemon juice, rosemary, shallot powder, salt, pepper, and turmeric. Stir well. Make 12 balls out of the mixture and smash them lightly with your hands to make patties. Place them in the greased frying basket, and Air Fry for 10-12 minutes, flipping once, until golden and cooked through. Serve.

## Vietnamese Gingered Tofu

**Ingredients** for 4 servings

1 (8-oz) package tofu, cubed
4 tsp shoyu
1 tsp onion powder
½ tsp garlic powder
½ tsp ginger powder
½ tsp turmeric powder
Black pepper to taste
2 tbsp nutritional yeast
1 tsp dried rosemary
1 tsp dried dill
2 tsp cornstarch
2 tsp sunflower oil

**Directions** and Total Time: 25 minutes

Sprinkle the tofu with shoyu and toss to coat. Add the onion, garlic, ginger, turmeric, and pepper. Gently toss to coat. Add the yeast, rosemary, dill, and cornstarch. Toss to coat. Dribble with the oil and toss again. Preheat air fryer to 390°F. Spray the fryer basket with oil, put the tofu in the basket and Bake for 7 minutes. Remove, shake gently, and cook for another 7 minutes or until the tofu is crispy and golden. Serve warm.

## Morning Apple Biscuits

**Ingredients** for 6 servings

1 apple
1 cup oat flour
2 tbsp maple syrup
¼ cup butter
1/3 cup raisins
½ tsp ground cinnamon

**Directions** and Total Time: 15 minutes

Preheat air fryer to 350°F. Grate the apple with a grater. Combine apple, flour, maple syrup, butter, raisins, and cinnamon in a bowl until combined. Make balls out of the mixture. Place them onto parchment paper and flatten them. Bake for 9 minutes until slightly brown.

## Blueberry Pudding with Chia & Walnuts

**Ingredients** for 2 servings

¾ cup milk
½ tsp vanilla extract
½ cup blueberries
2 tbsp chia seeds
Chopped walnuts to garnish

**Directions** and Total Time: 5 minutes + chilling time

In a blender, pour the milk, vanilla extract, and half of the blueberries. Process the ingredients at high speed until the blueberries are incorporated into the liquid. Open the blender and mix in the chia seeds. Share the mixture into two breakfast jars, cover, and refrigerate for 4 hours to allow the mixture to gel. Garnish the pudding with the remaining blueberries and walnuts.

## Berry Muesli Bowl

**Ingredients** for 5 servings

1 cup rolled oats
1 cup quinoa flakes
2 cups puffed cereal
¼ cup sunflower seeds
¼ cup walnuts
¼ cup raisins
¼ cup dried pitted cherries
¼ cup chopped dried figs
¼ cup shredded coconut
¼ cup chocolate chips
1 tsp ground cinnamon
½ cup applesauce
½ cup berries

**Directions** and Total Time: 20 minutes

Place the rolled oats, quinoa flakes, puffed cereal, sunflower seeds, walnuts, raisins, cherries, figs, coconut, chocolate chips, and cinnamon in a container and shake. Transfer the muesli to a bowl and add in with applesauce and berries. Stir to combine, then serve.

## Broccoli Sprout Smoothie

**Ingredients** for 2 servings

1 banana
2 cups kale, chopped
½ cup frozen strawberries
½ cup milk
1 cup broccoli sprouts
2 soft Medjool dates, pitted
1 tbsp hemp hearts
¼ tsp ground cinnamon
¼ tsp ground cardamom
1 tbsp grated fresh ginger

**Directions** and Total Time: 15 minutes

Place all ingredients in your blender, adding 1 cup of water or more for a lighter version. Serve immediately

## Watermelon & Raspberry Smoothie

**Ingredients** for 2 servings

1 cup strawberries
1 cup chopped watermelon
1 cup raspberries
1 tbsp chia seeds
½ cup milk
2 tbsp fresh mint, chopped

**Directions** and Total Time: 15 minutes

Place all the ingredients in your blender, add 1 cup of water and blitz until smooth. Serve and enjoy!

## Refresh Smoothie

**Ingredients** for 2 servings

1 peeled apple, chopped
1 cup apple juice
1 cup strawberries
1 cup chopped cucumber
½ cup coconut water
1 cup water
½ cup ice
1 cup chopped spinach
¼ cup fresh mint, chopped

**Directions** and Total Time: 15 minutes

Put all ingredients in your blender and blitz until you obtain the desired consistency. Pour the smoothie into glasses and serve immediately.

## Work-Out Smoothie

**Ingredients** for 2 servings

1 banana
1 tbsp butter
¼ tsp ground cinnamon
¼ tsp ground nutmeg
2 tbsp raisins
1 tsp maple syrup
1 tbsp ground flaxseed
1 ½ cups orange juice

**Directions** and Total Time: 15 minutes

Blitz all the ingredients in your blender until smooth. Serve chilled.

## Chocolate-Oat Cookies

**Ingredients** for 5 servings

1 egg, beaten
2 tbsp butter
2 tbsp date syrup
1 peeled apple, shredded
1 tsp ground cinnamon
¼ tsp ground nutmeg
A pinch of salt
½ cup rolled oats
¼ cup dark chocolate chips

**Directions** and Total Time: 30 minutes

Preheat oven to 350°F. Beat butter with date syrup in a bowl until creamy, then add the apple. Pour in the egg. Sift the cinnamon, nutmeg, and salt into a separate bowl, then stir into the wet mixture. Fold in the oats and chocolate chips. Scoop out about 10 balls of dough and press lightly to flatten. Arrange the cookies on a parchment-lined baking sheet at least 2-3 inches apart. Bake for 12 minutes until golden brown. Cool the cookies on a wire rack. Keep for up to 3 days.

## Homemade Fruit & Nut Granola

**Ingredients** for 4 servings

2 cups rolled oats
¾ cup rice flour
1 tbsp ground cinnamon
1 tsp ground ginger
½ cup walnuts, chopped
½ cup almonds, chopped
½ cup pumpkin seeds
½ cup shredded coconut
1 ¼ cups apple juice
½ cup raisins
½ cup goji berries

**Directions** and Total Time: 60 minutes

Preheat the oven to 350°F. Combine oats, flour, cinnamon, ginger, walnuts, almonds, pumpkin seeds, and coconut. Pour juice over the oat mixture and stir until just combined. Arrange the granola on a large baking sheet. Bake for 15 minutes, then stir with a spatula to ensure even dryness. Bake for another 30 minutes or until crunchy. Remove the granola and toss in raisins and goji berries. Serve and enjoy. Once cooled, granola can be stored in an airtight container for 2 weeks.

## Soy Chorizo & Corn Grits with Cheddar

**Ingredients** for 6 servings

½ cup grated cheddar cheese
2 tbsp butter
1 cup quick-cooking grits
1 cup soy chorizo, chopped
1 cup corn kernels
2 cups vegetable broth
Salt to taste

**Directions** and Total Time: 25 minutes

Preheat oven to 380°F. Pour the broth in a pot and bring to a boil over medium heat. Stir in salt and grits. Lower the heat and cook until the grits are thickened, stirring often. Turn the heat off, put in the cheddar cheese, butter, soy chorizo, and corn; mix well. Spread the mixture into a greased baking dish and bake for 45 minutes until slightly puffed and golden brown.

## Pistachio-Pumpkin Cake

**Ingredients** for 4 servings

3 tbsp vegetable oil
2 eggs
¾ cup canned pumpkin puree
½ cup honey
3 tbsp sugar
1 ½ cups whole-wheat flour
½ tsp cinnamon powder
½ tsp baking powder
¼ tsp cloves powder
½ tsp allspice powder
½ tsp nutmeg powder
2 tbsp chopped pistachios

**Directions** and Total Time: 70 minutes

Preheat the oven to 350°F. In a bowl, whisk the vegetable oil, pumpkin puree, honey, sugar, and eggs. In another bowl, mix the flour, cinnamon powder, baking powder, cloves powder, allspice powder, and nutmeg powder. Add this mixture to the wet batter and mix until well combined. Pour the batter into a greased loaf pan, sprinkle the pistachios on top, and gently press the nuts onto the batter to stick.

Bake in the oven for 50-55 minutes or until a toothpick inserted into the cake comes out clean. Remove the cake onto a wire rack, allow cooling, slice, and serve.

## Almond Crêpes with Berry Cream

**Ingredients** for 4 servings

**For the berry cream:**
2 tbsp butter
2 tbsp sugar
1 tsp vanilla extract
½ cup fresh blueberries
½ cup fresh raspberries
½ cup cream

**For the crepes:**
3 tbsp butter
2 eggs
1 tsp vanilla extract
1 tsp sugar
¼ tsp salt
2 cups flour
1 ½ cups milk
1 ½ cups water

**Directions** and Total Time: 35 minutes

Melt 2 tbsp of butter in a saucepan over low heat. Mix in date sugar and vanilla. Cook until the sugar melts and then toss in berries. Allow softening for 2-3 minutes. Set aside to cool.

In a bowl, beat the eggs. Whisk in vanilla, sugar, and salt. Pour in ¼ cup of flour and whisk, then a quarter cup of milk, and mix until no lumps remain. Repeat the mixing process with the remaining almond flour and milk in the same quantities until exhausted.

Mix in 1 cup of water until the mixture is runny like that of pancakes, and add the remaining water until it is lighter. Brush a large non-stick skillet with some butter and place over medium heat to melt. Pour 1 tablespoon of the batter into the pan and swirl the skillet quickly and all around to coat the pan with the batter.

Cook until the batter is dry and golden brown beneath, about 30 seconds. Use a spatula to carefully flip the crepe and cook the other side until golden brown too. Fold the crepe onto a plate and set aside. Repeat making more crepes with the remaining batter until exhausted. Plate the crepes, top with the whipped coconut cream and the berry compote. Serve immediately.

## Strawberry-Coconut Porridge

**Ingredients** for 2 servings

2 tsp olive oil
5 tbsp heavy cream
1 egg
1 tbsp coconut flour
1 pinch ground chia seeds
8-10 strawberries

**Directions** and Total Time: 12 minutes

Warm the olive oil in a non-stick saucepan over low heat. Pour the egg, coconut flour, chia seeds, and heavy cream. Cook the mixture while stirring continuously until your desired consistency is achieved. Turn the heat off and spoon the porridge into serving bowls. Top with strawberries and serve immediately.

## Oat & Peach Smoothie

**Ingredients** for 4 servings

1 cup chopped peaches
1 banana
¼ cup rolled oats
1 tbsp chia seeds
1 cup raspberries
½ cup milk
1 cup water
2 tbsp parsley, chopped
1 cup chopped spinach
1 carrot, peeled
1 tbsp grated fresh ginger

**Directions** and Total Time: 15 minutes

Place all ingredients in your blender and purée until smooth. Serve in glasses and enjoy!

## Morning Oats

**Ingredients** for 1 serving

½ cup rolled oats
1 tbsp chia seeds
1 tbsp date syrup
¼ tsp ground cinnamon
1 tbsp hazelnuts, chopped
1 banana, sliced

**Directions** and Total Time: 10 minutes + soaking time

In a mixing bowl, place the oats, chia seeds, date syrup, and cinnamon. Pour enough cool water over the oats to submerge them, and stir to combine. Leave to soak for 1 hour. Top with banana and hazelnuts before serving.

## Creole Kale & Tofu Scramble

**Ingredients** for 4 servings

¼ cup grated Parmesan
2 tbsp butter
1 (14-oz) pack tofu, crumbled
1 red bell pepper, chopped
1 green bell pepper, chopped
1 tomato, finely chopped
2 tbsp chopped green onions
Salt and black pepper to taste
1 tsp turmeric powder
1 tsp Creole seasoning
½ cup chopped baby kale

**Directions** and Total Time: 20 minutes

Melt butter in a skillet over medium heat. Add tofu. Cook stirring until the tofu is light golden brown while making sure not to break the tofu into tiny bits but to have scrambled resemblance, 5 minutes. Stir in the bell peppers, tomato, green onions, salt, black pepper, turmeric powder, and Creole seasoning. Sauté for 5 minutes. Mix in the kale to wilt, 3 minutes and then half of the Parmesan cheese. Allow melting for 2 minutes and then turn the heat off. Top with the remaining cheese and serve.

## Sweet Corn Bread

**Ingredients** for 6 servings

1 mashed banana
½ cup cornmeal
½ cup pastry flour
1/3 cup sugar
1 tsp lemon zest
½ tbsp baking powder
¼ tsp baking soda
½ tbsp lemon juice
½ cup milk
¼ cup sunflower oil

**Directions** and Total Time: 35 minutes

Preheat air fryer to 350°F. Add the cornmeal, flour, lemon zest, baking powder, salt, and baking soda in a bowl. Stir with a whisk until combined. Add the mashed banana, lemon juice, milk, and oil to another bowl and stir well. Add the wet mixture to the dry mixture and stir gently until combined. Spray a baking pan with oil. Pour the batter in and Bake in the fryer for 25 minutes or until golden and a knife inserted in the center comes out clean. Cut into wedges and serve.

## Pumpkin Crumble Muffins

**Ingredients** for 6 servings

2 tbsp butter
1 ½ cups pumpkin purée
1/3 cup coconut sugar
½ cup milk
2 tbsp ground flaxseed
1 tsp apple cider vinegar
1 tsp pure vanilla extract
2 cups whole-grain flour
1 tsp baking powder
1 tsp ground cinnamon
A pinch of salt
½ cup walnuts, chopped
¼ cup dark chocolate chips

**Directions** and Total Time: 35 minutes

Preheat the oven to 350°F. Lightly spray 12-cup muffin tin with cooking oil. Add butter, pumpkin puree, coconut sugar, milk, flaxseed, vinegar, and vanilla in a blender jar. Puree until well mixed. Sift flour, baking powder, cinnamon, salt, and chopped walnuts into a large bowl. Stir in the wet ingredients until it just comes together. Divide the batter between the muffin cups. Top with chocolate chips and coconut sugar. Bake for 15-20 minutes until a toothpick in the middle of the muffin comes out clean. Let cool for a few minutes. Serve.

## Raspberry-Coconut Smoothie

**Ingredients** for 1 serving

¼ cup raspberries
1 cup milk
½ tsp vanilla extract
1 tsp heavy cream
1 tbsp date sugar

**Directions** and Total Time: 5 minutes

Put the blueberries, milk, vanilla, heavy cream, and date sugar in a blender. Blend for 30-60 seconds. Serve.

## Mediterranean Sandwiches

**Ingredients** for 2 servings

1 tbsp wholegrain mustard
1 tbsp umeboshi vinegar
1 (15-oz) can garbanzo beans
¼ cup mayonnaise
1 celery stalk, thinly sliced
2 tbsp minced red onions
1 tbsp capers, minced
1 tsp caper juice
Salt and black pepper to taste
4 bread slices, toasted

**Directions** and Total Time: 20 minutes

Mash garbanzo beans, mustard, vinegar, mayonnaise, celery, red onion, capers, caper juice, salt, and pepper in a large bowl. Spread ½ of the mixture over one piece of toast, then top with another piece of toast. Repeat for the other sandwich. Serve and enjoy.

## Cinnamon-Coconut Doughnuts

**Ingredients** for 6 servings

¼ cup applesauce
¼ cup milk
2 tbsp safflower oil
1 ½ tsp vanilla
½ tsp lemon zest
1 ½ cups all-purpose flour
¾ cup coconut sugar
2 ½ tsp cinnamon
½ tsp ground nutmeg
¼ tsp salt
¾ tsp baking powder

**Directions** and Total Time: 35 minutes

Preheat air fryer to 350°F. Add applesauce, milk, oil, vanilla, and lemon zest. Stir well. In a different bowl, combine flour, ½ cup coconut sugar, ½ tsp cinnamon, nutmeg, salt, and baking powder. Stir well. Add the mixture to the wet mix and blend. Pull off bits of the dough and roll into balls. Place in the greased frying basket, leaving room between as they get bigger. Spray the tops with oil. Air Fry for 8-10 minutes, flipping once.

During the last 2 minutes of frying, place 4 tbsp of coconut sugar and 2 tsp of cinnamon in a bowl and stir to combine. After frying, coat each donut by spraying with oil and toss in the cinnamon-sugar mix. Serve.

## Date-Apple French Toast

**Ingredients** for 2 servings

2 tsp coconut oil
½ tsp ground cinnamon
½ tsp orange zest
1 tbsp maple date syrup
1 apple, cored and thinly sliced
2 slices whole-grain bread

**Directions** and Total Time: 40 minutes

Preheat the oven to 350°F. Combine coconut oil, cinnamon, orange zest, and date syrup in a large bowl. Toss in apple slices and coat. Transfer the apples to a medium skillet over medium heat. Cook until it has softened, or about 5 minutes. Place the apples on a plate and cook the bread in the same skillet. Cook for 2 or 3 minutes, then flip the bread. Cook for another 2 to 3 minutes. Arrange the cooked bread on a baking sheet and top with the apples. Bake for 15-20 minutes. Serve.

## Chia & Coconut Pudding with Nectarines

**Ingredients** for 4 servings

1 cup milk
½ tsp vanilla extract
3 tbsp chia seeds
½ cup granola
2/3 cup chopped nectarine

**Directions** and Total Time: 5 minutes+ cooling time

In a medium bowl, mix the milk, vanilla, and chia seeds until well combined. Divide the mixture between 4 breakfast cups and refrigerate for at least 4 hours to allow the mixture to gel. Top with granola and nectarine.

### Yummy Almond Waffles

**Ingredients** for 4 servings

2 tbsp olive oil
½ cup butter, melted
2 eggs
2/3 cup flour
2 ½ tsp baking powder
A pinch of salt
1 ½ cups milk
2 tbsp pure maple syrup
1 tsp fresh lemon juice

**Directions** and Total Time: 20 minutes

In a medium bowl, mix the eggs, flour, baking powder, salt, and milk. Mix until well combined. Preheat a waffle iron and brush with some olive oil. Pour in a quarter cup of the batter, close the iron and cook until the waffles are golden and crisp, 2-3 minutes. Transfer the waffles to a plate and make more waffles using the same process and ingredient proportions. In a bowl, mix the butter with maple syrup and lemon juice. Spread the top with the butter-lemon mixture and serve.

### Homemade English Muffins

**Ingredients** for 4 servings

3 tbsp butter
2 eggs, beaten
2 tbsp flour
½ tsp baking powder
1 pinch of salt

**Directions** and Total Time: 20 minutes

In a bowl, evenly combine the flour, baking powder, and salt. Then, pour in the eggs and whisk again. Melt the butter in a frying pan over medium heat and add the mixture in four dollops. Fry until golden brown on one side, then flip the bread and fry further until golden brown.

### Cinnamon Almond Buckwheat

**Ingredients** for 4 servings

1 cup milk
1 cup water
1 cup buckwheat groats
1 tsp cinnamon
¼ cup chopped almonds
2 tbsp honey

**Directions** and Total Time: 20 minutes

Place the milk, water, and buckwheat in a pot over medium heat and bring to a boil. Lower the heat and simmer covered for 15 minutes. Allow sitting covered for 5 minutes. Mix in cinnamon, almonds, and honey.

### Tofu Avocado "Sandwich"

**Ingredients** for 2 servings

2 tsp butter, softened
1 avocado, sliced
1 large red tomato, sliced
2 oz gem lettuce leaves
1 oz tofu, sliced
1 tbsp chopped parsley

**Directions** and Total Time: 10 minutes

Put the avocado on a plate and place the tomato slices by the avocado. Arrange the lettuce (with the inner side facing you) on a flat plate to serve as the base of the sandwich.

To assemble the sandwich, smear each leaf of the lettuce with butter, and arrange some tofu slices in the leaves. Then, share the avocado and tomato slices on each tofu. Garnish with parsley and serve.

### Mozzarella & Pesto Twists

**Ingredients** for 6 servings

1 ½ cups grated mozzarella
5 eggs
1 tbsp flax seed powder
4 tbsp coconut flour
½ cup almond flour
½ tsp salt
1 tsp baking powder
2 oz pesto
Olive oil for brushing

**Directions** and Total Time: 35 minutes

Preheat oven to 350°F. In a bowl, combine coconut flour, almond flour, salt, and baking powder. Melt the butter and cheese in a deep skillet over medium heat. Stir in the eggs. Mix in the flour mixture until a firm dough forms. Turn the heat off, transfer the mixture in between two parchment papers, and then use a rolling pin to flatten out the dough of about an inch's thickness.

Remove the parchment paper on top and spread the pesto all over the dough. Now, use a knife to cut the dough into strips, twist each piece, and place it on the baking sheet. Brush with olive oil and bake for 15 to 20 minutes until golden brown. Remove the bread twist; allow cooling for a few minutes, and serve.

### Seedy Bread

**Ingredients** for 6 servings

½ cup olive oil
3 eggs
¾ cup coconut flour
1 cup almond flour
3 tsp baking powder
5 tbsp sesame seeds
½ cup chia seeds
1 tsp ground caraway seeds
1 tsp hemp seeds
¼ cup psyllium husk powder
1 tsp salt
2/3 cup cream cheese
¾ cup heavy cream
1 tbsp poppy seeds

**Directions** and Total Time: 55 minutes

Preheat oven to 350°F. In a bowl, evenly combine the coconut flour, almond flour, baking powder, sesame seeds, chia seeds, ground caraway seeds, hemp seeds, psyllium husk powder, and salt. In another bowl, use an electric hand mixer to whisk the cream cheese, olive oil, heavy cream, and eggs. Pour the liquid ingredients into the dry ingredients, and continue whisking with the hand mixer until a dough forms. Transfer the dough to a parchment-lined loaf pan, sprinkle with poppy seeds, and bake in the oven for 45 minutes or until a knife inserted into the bread comes out clean. Remove the parchment paper with the bread, and allow cooling on a rack.

### Pineapple French Toasts

**Ingredients** for 4 servings

2 tbsp maple syrup + extra for drizzling
2 eggs
1 ½ cups milk
½ cup flour
2 pinches of salt
½ tbsp cinnamon powder
½ tsp fresh lemon zest
1 tbsp fresh pineapple juice
8 whole-grain bread slices

**Directions** and Total Time: 55 minutes

Preheat the oven to 400°F. In a bowl, whisk the eggs. Add the milk, flour, maple syrup, salt, cinnamon powder, lemon zest, and pineapple juice and whisk well.

Soak the bread on both sides in the milk mixture and allow sitting on a plate for 3 minutes.

Heat a large skillet over medium heat and place the bread in the pan. Cook until golden brown on the bottom side. Flip the bread and cook further until golden brown on the other side, 4 minutes in total. Transfer to a plate, drizzle some maple syrup on top and serve immediately.

### Exotic Pancakes

**Ingredients** for 4 servings

2 tsp butter
2 eggs
½ cup milk
¼ cup raspberries, mashed
½ cup oat flour
1 tsp baking soda
A pinch salt
1 tbsp coconut sugar
2 tbsp pure date syrup
½ tsp cinnamon powder
2 tbsp coconut flakes
1 cup raspberries

**Directions** and Total Time: 25 minutes

In a medium bowl, mix the eggs, milk, and raspberries. Add the oat flour, baking soda, salt, coconut sugar, date syrup, and cinnamon powder. Fold in the coconut flakes until well combined.

Working in batches, melt a quarter of the butter in a non-stick skillet and add ¼ cup of the batter. Cook until set beneath and golden brown, 2 minutes. Flip the pancake and cook on the other side until set and golden brown, 2 minutes. Transfer to a plate and make the remaining pancakes using the rest of the ingredients in the same proportions. Garnish the pancakes with some raspberries and serve warm!

### Raspberry Muffins with Orange Glaze

**Ingredients** for 4 servings

½ cup butter, softened
2 eggs
2 cups whole-wheat flour
1 ½ tsp baking powder
A pinch salt
2 cups sugar
½ cup milk
2 tsp vanilla extract
1 lemon, zested
1 cup dried raspberries
2 tbsp orange juice

**Directions** and Total Time: 40 minutes

Preheat oven to 400°F. Grease 6 muffin cups with cooking spray. In a medium bowl, mix the flour, baking powder, and salt. In another bowl, cream the butter, half of the sugar, and eggs. Mix in the milk, vanilla, and lemon zest. Combine both mixtures, fold in raspberries, and fill muffin cups two-thirds way up with the batter. Bake for 20-25 minutes. In a medium bowl, whisk orange juice and remaining sugar until smooth. Remove the muffins when ready and transfer to them a wire rack to cool. Drizzle the glaze on top to serve.

### Carrot Bread with Chocolate Chips

**Ingredients** for 4 servings

¼ cup olive oil
1 ½ cup whole-wheat flour
¼ cup almond flour
¼ tsp salt
¼ tsp cloves powder
¼ tsp cayenne pepper
1 tbsp cinnamon powder
½ tsp nutmeg powder
1 ½ tsp baking powder
2 eggs
½ cup sugar
¼ cup maple syrup
¾ tsp almond extract
1 tbsp grated lemon zest
½ cup applesauce
4 carrots, shredded
3 tbsp chocolate chips
2/3 cup black raisins

**Directions** and Total Time: 75 minutes

Preheat oven to 375°F. In a bowl, mix all the flour, salt, cloves powder, cayenne pepper, cinnamon powder, nutmeg powder, and baking powder. In another bowl, beat the eggs. Mix in the sugar, maple syrup, almond extract, lemon zest, applesauce, and olive oil.

Combine both mixtures until smooth and fold in the carrots, chocolate chips, and raisins. Pour the mixture into a baking paper-lined loaf pan and bake in the oven until golden brown on top or a toothpick inserted into the bread comes out clean, 45-50 minutes. Remove from the oven, transfer the bread onto a wire rack to cool, slice, and serve.

### Morning Corn Cakes

**Ingredients** for 4 servings

4 tbsp olive oil
1 egg
2 cups yellow cornmeal
1 tsp salt
2 tsp baking powder
1 cup mayonnaise

**Directions** and Total Time: 35 minutes

In a bowl, whisk the egg. Mix in 1 cup of water and then whisk in the cornmeal, salt, and baking powder until soup texture forms but not watery. Heat a quarter of the olive oil in a griddle pan and pour in a quarter of the batter. Cook until set and golden brown beneath, 3 minutes. Flip the cake and cook the other side until set and golden brown too. Plate the cake and make three more with the remaining oil and batter. Top the cakes with mayonnaise.

### Avocado & Mushroom Panini

**Ingredients** for 4 servings

1 cup sliced button mushrooms
4 oz sliced Parmesan cheese
1 tbsp olive oil
Salt and black pepper to taste
1 ripe avocado, sliced
2 tbsp lemon juice
½ tsp pure maple syrup
8 slices whole-wheat ciabatta

**Directions** and Total Time: 30 minutes

Heat the olive oil in a medium skillet over medium heat and sauté the mushrooms until softened, 5 minutes. Season with salt and black pepper. Turn the heat off.

Preheat a panini press to medium heat, 3 to 5 minutes. Mash the avocado in a medium bowl and mix in the lemon juice and maple syrup. Spread the mixture on 4 bread slices, divide the mushrooms and Parmesan cheese on top. Cover with the other bread slices and brush the top with olive oil. Grill the sandwiches one after another in the heated press until golden brown, and the Parmesan cheese is melted. Serve.

## Cauliflower & Potato Hash Browns

**Ingredients** for 4 servings

4 tbsp butter
3 eggs
2 large potatoes, shredded
1 big head cauliflower, riced
½ white onion, grated
Salt and black pepper to taste

**Directions** and Total Time: 35 minutes

In a bowl, beat the eggs. Add the potatoes, cauliflower, onion, salt, and black pepper and mix until well combined. Melt 1 tbsp of butter in a non-stick skillet over medium heat and add 4 scoops of the hashbrown mixture. Make sure to have 1-inch intervals between each scoop.

Use a spoon to flatten the batter and cook until compacted and golden brown on the bottom part, 2 minutes. Flip the hashbrowns and cook further for 2 minutes or until the vegetable cook and is golden brown. Transfer to a paper-towel-lined plate to drain grease. Make the remaining hashbrowns using the remaining ingredients.

## Mango Naan Bread

**Ingredients** for 4 servings

1/3 cup olive oil
2 tbsp butter
¾ cup flour
1 tsp salt
1 tsp baking powder
2 cups boiling water
4 cups chopped mangoes
1 cup honey
1 lemon, juiced
A pinch of saffron powder
1 tsp cardamom powder

**Directions** and Total Time: 40 minutes

In a large bowl, mix the flour, salt, and baking powder. Mix in the olive oil and boiling water until smooth, thick batter forms. Allow the dough to rise for 5 minutes. Form balls out of the dough, place each on a baking paper, and use your hands to flatten the dough.

Melt the butter in a large skillet over medium heat and fry the dough on both sides until set and golden brown on each side, 4 minutes per bread. Transfer to a plate and set aside. Add mangoes, honey, lemon juice, and 3 tbsp water in a pot and cook until boiling, 5 minutes.

Mix in saffron and cardamom powders and cook further over low heat until the mangoes soften. Mash the mangoes with the back of the spoon until relatively smooth with little chunks of mangoes in a jam. Cool completely. Spoon the jam into sterilized jars and serve with the naan bread.

## Cinnamon-Apple Muffins

**Ingredients** for 4 servings

**For the muffins:**
1 egg, beaten
1/3 cup melted butter
1 ½ cups whole-wheat flour
¾ cup sugar
2 tsp baking powder
¼ tsp salt
1 tsp cinnamon powder
1/3 cup milk
2 apples, chopped

**For topping:**
½ cup cold butter, cubed
1/3 cup whole-wheat flour
½ cup pure date sugar
1 ½ tsp cinnamon powder

**Directions** and Total Time: 40 minutes

Preheat oven to 400°F. and grease 6 muffin Gcups with cooking spray. In a bowl, mix flour, sugar, baking powder, salt, and cinnamon powder. Whisk in the melted butter, egg, milk, and fold in the apples. Fill the muffin cups two-thirds way up with the batter.

In a bowl, mix remaining flour, sugar, cold butter, and cinnamon powder. Sprinkle the mixture on the muffin batter. Bake for 20 minutes. Remove the muffins onto a wire rack, allow cooling, and serve.

## Zucchini Hash Browns

**Ingredients** for 4 servings

2 shredded zucchinis
2 tbsp nutritional yeast
1 tsp allspice
1 egg white

**Directions** and Total Time: 20 minutes

Preheat air fryer to 400°F. Combine zucchinis, nutritional yeast, allspice, and egg white in a bowl. Make 4 patties out of the mixture. Cut 4 pieces of parchment paper, put a patty on each foil, and fold in all sides to create a rectangle. Using a spatula, flatten them and spread them. Then unwrap each foil and remove the hash browns onto the fryer and Air Fry for 12 minutes until golden brown and crispy, turning once. Serve right away.

## Banana French Toasts with Berry Syrup

**Ingredients** for 8 servings

1 banana, mashed
1 cup milk
1 tsp pure vanilla extract
¼ tsp ground nutmeg
½ tsp ground cinnamon
1 ½ tsp arrowroot powder
A pinch of salt
8 slices whole-grain bread
1 cup strawberries
2 tbsp water
2 tbsp maple syrup

**Directions** and Total Time: 40 minutes

Preheat oven to 350°F. In a bowl, stir banana, milk, vanilla, nutmeg, cinnamon, arrowroot, and salt. Dip each bread slice in the banana mixture and arrange on a baking tray. Spread the remaining banana mixture over the top. Bake for 30 minutes until the tops are lightly browned. In a pot over medium heat, put the strawberries, water, and maple syrup. Simmer for 15-10 minutes until the berries break up and the liquid is reduced. Serve topped with strawberry syrup.

## Cherry-Carrot Muffins

**Ingredients** for 6 servings

2 tbsp butter, softened
¼ cup milk
1 orange, chopped
1 carrot, coarsely chopped
2 tbsp chopped dried cherries
3 tbsp molasses
2 tbsp ground flaxseed
1 tsp apple cider vinegar
1 tsp pure vanilla extract
½ tsp ground cinnamon
½ tsp ground ginger
¼ tsp ground nutmeg
¼ tsp allspice
¾ cup whole-wheat flour
1 tsp baking powder
½ tsp baking soda
½ cup rolled oats
2 tbsp raisins
2 tbsp sunflower seeds

**Directions** and Total Time: 45 minutes

Preheat oven to 350 F. In a food processor, add the butter, milk, orange, carrot, cherries, molasses, flaxseed, vinegar, vanilla, cinnamon, ginger, nutmeg, and allspice and blend until smooth. In a bowl, combine the flour, baking powder, and baking soda. Fold in the wet mixture and gently stir to combine. Mix in the oats, raisins, and sunflower seeds. Divide the batter between 6 greased muffin cups. Put in a baking tray and bake for 30 minutes. Let cool and serve.

## Creamy Pimiento Biscuits

**Ingredients** for 4 servings

¼ cup butter, cold and cubed
1 cup shredded cheddar
1 tbsp melted butter
2 cups whole-wheat flour
2 tsp baking powder
1 tsp salt
½ tsp baking soda
½ tsp garlic powder
¼ tsp black pepper
¾ cup milk
1 (4 oz) jar chopped pimientos,

**Directions** and Total Time: 30 minutes

Preheat the oven to 450°F. In a medium bowl, mix the flour, baking powder, salt, baking soda, garlic powder, and black pepper. Add the cold butter using a hand mixer until the mixture is the size of small peas. Pour in ¾ of the milk and continue whisking. Continue adding the remaining milk, a tablespoonful at a time, until dough forms. Mix in the cheddar cheese and pimientos. Place the dough on a lightly floured surface and flatten the dough into ½-inch thickness.

Use a 2 ½-inch round cutter to cut out biscuits' pieces from the dough. Gather, re-roll the dough once and continue cutting out biscuits. Arrange the biscuits on a parchment-lined baking pan and brush the tops with melted butter. Bake for 12-14 minutes, or until the biscuits are golden brown. Cool and serve.

## Home-Style Cinnamon Rolls

**Ingredients** for 4 servings

½ (16-oz) pizza dough
1/3 cup dark brown sugar
¼ cup butter, softened
½ tsp ground cinnamon

**Directions** and Total Time: 40 minutes

Preheat air fryer to 360°F. Roll out the dough into a rectangle. Using a knife, spread the brown sugar and butter, covering all the edges, and sprinkle with cinnamon. Fold the long side of the dough into a log, then cut it into 8 equal pieces, avoiding compression. Place the rolls, spiral-side up onto a parchment-lined sheet. Let rise for 20 minutes. Grease the rolls with cooking spray and Bake for 8 minutes until golden brown. Serve right away.

## Pear & Pecan Farro Breakfast

**Ingredients** for 4 servings

1 tbsp butter
2 cups water
½ tsp salt
1 cup farro
2 peeled pears, chopped
¼ cup chopped pecans

**Directions** and Total Time: 20 minutes

Bring water to a boil in a pot over high heat. Stir in salt and farro. Lower the heat, cover, and simmer for 15 minutes until the farro is tender and the liquid has absorbed. Turn the heat off and add in the butter, pears, and pecans. Cover and rest for 12-15 minutes. Serve.

## Collard Green & Feta Crêpes with Mushrooms

**Ingredients** for 4 servings

2 tbsp extra-virgin olive oil
1 cup whole-wheat flour
1 tsp onion powder
½ tsp baking soda
¼ tsp salt
1 cup crumbled feta
1/3 cup milk
¼ cup lemon juice
½ cup chopped mushrooms
½ cup finely chopped onion
2 cups collard greens

**Directions** and Total Time: 25 minutes

Combine the flour, onion powder, baking soda, and salt in a bowl. Blitz the feta, milk, lemon juice, and oil in a food processor over high speed for 30 seconds. Pour over the flour mixture and mix to combine well. Add in the mushrooms, onion, and collard greens.

Heat a skillet and grease with cooking spray. Lower the heat and spread a ladleful of the batter across the surface of the skillet. Cook for 4 minutes on both sides or until set. Remove to a plate. Repeat the process until no batter is left, greasing with a little more oil, if needed. Serve.

## Orange Crêpes

**Ingredients** for 4 servings

½ cup melted butter
3 tbsp olive oil
2 eggs
1 tsp vanilla extract
1 tsp sugar
¼ tsp salt
2 cups flour
1 ½ cups milk
3 tbsp fresh orange juice
2 tbsp maple syrup

**Directions** and Total Time: 30 minutes

In a medium bowl, whisk the eggs with vanilla, sugar, and salt. Pour in a quarter cup of flour and whisk, then a quarter cup of milk, and mix until no lumps remain.

Repeat the mixing process with the remaining flour and milk in the same quantities until exhausted. Mix in the melted butter, orange juice, and half of the water until the mixture is runny like pancakes. Add the remaining milk until the mixture is lighter. Brush a non-stick skillet with some olive oil and place over medium heat to melt.

Pour 1 tbsp of the batter into the pan and swirl the skillet quickly and all around to coat the pan with the batter. Cook until the batter is dry and golden brown beneath, about 30 seconds.

Flip the crepe and cook the other side until golden brown too. Fold the crepe onto a plate and set aside. Repeat with the remaining batter until exhausted. Drizzle maple syrup on the crepes and serve.

# SALADS

## Greek-Style Salad

**Ingredients** for 2 servings

10 cherry tomatoes, halved
1 cucumber, diced
½ cup green olives, halved
1 tsp Greek seasoning
2 tbsp extra-virgin olive oil
Salt and black pepper to taste
½ head iceberg lettuce, halved

**Directions** and Total Time: 10 minutes

Put the cherry tomatoes, cucumber, green olives, Greek seasoning, and a tablespoon of olive oil in a bowl. Add some salt and pepper and combine by tossing. Put wedges of lettuces on plates and add the mix on top. Drizzle the rest of the olive oil and add a bit of salt. Serve.

## Radish-Cucumber Salad

**Ingredients** for 2 servings

¼ cup milk
1 garlic clove, minced
1 lemon wedge, juiced
2 cucumbers, diced
4 radishes, sliced thin
Salt and black pepper to taste
2 tbsp chopped parsley

**Directions** and Total Time: 5 minutes

Combine the milk, garlic, and lemon juice in a bowl. In a separate bowl, add the cucumbers and radishes, then sprinkle with salt and pepper. Put the resulting dressing on top of the veggies and stir until coated. Add some parsley on top and serve.

## Minty Tofu Salad with Avocado

**Ingredients** for 2 servings

2 tbsp extra-virgin olive oil
1 tbsp lime juice
2 cucumbers, diced
2 avocados, diced
8 cherry tomatoes, halved
¼ cup crumbled tofu
¼ cup chopped fresh mint
Salt and black pepper to taste

**Directions** and Total Time: 5 minutes

Combine the olive oil and lime juice in a bowl. In a separate bowl, combine the cucumbers, avocados, and cherry tomatoes, then sprinkle with salt and pepper. Ladle the dressing over the cucumber mix and stir, making sure everything is well-coated. Toss in the tofu and mint, then shake the bowl.

## German-Style Potato Salad

**Ingredients** for 4 servings

6 medium potatoes, scrubbed and chopped
2 celery sticks, chopped
¼ cup chopped parsley
1 tsp Dijon mustard
Salt and black pepper to taste
5 radishes, chopped
1 bell pepper, chopped
1 tbsp chopped chives

**Directions** and Total Time: 35 minutes

Bring about a quarter of a large pot of water to a boil. Add potatoes and continue boiling for 10 minutes. Add celery and boil for 10 minutes. Reserve 1 cup of cooking liquid. Drain the rest of the water. Set vegetables aside. When cooled, transfer ½ cup potatoes to the blender. Pour in cooking liquid, then add parsley, mustard, salt, and pepper. Puree until no longer chunky. In a large bowl, combine potatoes and celery along with radishes, pepper, and chives. Top with the mustard dressing and toss to coat. Serve and enjoy.

## Mediterranean Eggplant Salad

**Ingredients** for 2 servings

1 tsp olive oil
1 eggplant, diced
½ tsp ground cumin
½ tsp ground ginger
¼ tsp turmeric
¼ tsp ground nutmeg
Sea salt to taste
½ lemon, zested and juiced
2 lemon wedges
2 tbsp capers
1 tbsp chopped green olives
1 garlic clove, pressed
1 tsp mint, finely chopped
2 cups spinach, chopped
1 cucumber, cut into chunks
4 cherry tomatoes, halved

**Directions** and Total Time: 30 minutes

Saute eggplant in oil in a large skillet over medium heat. After 5 minutes, stir in cumin, ginger, turmeric, nutmeg, and salt. Continue cooking for 10 minutes or until the eggplant is very soft. Stir in lemon zest, lemon juice, capers, olives, garlic, and mint. Cook for another two minutes, stirring occasionally. Divide the spinach between the plates. Top with eggplant mixture, cucumber, and tomatoes. Garnish with a wedge of lemon to squeeze over the greens. Serve warm and enjoy.

## Moroccan Garbanzo Bean Salad

**Ingredients** for 2 servings

1 tbsp olive oil
2 tbsp balsamic vinegar
1 tsp minced scallions
1 garlic clove, minced
1 tbsp basil, chopped
1 tbsp oregano, chopped
Salt to taste
1 (14-oz) can garbanzo beans
6 mushrooms, thinly sliced
1 zucchini, diced
2 carrots, diced

**Directions** and Total Time: 25 minutes

Whisk all the ingredients together in a large bowl, except for beans, mushrooms, zucchini and carrots, to make the dressing. Add all the veggies to a big bowl. Stir in the dressing and shake vigorously. Let it marinate for 15 minutes before serving.

## Lettuce Wraps with Vegetables & Walnuts

**Ingredients** for 4 servings

1 cup walnuts, chopped
8 sun-dried tomatoes, diced
2 carrots, peeled and grated
1 celery stalk, thinly sliced
¼ cup chopped parsley
2 tsp taco seasoning
½ lime, zested and juiced
2 tsp olive oil
2 tsp maple syrup
Salt to taste
8 large lettuce leaves
2 spring onions, thinly sliced

**Directions** and Total Time: 25 minutes

Combine walnuts, tomatoes, carrots, celery, parsley, taco seasoning, lime juice, lime zest, oil, maple syrup, and salt in a large bowl. Spoon mixture among the lettuce leaves and garnish with spring onions. Serve and enjoy.

## Tri-Color Salad Bowl

**Ingredients** for 6 servings

1 cup baby bella mushrooms, sliced
1 tbsp olive oil
1 onion, chopped
12 diced sun-dried tomatoes
6 garlic cloves, minced
Salt and black pepper to taste
¼ tsp red pepper flakes
½ cup vegetable broth
2 cups spinach, chopped
3 cups penne, cooked
1 (15-oz) can cannellini beans
3 tbsp Parmesan cheese
2 tbsp chopped parsley

**Directions** and Total Time: 25 minutes

In a large skillet, heat oil over medium heat. Sauté onion, tomatoes, and mushrooms for about 5 minutes or until the onion is soft and the mushrooms have reduced. Stir in garlic, salt, black pepper, and red pepper flakes. Cook for 1 minute until aromatic. Pour in broth slowly and stir in spinach. Let simmer covered for 5 minutes to wilt the spinach. Stir in pasta and bean and heat through for about 2 minutes. Divide among 6 bowls. Top with Parmesan and chopped parsley. Serve warm and enjoy.

## Fall Bowls

**Ingredients** for 4 servings

2 russet potatoes, cubed
2 tbsp olive oil
Salt and black pepper to taste
2 cups broccoli florets
4 cups grated purple cabbage
1 tbsp tamari
2 cups cooked chickpeas
3 tbsp ranch dressing
¼ cup sunflower seeds
¼ cup thinly sliced scallions

**Directions** and Total Time: 35 minutes

Preheat the oven to 425°F. Use parchment paper to line a baking sheet. Toss potato and 1 tablespoon olive oil in a large bowl. Season with salt and pepper. Arrange the potatoes in a single layer on the baking sheet. Bake for 15 minutes. Using the same bowl, toss broccoli, cabbage, tamari, and 1 tablespoon of olive oil. Season with salt and pepper. After 15 minutes, toss the potatoes on the baking sheet. Arrange the broccoli-cabbage mixture over the potatoes and bake for 10 minutes when the potatoes are fork-tender. Toss and combine. Portion the chickpeas among 4 bowls, then add the vegetables over them. Drizzle with ranch dressing and garnish with sunflower seeds and scallions. Serve warm and enjoy.

## Tofu Caesar Salad with Pears

**Ingredients** for 4 servings

1 (14-oz) block tofu, cubed
2 cups chopped ripe pears
2 minced green onions
¼ cup thinly sliced celery
1 tbsp chopped fresh parsley
¾ tsp dried dill
½ tsp garlic powder
½ tsp onion powder
½ cup mayonnaise
½ head Iceberg lettuce, torn
Salt and black pepper to taste

**Directions** and Total Time: 20 minutes

Toss tofu, pears, onions, celery, parsley, dill, garlic powder, and onion powder in a large bowl. Gently stir in mayonnaise and season with salt and pepper. Serve on bed of lettuce in a salad platter and enjoy.

## Pizza-Style Mushroom & Spinach Bowls

**Ingredients** for 4 servings

1 tbsp olive oil
1 carrot, sliced
½ red onion, thinly sliced
1 cup bella mushrooms, sliced
1 tsp Italian garlic seasoning
2 cups marinara sauce
5 oz baby spinach
2 cups cooked cannellini beans
1 cup black olives, sliced
½ tsp Red pepper flakes
2 tbsp Parmesan cheese
1 tbsp chopped basil

**Directions** and Total Time: 15 minutes

In a large skillet, heat oil over medium heat. Stir in carrot, red onion, mushrooms, and Italian seasoning. Sauté for 3 to 5 minutes to soften the onion. Add garlic and sauté for another minute until aromatic. In each bowl, add ¼ cup marinara sauce, then a layer of spinach. Top with ¼ cup beans and ¼ of the vegetable mixture. Finish with the rest of the sauce and black olives. Top with red pepper flakes, Parmesan, and basil. Serve warm

## Vegan Bacon & Avocado Salad

**Ingredients** for 4 servings

6 oz baby greens salad
10 cherry tomatoes, halved
1 avocado, diced
1 cup corn kernels
1 peeled cucumber, diced
2 oz vegan bacon
4 scallions, thinly sliced
4 tbsp ranch dressing

**Directions** and Total Time: 25 minutes

Divide the baby greens among 4 bowls. Arrange each ingredient in a line across the greens: tomatoes, avocado, corn, cucumber, and vegan bacon. Top with scallions and ranch dressing. Serve and enjoy.

## Hall of Fame Salad

**Ingredients** for 4 servings

1 lemon, juiced
2 tbsp olive oil
1 tbsp maple syrup
Salt to taste
5 oz package arugula
1 cup corn kernels
½ red onion, thinly sliced
2 cored Fuji apples, sliced
½ cup chopped hazelnuts
¼ cup raisins

**Directions** and Total Time: 20 minutes

Mix lemon juice, oil, maple syrup, and salt in a small bowl. Toss arugula, corn, red onion, and apples in a large bowl. Add dressing and toss. Serve salad among 4 plates. Sprinkle it with hazelnuts and raisins. Serve and enjoy.

## Rich Multi-Grain Bowls

**Ingredients** for 2 servings

2 tsp olive oil
1 cup cooked quinoa
1 (15-oz) can pink beans
1 bunch spinach, chopped
1 tbsp tamari
Salt and black pepper to taste

**Directions** and Total Time: 15 minutes

Heat oil in a large skillet over medium heat. Stir in quinoa, beans, and spinach and continue stirring until the spinach is wilted. Cook for 3 to 5 minutes for everything to be heated through. Stir in tamari and season with salt and pepper. Divide between bowls. Serve warm and enjoy.

## Asian Edamame & Rice Salad

**Ingredients** for 4 servings

1 cup rice
Salt to taste
1 large sweet potato
1 tsp olive oil
1 cup shelled edamame
1 red bell pepper, chopped
½ head red cabbage, shredded
4 scallions, chopped
2 tbsp cilantro, chopped
1 tbsp sesame seeds
½ cup pure orange juice
1 tbsp tamari
1 tbsp rice vinegar
2 tsp agave nectar
2 tsp sesame oil

**Directions** and Total Time: 65 minutes

Preheat the oven to 400°F. Place 2 cups of salted water in a pot over high heat. When the water comes to a boil, add the rice, reduce the heat, and cover. Simmer for 30 minutes. Peel sweet potatoes and dice vinegar into small cubes. Toss with olive oil, then arrange in a baking dish. Roast for 15-20 minutes while the rice is cooking. When the rice and potato are done cooking, set aside to cool slightly. Add the orange juice, tamari, rice vinegar, agave nectar, and sesame oil to a jar Cover and shake well. Assemble the salad by combining rice, sweet potato, edamame, bell pepper, red cabbage and scallions in a large bowl. Top with dressing and toss to coat. Garnish with cilantro and sesame seeds. Serve and enjoy.

## Lentil Salad

**Ingredients** for 4 servings

2 tbsp olive oil
1 shallot, diced
1 garlic clove, minced
1 carrot, diced
1 cup lentils
1 tbsp dried basil
1 tbsp dried oregano
1 tbsp balsamic vinegar
¼ cup white wine vinegar
Salt to taste
2 cups chopped mustard greens
2 cups torn red leaf lettuce

**Directions** and Total Time: 60 minutes

Saute shallot and garlic in 1 teaspoon of oil in a large pot over medium heat. After 5 minutes, saute carrot until slightly cooked. Three minutes later, combine vegetables with lentils, basil, oregano, balsamic vinegar, and 2 cups of water. Bring the soup to a boil, then reduce the heat. Simmer uncovered for 20 to 30 minutes or until the lentils are soft but not mushy.

Mix together white wine vinegar, olive oil, and salt in a small bowl. Set aside. When the lentils are ready, drain all remaining liquid. Stir in about ¾ of the white wine vinegar dressing and mustard greens. Cook on low for 10 minutes, stirring occasionally. Toss red leaf lettuce with the rest of the dressing. Divide the lettuce among the plates, then spoon over the lentil mixture. Serve warm.

## Easy Sushi Bowl

**Ingredients** for 1 serving

½ cup green beans
¾ cup cooked brown rice
½ cup chopped spinach
¼ cup sliced avocado
¼ cup shredded carrots
¼ cup fresh cilantro, chopped
1 scallion, chopped
¼ nori sheet
1 tbsp tamari
1 tbsp sesame seeds

**Directions** and Total Time: 15 minutes

Steam the green beans. Arrange the beans, rice, spinach, avocado, carrots, cilantro, and scallions in a bowl. Use scissors to cut the nori into small ribbons. Drizzle tamari over the bowl and garnish with nori and sesame seeds.

## Curried Potato Samosas

**Ingredients** for 4 servings

4 small potatoes
1 tsp coconut oil
1 shallot, finely chopped
2 garlic cloves, minced
1 small piece ginger, grated
2 tsp curry powder
Salt and black pepper to taste
2 carrots, grated
¼ cup green peas
¼ cup parsley, chopped

**Directions** and Total Time: 60 minutes

Preheat the oven to 350°F. Poke the potatoes all around with a fork. Wrap each potato with foil and bake for 30 minutes. Add oil to a medium skillet of medium heat. Saute shallot for 5 minutes, then add garlic and ginger for another 3 minutes until all of the ingredients have softened. Stir in curry powder, salt, and pepper. Remove from the heat. When the potatoes are ready, remove the foil and slice it in half. When they are cool enough to handle, scoop out enough flesh while maintaining the stability of the skin. Add the flesh to the shallot mixture and carrots, peas, and parsley. Scoop the mixture back into the potato skins, then transfer to a baking dish. Bake at the same temperature for 10 minutes. Serve.

## Green Salad with Almond Crunch

**Ingredients** for 4 servings

3 tbsp tahini
2 tbsp Dijon mustard
3 tsp maple syrup
1 tbsp lemon juice
Salt to taste
½ cup chopped almonds
6 radishes, finely sliced
1 lb kale, roughly chopped
1 cored green apple, sliced

**Directions** and Total Time: 20 minutes

Preheat the oven to 325°F. Line a baking sheet with parchment paper. In a small bowl, combine 2 tablespoons tahini, mustard, 2 teaspoon maple syrup, lemon juice, and salt until well mixed. Set to the side. In a medium bowl, combine chopped almonds, salt and the rest of the tahini and maple syrup. Spread out the mixture onto the baking sheet and bake for 5 to 7 minutes. When the almond mixture is crunchy and just darker, let cool for 3 minutes. Toss radishes, kale, and apples in a large bowl with the dressing. Sprinkle over almond crunch. Serve.

## Authentic Caesar Salad

**Ingredients** for 4 servings

4 oz shaved Parmesan cheese
½ cup walnuts
3 tbsp olive oil
½ lime, juiced
1 tbsp white miso paste
1 tsp soy sauce
1 tsp Dijon mustard
1 tsp garlic powder
1 tbsp capers, minced
Salt and black pepper to taste
2 heads romaine lettuce, torn
1 cup cherry tomatoes, halved
2 oz whole-wheat croutons

**Directions** and Total Time: 20 minutes

Add walnuts, olive oil, lime juice, miso paste, soy sauce, mustard, garlic powder, capers, salt, pepper, and ½ cup water to a blender jar. Puree for about 2 minutes or until nearly smooth. Toss romaine and half of the dressing in a large bowl. Plate the salad for each portion, then top with tomatoes, Parmesan, and croutons. Have the rest of the dressing on the side. Serve and enjoy.

## Daikon Radish Salad

**Ingredients** for 4 servings

1 peeled daikon radish, grated
1 carrot, shredded
2 tbsp parsley, chopped
1 scallion, chopped
Salt and black pepper to taste
2 tsp white wine vinegar
2 tbsp extra-virgin olive oil
2 tbsp chopped cashews

**Directions** and Total Time: 75 minutes

Whisk the olive oil, vinegar, salt, and pepper in a bowl. Add the daikon radish and carrot and stir to coat. Place covered in the fridge for 1 hour. Serve topped with chopped cashews, parsley and scallion.

## Lebanese-Inspired Tabbouleh

**Ingredients** for 4 servings

1 cup whole-wheat couscous
1 lime, zested and juiced
1 garlic clove, pressed
Salt to taste
1 tbsp olive oil
½ cucumber, diced
1 tomato, diced
1 cup parsley, chopped
¼ cup fresh mint, chopped
2 scallions, finely chopped
4 tbsp pomegranate seeds

**Directions** and Total Time: 20 minutes

Cover couscous in 1 cup boiling water in a medium bowl. Cover the bowl and set to the side. In a large bowl, stir lime zest, lime juice, garlic, salt, and olive oil. Add cucumber, tomato, parsley, mint, and scallions. Toss in the dressing until coated. Fluff the couscous with a fork, then toss into the salad until coated with dressing. Garnish with pomegranate seeds. Serve and enjoy.

## Tijuana-Inspired Salad

**Ingredients** for 4 servings

1 lemon, juiced
2 tbsp olive oil
1 tbsp agave syrup
¼ tsp salt
2 cups cooked quinoa
1 tbsp taco seasoning
2 heads romaine lettuce, torn
1 (15-oz) can black beans
1 cup grape tomatoes, halved
1 cup corn kernels
1 avocado, diced
2 green onions, sliced
12 tortilla chips, crushed

**Directions** and Total Time: 25 minutes

To make the vinaigrette, whisk lemon juice, olive oil, agave syrup, and salt in a small bowl. Set to the side. Combine quinoa and taco seasoning in a medium bowl. Toss lettuce and vinaigrette in a large bowl, then serve among four bowls. Top the lettuce with equal portions of quinoa, beans, tomatoes, corn, avocado, green onions, and crushed tortilla chips. Serve and enjoy.

## Corn & Asparagus Salad

**Ingredients** for 4 servings

2 heads romaine lettuce, halved lengthwise
2 tbsp cottage cheese
1 tsp garlic powder
2 bread slices
1 cup corn kernels
1 lb asparagus, trimmed
16 cherry tomatoes, halved
½ sliced red onion
½ cup Ranch dressing

**Directions** and Total Time: 30 minutes

Preheat air fryer to 400°F. Combine cottage cheese and garlic in a bowl. Spread one side of each bread slice with half of the mixture and place them, spread-side up, in the frying basket. Grill for 2 minutes until toasted. Let cool completely before slicing into croutons. Set aside. Put the corn kernels in a baking dish in the air fryer. Grill for 4 minutes. Slice each asparagus into 3 pieces and Grill in the air fryer for 6-8 minutes until crisp-tender. Set aside. Put the lettuce halves, cut-side up, in the fryer and Grill for 3 minutes until golden brown. Divide the lettuce halves between serving plates and add the croutons, corn, asparagus, tomatoes, and red onion. Sprinkle each with Ranch dressing and serve right away.

## Italian Salad with Roasted Veggies

**Ingredients** for 4 servings

1 ½ cups quartered mushrooms
1 cup cherry tomatoes
1 green onion, thinly sliced
1 tbsp allspice
10 oz green beans, thawed
2 cups fingerling potatoes
½ lb baby spinach
½ cup Italian dressing
¼ cup pepitas

**Directions** and Total Time: 35 minutes

Preheat air fryer to 380°F. Combine mushrooms, tomatoes, green onion, and allspice in a bowl. Set aside. Arrange the green beans on a baking pan, then put in the veggie mixture, and finally top with potatoes. Roast for 25 minutes until the potatoes are tender. Let cool completely before removing to a bowl; toss to combine. Stir in spinach, drizzle with Italian dressing, and scatter with pepitas; toss to combine. Serve right away.

## Tofu-Beet Salad

**Ingredients** for 4 servings

2 tbsp butter
8 oz red beets
2 oz tofu, chopped into bits
½ red onion
1 cup mayonnaise
1 small romaine lettuce, torn
Freshly chopped chives
Salt and black pepper to taste

**Directions** and Total Time: 50 minutes

Put beets in a pot, cover with water, and bring to a boil for 40 minutes. Melt butter in a non-stick pan over medium heat and fry tofu until browned. Set aside to cool. When the bits are ready, drain through a colander and allow cooling. Slip the skin off after and slice them. In a salad bowl, combine the beets, tofu, red onions, lettuce, salt, pepper, and mayonnaise and mix until the vegetables are adequately coated with the mayonnaise. Garnish with chives and serve.

## Arizona-Inspired Bean & Avocado Salad

**Ingredients** for 4 servings

1 head romaine lettuce, torn
1 (15-oz) can pinto beans
1 cup grape tomatoes, halved
1 ½ cups corn kernels
1 avocado, diced
¼ cup chopped fresh cilantro
1 lime, juiced
1 tbsp agave syrup
1 tbsp olive oil
Salt and black pepper to taste

**Directions** and Total Time: 20 minutes

Combine lettuce, beans, tomatoes, corn, avocado, and cilantro in a large bowl. Stir in lime juice, agave syrup, oil, salt, and pepper. Serve and enjoy.

## Kidney Bean Salad

**Ingredients** for 6 servings

1 (15-oz) can kidney beans
1 cucumber, peeled and diced
1 red onion, sliced
4 radishes, diced
Salt and black pepper to taste
3 tbsp extra-virgin olive oil
2 tsp lemon juice

**Directions** and Total Time: 15 minutes

To a large bowl, toss in all the ingredients together. Serve right away or refrigerate before serving.

## Chickpea-Kale Salad Bowls with Pine Nuts

**Ingredients** for 4 servings

2 tbsp green goddess dressing
1 (15-oz) can chickpeas
2 tbsp olive oil, divided
1 tbsp ground coriander
1 tbsp ground cumin
Salt and black pepper to taste
5 oz curly kale, chopped
1 cup thinly sliced cucumber
1 pint grape tomatoes, halved
½ red onion, thinly sliced
½ cup chopped cilantro
¼ cup chopped parsley
¼ cup chopped mint
2 tbsp toasted pine nuts

**Directions** and Total Time: 40 minutes

Preheat the oven to 425°F. Line a baking sheet with parchment paper. Toss chickpeas with 1 ½ tablespoon olive oil, coriander, cumin, salt, and pepper in a medium bowl. Arrange on the baking sheet in a single layer and roast for 20 minutes, tossing halfway through. When the chickpeas are brown and crisp, remove from the oven to cool for 5 minutes. While you are waiting on the chickpeas to cool, add kale and ½ tablespoon olive oil in a large bowl. Massage the oil into the kale for 2 minutes or until soft. Toss in cucumber, tomatoes, red onion, cilantro, parsley, and mint. To serve, portion the salad among 4 plates, then top with roasted chickpeas. Drizzle with dressing and garnish with toasted pine nuts. Serve.

## Spring Lentil Salad

**Ingredients** for 4 servings

2 tbsp olive oil
1 onion, chopped
2 garlic cloves, minced
½ red bell pepper, diced
½ zucchini, julienned
2 celery stalks, thinly sliced
1 tsp dried thyme
1 (15-oz) can lentils
1 tbsp apple cider vinegar
Salt and black pepper to taste
½ tsp red chili flakes
5 oz mixed spring greens

**Directions** and Total Time: 20 minutes

In a medium skillet, heat oil over medium heat. Sauté onions for 3 minutes until softened. Add garlic and stir for 1 minute until aromatic. Stir in bell pepper, zucchini, celery and thyme. Cook for 3 to 5 minutes, stirring occasionally. When the pepper is tender, stir in lentils and vinegar. Season with salt, pepper, and chili flakes. Cook for 2 minutes, stirring occasionally. To serve, fill 4 bowls with greens and top with lentils. Serve warm.

## Honolulu Tofu Bowls

**Ingredients** for 4 servings

1 red onion, sliced
1 red bell pepper, sliced
3 tsp olive oil
1 (14-oz) block tofu, cubed
1 sliced pineapple
1 cup barbecue sauce
5 oz baby spinach
1 cup cooked quinoa
1 avocado, sliced
2 tbsp chopped cilantro
1 tbsp coconut flakes

**Directions** and Total Time: 30 minutes

Preheat the oven to 425°F. Line a baking sheet with parchment paper. In a medium bowl, toss onion and bell pepper with 2 teaspoons olive oil. Arrange the vegetables in a single layer on one side of the baking sheet and the tofu on the other side. Bake for 10 minutes, then toss with a spatula. Bake for another 10 minutes until the tofu is golden. While the tofu is baking, add 1 teaspoon oil in a large skillet over medium heat. Sauté the pineapple slices until it is caramelized and dark brown. Transfer the tofu to a bowl with barbecue sauce and toss until coated. To prepare the bowls, layer spinach, avocado, and quinoa among 4 bowls. Next, add vegetables, tofu, and pineapple. Top with cilantro and coconut flakes.

## Power Green Salad

**Ingredients** for 4 servings

½ cup green goddess dressing
8 asparagus spears, cut into 2-inch pieces
1 head Romaine lettuce
1 celery stick, finely sliced
1 cored green apple, sliced
1 seedless cucumber, sliced
1 zucchini, cut into ribbons
2 scallions, thinly sliced

**Directions** and Total Time: 20 minutes

Boil the asparagus for 1-2 minutes in boiling water, then drain, run under cold water to cool, then drain again. Divide the lettuce leaves between 4 plates. Top each with asparagus, celery, cucumber, zucchini, and apple. Drizzle with dressing and scatter with scallions.

## Kale & Quinoa Salad with Avocado Dressing

**Ingredients** for 4 servings

1 avocado, peeled and pitted
1 tbsp lime juice
½ tsp ground coriander
1 garlic clove, minced
1 scallion, chopped
Salt to taste
¼ cup water
8 kale leaves, chopped
½ cup chopped snap beans
1 cup cherry tomatoes, halved
1 bell pepper, chopped
1 green onion, chopped
2 cups cooked quinoa
1 tbsp hummus

**Directions** and Total Time: 20 minutes

Add the avocado, lime juice, ground coriander, garlic, scallion, salt, and ¼ cup of water in a blender or food processor. Puree until the dressing is smooth. Add water a little bit at a time to thin it out if necessary. Check for seasoning. Prepare the salad by adding the kale, snap beans, cherry tomatoes, bell pepper, green onion, quinoa, and hummus in a large bowl. Toss with dressing until evenly coated. Divide the salad among the plates and garnish with a spoonful of hummus. Serve and enjoy.

## Tricolor Quinoa Salad

**Ingredients** for 6 servings

3 tbsp olive oil
1 lemon, juiced
1 tsp garlic powder
½ tsp dried oregano
1 bunch curly kale, chopped
2 cups cooked tricolor quinoa
1 English cucumber
1 avocado, cubed
1 red bell pepper, diced
½ red onion, thinly sliced
10 sundried tomatoes, diced
½ cup slivered almonds

**Directions** and Total Time: 15 minutes

Whisk oil, lemon juice, garlic powder, and oregano in a small bowl. Pour the dressing over kale in a large bowl and massage until coated and soft. Toss in quinoa, cucumber, avocado, bell pepper, and red onion. Transfer to a serving bowl and top with tomatoes and almonds.

## Kale & Tofu Bowls with Pesto

**Ingredients** for 4 servings

1 (14-oz) block tofu, cubed
1 tbsp olive oil
½ cup sliced red onions
10 oz curly kale, chopped
½ cup shelled cooked edamame
Salt and black pepper to taste
1 cup pesto
2 cups cooked brown rice

**Directions** and Total Time: 30 minutes

Preheat the oven to 425°F. Arrange the tofu in a single layer on a parchment-lined baking sheet and bake for 10 minutes. Flip the tofu and bake for another 10 minutes until golden. In a large skillet, heat oil over medium heat. Sauté onions for 3 minutes until softened. Stir in kale and edamame and sauté for another 3 minutes. Continue stirring until wilted. Add salt and pepper to taste. Add tofu and pesto to a large bowl and toss to coat. Add rice to 4 bowls, then top with the kale mixture. Finish it off with the pesto tofu. Serve warm and enjoy.

## Broccoli & Tempeh Salad with Cranberries

**Ingredients** for 4 servings

3 oz butter
¾ lb tempeh slices, cubed
1 lb broccoli florets
Salt and black pepper to taste
2 oz almonds
½ cup frozen cranberries

**Directions** and Total Time: 15 minutes

In a skillet, melt the butter over medium heat until no longer foaming, and fry the tempeh cubes until brown on all sides. Add the broccoli and stir-fry for 6 minutes. Season with salt and pepper. Turn the heat off. Stir in the almonds and cranberries to warm through. Serve.

## Caramelized Onion & Daikon Salad

**Ingredients** for 4 servings

2 tsp olive oil
1 lb daikon, peeled
2 cups sliced sweet onions
Salt to taste
1 tbsp rice vinegar

**Directions** and Total Time: 50 minutes

Place the daikon in a pot with salted water and cook 25 minutes, until tender. Drain and let cool. In a skillet over low heat, warm olive oil and add the onion. Sauté for 10-15 minutes until caramelized. Sprinkle with salt. Remove to a bowl. Chop the daikon into wedges and add to the onion bowl. Stir in the vinegar. Serve.

## Cherry Millet & Bean Salad

**Ingredients** for 4 servings

¼ cup grapeseed oil
1 cup millet
1 (15.5-oz) can navy beans
1 celery stalk, finely chopped
1 carrot, shredded
3 green onions, minced
8 chopped kalamata olives
½ cup dried cherries
½ cup toasted pecans, chopped
½ cup minced fresh parsley
1 garlic clove, pressed
3 tbsp sherry vinegar

**Directions** and Total Time: 40 minutes

Cook the millet in salted water for 30 minutes. Remove to a bowl. Mix in beans, celery, carrot, green onions, olives, cherries, pecans, and parsley. In another bowl, whisk the garlic, grapeseed oil, vinegar, salt, and pepper until well mixed. Pour over the millet mixture and toss to coat.

## Balsamic Beet-Cucumber Salad

**Ingredients** for 2 servings

1 tsp olive oil
3 beets, peeled and sliced
1 cucumber, sliced
2 cups mixed greens
4 tbsp balsamic dressing
2 tbsp chopped almonds

**Directions** and Total Time: 40 minutes

Preheat oven to 390°F. In a bowl, stir the beets, oil, and salt. Toss to coat. Transfer to a baking dish and roast for 20 minutes, until golden brown. Once the beets are ready, divide between 2 plates and place a cucumber slice on each beet. Top with mixed greens. Pour over the dressing and garnish with almonds to serve.

## Lebanese-Style Salad

**Ingredients** for 4 servings

1 tbsp olive oil
1 cup cooked bulgur
Zest and juice of 1 lemon
1 garlic clove, pressed
Sea salt to taste
½ cucumber, sliced
1 tomato, sliced
1 cup fresh parsley, chopped
¼ cup fresh mint, chopped
2 scallions, chopped
4 tbsp sunflower seeds

**Directions** and Total Time: 25 minutes

In a bowl, mix the lemon juice, lemon zest, garlic, salt, and olive oil. Stir in cucumber, tomato, parsley, mint, and scallions. Toss to coat. Fluff the bulgur and stir it into the cucumber mix. Top with sunflower seeds and serve.

## White Bean Falafel Salad

**Ingredients** for 4 servings

1 (15.5-oz) can white beans
½ sliced red onion
2 tbsp chopped cilantro
2 tbsp lemon juice
1 tsp garlic powder
1 tsp ground cumin
¼ cup chickpea flour
2 cups torn romaine lettuce
1 cup cherry tomatoes, halved
1 peeled cucumber, sliced
¼ cup Italian dressing

**Directions** and Total Time: 30 minutes

Preheat air fryer to 375°F. Using a fork, mash the white beans until smooth. Stir in ¼ cup of red onion, cilantro, lemon juice, garlic, cumin, and chickpea flour until well combined. Make 8 equal patties out of the mixture and Bake for 12 minutes until golden brown, turning once. Let cool slightly. Combine the lettuce, tomatoes, cucumber, and the remaining red onion in a bowl. Add in falafels and drizzle with Italian dressing; toss to combine.

## Picante Chickpea Salad

**Ingredients** for 2 servings

3 tbsp chipotle hot sauce
1 tsp garlic powder
1 (15.5-oz) can chickpeas
12 cherry tomatoes
2 cups torn romaine lettuce
1 cucumber, sliced
3 radishes, sliced
2 celery stalks, chopped
2 scallions, sliced
¼ cup Ranch dressing

**Directions** and Total Time: 20 minutes

Preheat air fryer to 360°F. Whisk chipotle hot sauce and garlic in a bowl. Add in chickpeas and toss to coat. Bake chickpeas and tomatoes, in a single layer, for 8-10 minutes until tomatoes are blistered. In the meantime, combine lettuce, cucumber, celery, radishes, and scallions in a bowl. Drizzle with Ranch dressing and toss to combine. Mix in Baked chickpeas and tomatoes and serve.

## Brussels Sprout & Roasted Chickpea Salad

**Ingredients** for 4 servings

1 lb Brussels sprouts, sliced
1 (15-oz) can chickpeas
2 tbsp olive oil
1 tbsp apple cider vinegar
Salt and black pepper to taste
1/3 cup sunflower seeds
2 tbsp Parmesan cheese

**Directions** and Total Time: 30 minutes

Preheat the oven to 400°F. Prepare a baking sheet by lining it with parchment paper. Toss Brussels sprouts, chickpeas, oil, apple cider vinegar, salt, and pepper in a large bowl. Arrange on the baking sheet in a single layer and roast for 15 minutes. Stir in sunflower seeds and roast for 10 minutes. Top with Parmesan. Serve.

## Mozzarella Salad

**Ingredients** for 2 servings

4 tbsp olive oil
½ yellow bell pepper, diced
3 tomatoes, diced
½ cucumber, chopped
½ red onion, peeled and sliced
½ cup mozzarella, cubed
10 Kalamata olives, pitted
½ tbsp red wine vinegar
2 tsp dried oregano
Salt and black pepper to taste

**Directions** and Total Time: 10 minutes

Pour the bell pepper, tomatoes, cucumber, red onion, mozzarella cheese, and olives into a salad bowl. Drizzle the red wine vinegar and olive oil over the vegetables. Season with salt, black pepper, and oregano, and toss the salad with two spoons. Share the salad into bowls and serve.

## Dilly Green Squash Salad

**Ingredients** for 4 servings

2 tbsp butter
2 lb green squash, cubed
Salt and black pepper to taste
3 oz fennel, sliced
2 oz chopped green onions
1 cup mayonnaise
2 tbsp chives, finely chopped
A pinch of mustard powder
Chopped dill to garnish

**Directions** and Total Time: 20 minutes

Put a pan over medium heat and melt butter. Fry in squash cubes until slightly softened but not browned, about 7 minutes. Allow the squash to cool. In a salad bowl, mix the cooled squash, fennel slices, green onions, mayonnaise, chives, salt, pepper, and mustard powder. Garnish with dill and serve.

## Peanut & Mango Rice Salad with Lime Dressing

**Ingredients** for 4 servings

1/3 cup grapeseed oil
3 ½ cups cooked brown rice
½ cup chopped roasted peanuts
½ cup sliced mango
4 green onions, chopped
3 tbsp fresh lime juice
2 tsp agave nectar
1 tsp grated fresh ginger
Salt and black pepper to taste

**Directions** and Total Time: 15 minutes

In a bowl, mix the rice, peanuts, mango, and green onions. Set aside. In another bowl, whisk the lime juice, agave nectar, and ginger. Add oil, salt, and pepper and stir to combine. Pour over the rice bowl and toss to coat.

## Bean & Ricotta Pasta Salad

**Ingredients** for 4 servings

1 tbsp olive oil
2 ½ cups bow tie pasta
1 medium zucchini, sliced
2 garlic cloves, minced
2 large tomatoes, chopped
1 (15 oz) can cannellini beans
10 can green olives, sliced
½ cup crumbled ricotta cheese

**Directions** and Total Time: 35 minutes

Cook the pasta until al dente, 10 minutes. Drain and set aside. Heat olive oil in a skillet and sauté zucchini and garlic for 4 minutes. Stir in tomatoes, beans, and olives. Cook until the tomatoes soften, 10 minutes. Mix in pasta. Allow warming for 1 minute. Stir in ricotta cheese. Serve.

## Green Bean Salad with Roasted Mushrooms

**Ingredients** for 4 servings

1 lb cremini mushrooms, sliced
3 tbsp melted butter
½ cup green beans
Salt and black pepper to taste
Juice of 1 lemon
4 tbsp toasted hazelnuts

**Directions** and Total Time: 25 minutes

Preheat oven to 450°F. Arrange the mushrooms and green beans in a baking dish, drizzle butter over, and sprinkle with salt and black pepper. Use your hands to rub the vegetables with the seasoning and roast in the oven for 20 minutes or until they are soft. Transfer the vegetables into a salad bowl, drizzle with the lemon juice, and toss the salad with hazelnuts. Serve immediately.

## Dijon Kale Salad

**Ingredients** for 4 servings

2 tbsp olive oil
2 tbsp Dijon mustard
¼ cup fresh orange juice
1 tsp agave nectar
2 tbsp minced fresh parsley
1 tbsp minced green onions
4 cups fresh kale, chopped
1 peeled orange, segmented
½ red onion, sliced paper-thin
Salt and black pepper to taste

**Directions** and Total Time: 10 minutes

In a food processor, place the mustard, oil, orange juice, agave nectar, salt, pepper, parsley, and green onions. Blend until smooth. In a bowl, combine the kale, orange, and onion. Coat the salad with dressing. Serve and enjoy!

## Farro & Bean Salad

**Ingredients** for 4 servings

4 cups watercress and arugula mix
2 tsp olive oil
1 (14-oz) can black beans
1 cup corn kernels
¼ cup fresh cilantro, chopped
Zest and juice of 1 lime
3 tsp chili powder
Salt and black pepper to taste
8 cherry tomatoes, halved
1 red bell pepper, chopped
2 scallions, chopped
4 large whole-grain tortillas
1 tbsp oregano
1 tsp cayenne pepper
¾ cup cooked faro
¼ cup chopped avocado
¼ cup mango salsa

**Directions** and Total Time: 20 minutes

Combine black beans, corn, cilantro, lime juice, lime zest, chili powder, salt, pepper, cherry tomatoes, bell peppers, and scallions in a bowl. Set aside. Brush the tortillas with olive oil and season with salt, pepper, oregano, and cayenne pepper. Slice into 8 pieces. Line with parchment paper a baking sheet. Arrange tortilla pieces and bake for 3-5 minutes until browned. On a serving platter, put the watercress and arugula mix, top with faro, bean mixture, avocado, and sprinkle with mango salsa all over to serve.

## Carrot Salad

**Ingredients** for 4 servings

¼ cup olive oil
1 lb carrots, shredded
2 oranges, chopped
½ cup roasted walnuts
¼ cup chopped fresh parsley
2 tbsp fresh orange juice
2 tbsp fresh lime juice
2 tsp pure date sugar
Salt and black pepper to taste

**Directions** and Total Time: 15 minutes

In a bowl, mix the carrots, oranges, walnuts, and parsley. Set aside. In another bowl, whisk the orange juice, lime juice, sugar, salt, pepper, and oil. Mix until blended. Pour over the carrot mixture and toss to coat. Serve and enjoy!

## Couscous & Bean Salad

**Ingredients** for 4 servings

¼ cup olive oil
1 shallot, minced
½ tsp ground coriander
½ tsp turmeric
¼ tsp ground cayenne
1 cup couscous
2 cups vegetable broth
1 yellow bell pepper, chopped
1 carrot, shredded
½ cup chopped dried apricots
¼ cup golden raisins
¼ cup chopped roasted cashews
1 (15.5-oz) can white beans
2 tbsp minced cilantro leaves
2 tbsp fresh lemon juice

**Directions** and Total Time: 15 minutes

Heat 1 tbsp of oil in a pot over medium heat. Place in shallot, coriander, turmeric, cayenne pepper, and couscous. Cook for 2 minutes, stirring often. Add in broth and salt. Bring to a boil. Turn the heat off and let sit covered for 5 minutes. Remove to a bowl and stir in bell pepper, carrot, apricots, raisins, cashews, beans, and cilantro. Set aside. In another bowl, whisk the remaining oil with lemon juice until blended. Pour over the salad and toss to combine. Serve immediately.

## Spinach Salad a la Puttanesca with Seitan

**Ingredients** for 4 servings

3 cups baby spinach, cut into strips
4 tbsp olive oil
8 oz seitan, cut into strips
2 garlic cloves, minced
½ cup Kalamata olives, halved
½ cup green olives, halved
2 tbsp capers
10 cherry tomatoes, halved
2 tbsp balsamic vinegar
2 tbsp torn fresh basil leaves
2 tbsp minced fresh parsley
1 cup pomegranate seeds

**Directions** and Total Time: 15 minutes

Heat half of the olive oil in a skillet over medium heat. Place the seitan and brown for 5 minutes on all sides. Add in garlic and cook for 30 seconds. Remove to a bowl and let cool. Stir in olives, capers, spinach, and tomatoes. Set aside. In another bowl, whisk the remaining oil, vinegar, salt, and pepper until well mixed. Pour this dressing over the seitan salad and toss to coat. Top with basil, parsley, and pomegranate seeds. Serve and enjoy!

## Quinoa & Tomato Salad with Sweet Onions

**Ingredients** for 4 servings

2 tbsp extra-virgin olive oil
1 ½ cups dry quinoa, drained
2 ¼ cups water
1/3 cup white wine vinegar
1 tbsp chopped fresh dill
Salt and black pepper to taste
2 cups sliced sweet onions
2 tomatoes, sliced
4 cups shredded lettuce

**Directions** and Total Time: 25 minutes

Place the quinoa in a pot with salted water. Bring to a boil. Lower the heat and simmer covered for 15 minutes. Turn the heat off and let sit for 5 minutes. Using a fork, fluff the quinoa and set aside. In a small bowl, whisk the vinegar, olive oil, dill, salt, and pepper; set aside. In a serving plate, combine onions, tomatoes, quinoa, and lettuce. Pour in the dressing and toss to coat. Serve.

## Red Cabbage & Chickpea Salad with Avocado

**Ingredients** for 4 servings

1 yellow bell pepper, cut into sticks
¼ cup olive oil
1 carrot, shredded
1 cup shredded red cabbage
1 cup cherry tomatoes, halved
1 (15.5-oz) can chickpeas
¼ cup capers
1 avocado, sliced
1 ½ tbsp fresh lemon juice
Salt and black pepper to taste

**Directions** and Total Time: 15 minutes

Combine carrot, cabbage, tomatoes, bell pepper, chickpeas, capers, and avocado in a bowl. In another bowl, mix oil, lemon juice, salt, and pepper until thoroughly combined. Pour over the cabbage mixture and toss to coat.

## Spinach-Zucchini Salad

**Ingredients** for 2 servings

1 lemon, half zested and juiced, half cut into wedges
1 tsp olive oil
1 zucchini, chopped
½ tsp ground cumin
½ tsp ground ginger
¼ tsp turmeric
¼ tsp ground nutmeg
A pinch of salt
2 tbsp capers
1 tbsp chopped green olives
1 garlic clove, pressed
2 tbsp fresh mint, chopped
2 cups spinach, chopped

**Directions** and Total Time: 20 minutes

Warm olive oil in a skillet over medium heat. Place the zucchini and sauté for 10 minutes. Stir in cumin, ginger, turmeric, nutmeg, and salt. Pour in lemon zest, lemon juice, capers, garlic, and mint, cook for 2 minutes. Divide the spinach between serving plates and top with the zucchini mixture. Garnish with lemon wedges and olives.

## Hot Brussel Sprout Salad with Seeds & Pecans

**Ingredients** for 4 servings

½ cup olive oil
1 tbsp butter
1 lb Brussels sprouts, grated
1 lemon, juiced and zested
1 tsp chili paste
2 oz pecans
1 oz pumpkin seeds
1 oz sunflower seeds
½ tsp cumin powder

**Directions** and Total Time: 20 minutes

Put Brussels sprouts in a salad bowl. In a small bowl, mix lemon juice, zest, olive oil, salt, and pepper, and drizzle the dressing over the Brussels sprouts. Toss and allow the vegetable to marinate for 10 minutes. Melt butter in a pan. Stir in chili paste and toss the pecans, pumpkin seeds, sunflower seeds, cumin powder, and salt in the chili butter. Sauté on low heat for 3-4 minutes just to heat the nuts. Allow cooling. Pour the nuts and seeds mix in the salad bowl, toss, and serve.

## Mustardy Collard & Tofu Salad

**Ingredients** for 2 servings

2 tbsp coconut oil
2 oz butter
¾ cup heavy cream
2 tbsp mayonnaise
A pinch of mustard powder
1 garlic clove, minced
Salt and black pepper to taste
1 cup collards, rinsed
4 oz tofu cheese

**Directions** and Total Time: 10 minutes

In a small bowl, whisk the heavy whipping cream, mayonnaise, mustard powder, coconut oil, garlic, salt, and black pepper until well mixed; set aside. Melt the butter in a large skillet over medium heat and sauté the collards until wilted and brownish. Season with salt and black pepper to taste. Transfer the collards to a salad bowl and pour the creamy dressing over. Mix the salad well and crumble the tofu cheese over. Serve.

## Herby Lentil Salad

**Ingredients** for 4 servings

2 tsp olive oil
1 red onion, diced
1 garlic clove, minced
1 carrot, diced
1 cup lentils
1 tbsp dried basil
1 tbsp dried oregano
1 tbsp balsamic vinegar
2 cups water
Sea salt to taste
2 cups chopped Swiss chard
2 cups torn curly endive

**Directions** and Total Time: 40 minutes

In a bowl, mix the balsamic vinegar, olive oil, and salt. Set aside. Warm 1 tsp of oil in a pot over medium heat. Place the onion, garlic, and carrot and cook for 5 minutes. Mix in lentils, basil, oregano, balsamic vinegar, and water and bring to a boil. Lower the heat and simmer for 20 minutes. Mix in two-thirds of the dressing. Add in the Swiss chard and cook for 5 minutes on low. Let cool. Coat the endive with the remaining dressing. Transfer to a plate and top with lentil mixture to serve.

## Summer Avocado Salad

**Ingredients** for 4 servings

1/3 cup olive oil
1 garlic clove, chopped
1 red onion, sliced
½ tsp dried basil
Salt and black pepper to taste
¼ tsp pure date sugar
3 tbsp white wine vinegar
1 head Iceberg lettuce, torn
12 ripe grape tomatoes, halved
½ cup frozen peas, thawed
8 black olives, pitted
1 avocado, sliced

**Directions** and Total Time: 15 minutes

In a food processor, place the garlic, onion, oil, basil, salt, pepper, sugar, and vinegar. Blend until smooth. Set aside. Place the lettuce, tomatoes, peas, and olives on a nice serving plate. Top with avocado slices and drizzle the previously prepared dressing all over. Serve.

## Chickpea & Corn Salad

**Ingredients** for 4 servings

¼ cup olive oil
1 cup corn kernels
1 (15.5-oz) can chickpeas
1 celery stalk, sliced
2 green onions, minced
2 tbsp chopped fresh cilantro
2 tbsp white wine vinegar
½ tsp ground cumin
Salt and black pepper to taste

**Directions** and Total Time: 10 minutes

Combine corn, chickpeas, celery, green onions, and cilantro in a bowl. In another bowl, mix the oil, vinegar, cumin, salt, and pepper. Pour over the salad and toss to coat.

## Potato & Green Bean Salad

**Ingredients** for 4 servings

1 tbsp extra-virgin olive oil
Salt and black pepper to taste
1 cup green beans, chopped
4 potatoes, quartered
2 carrots, sliced
1 tbsp lime juice
2 tsp dried dill
1 cup cashew cream

**Directions** and Total Time: 25 minutes

Pour salted water in a pot over medium heat. Add in potatoes, bring to a boil and cook for 8 minutes. Put in carrots and green beans and cook for 8 minutes. Drain and put in a bowl. Mix in olive oil, lime juice, dill, cashew cream, salt, and pepper. Toss to coat. Serve cooled.

## Asian Green Bean & Potato Salad

**Ingredients** for 4 servings

1 tbsp grapeseed oil
1/3 cup butter
1 ½ lb baby potatoes, unpeeled
1 cup green beans
½ cup shredded carrots
4 green onions, chopped
1 garlic clove, minced
½ tsp Asian chili paste
2 tbsp soy sauce
1 tbsp rice vinegar
¾ cup milk
3 tbsp chopped roasted peanuts

**Directions** and Total Time: 30 minutes

Place the potatoes in a pot with boiling salted water and cook for 20 minutes. Drain and let cool. Chop into chunks and place in a bowl. Stir in green beans, carrots, and green onions. Set aside.

Heat oil in a pot over medium heat. Place in garlic and cook for 30 seconds. Add butter, chili, soy sauce, vinegar, and milk. Cook for 5 minutes, stirring often. Pour over the potatoes and toss to coat. Garnish with peanuts.

## Southern Bean Salad

**Ingredients** for 4 servings

¼ cup salad dressing
1 tsp chili powder
2 (14.5-oz) cans kidney beans
2 cups frozen corn, thawed
1 cup cooked pearl barley
1 head torn Iceberg lettuce

**Directions** and Total Time: 15 minutes

Mix the salad dressing and chili powder in a bowl. Add in kidney beans, corn, barley, and lettuce. Serve.

## Green Bulgur Salad

**Ingredients** for 4 servings

1 avocado, peeled and pitted
1 tbsp fresh lemon juice
1 tbsp fresh dill
1 small garlic clove, pressed
1 scallion, chopped
Sea salt to taste
8 large kale leaves, chopped
½ cup chopped green beans
1 cup cherry tomatoes, halved
1 bell pepper, chopped
2 scallions, chopped
2 cups cooked bulgur

**Directions** and Total Time: 30 minutes

In a food processor, place the avocado, lemon juice, dill, garlic, scallion, salt, and ¼ cup water. Blend until smooth. Set aside the dressing. Put kale, green beans, cherry tomatoes, bell pepper, scallions, and bulgur in a serving bowl. Add in the dressing and toss to coat. Serve.

## Broccoli Rice Salad with Mango & Almonds

**Ingredients** for 4 servings

3 cups broccoli florets, blanched
1/3 cup roasted almonds, chopped
3 tbsp grapeseed oil
½ cup brown rice, rinsed
1 mango, chopped
1 small red bell pepper, diced
1 jalapeño, seeded and minced
1 tsp grated fresh ginger
2 tbsp fresh lemon juice

**Directions** and Total Time: 25 minutes

Place the rice in a bowl with salted water and cook for 18-20 minutes. Remove to a bowl. Stir in broccoli, mango, bell pepper, and chili. In another bowl, mix the ginger, lemon juice, and oil. Pour over the rice and toss to combine. Top with almonds to serve.

## Italian Chickpea & Pasta Salad

**Ingredients** for 4 servings

½ cup olive oil
8 oz whole-wheat pasta
1 (15.5-oz) can chickpeas
½ cup pitted black olives
10 minced sun-dried tomatoes
1(6-oz) jar dill pickles, sliced
2 roasted red peppers, diced
½ cup frozen peas, thawed
1 tbsp capers
3 tsp dried chives
¼ cup white wine vinegar
½ tsp dried basil
1 garlic clove, minced
Salt and black pepper to taste

**Directions** and Total Time: 15 minutes

Cook the pasta in salted water for 8-10 minutes until al dente. Drain and remove to a bowl. Stir in chickpeas, olives, tomatoes, dill pickles, roasted peppers, peas, capers, and chives. In another bowl, whisk oil, vinegar, basil, garlic, sugar, salt, and pepper. Pour over the pasta and toss to coat. Serve and enjoy!

## Radish Slaw with Tomatoes

**Ingredients** for 4 servings

¼ cup olive oil
2 tomatoes, sliced
6 small red radishes, sliced
2 ½ tbsp white wine vinegar
½ tsp chopped chervil
Salt and black pepper to taste

**Directions** and Total Time: 15 minutes

Mix tomatoes and radishes in a bowl. Set aside. In another bowl, whisk the vinegar,olive oil, chervil, salt, and pepper until mixed. Pour over the salad and toss to coat.

## Veggie & Quinoa Salad

**Ingredients** for 4 servings

¼ cup olive oil
2 cups cooked quinoa
½ red onion, diced
1 red bell pepper, diced
1 orange bell pepper, diced
1 carrot, diced
2 tbsp rice vinegar
1 tbsp soy sauce
1 garlic clove, minced
1 tbsp grated fresh ginger
Salt and black pepper to taste

**Directions** and Total Time: 15 minutes

Combine the quinoa, onion, bell peppers, and carrots in a bowl. In another bowl, mix the olive oil, rice vinegar, soy sauce, garlic, ginger, salt, and pepper. Pour over the quinoa and toss to coat. Serve and enjoy!

## Cannellini Bean & Veggie Salad

**Ingredients** for 2 servings

1 tbsp olive oil
2 tbsp balsamic vinegar
1 tsp minced fresh chives
1 garlic clove, minced
1 tbsp fresh rosemary, minced
1 tbsp fresh oregano, chopped
A pinch of salt
1 (14-oz) can cannellini beans
1 green bell pepper, sliced
1 zucchini, diced
2 carrots, diced
2 tbsp fresh basil, chopped

**Directions** and Total Time: 40 minutes

In a bowl, mix the olive oil, balsamic vinegar, chives, garlic, rosemary, oregano, and salt. Stir in the beans, bell pepper, zucchini, carrots, and basil. Serve.

## Raisin & Cashew Coleslaw with Haricots Verts

**Ingredients** for 4 servings

1/3 cup creamy butter
3 cups haricots verts, chopped
2 carrots, sliced
3 cups shredded cabbage
1/3 cup golden raisins
¼ cup roasted cashew
1 garlic clove, minced
1 medium shallot, chopped
1 ½ tsp grated fresh ginger
2 tbsp soy sauce
2 tbsp fresh lemon juice
Salt to taste
⅛ tsp ground cayenne
¾ cup milk

**Directions** and Total Time: 15 minutes

Place the haricots verts, carrots, and cabbage in a pot with water and steam for 5 minutes. Drain and transfer to a bowl. Add in raisins and cashew. Let cool. In a food processor, put the garlic, shallot, and ginger. Pulse until puréed. Add in butter, soy sauce, lemon juice, salt, and cayenne pepper. Blitz until smooth. Stir in milk. Sprinkle the salad with the dressing and toss to coat.

## Savory Green Salad

**Ingredients** for 4 servings

¼ cup extra-virgin olive oil
1 large grapefruit
2 cups coleslaw mix
2 cups green leaf lettuce, torn
2 cups baby spinach
1 bunch watercress
6 radishes, sliced
Juice of 1 lemon
2 tsp date syrup
1 tsp white wine vinegar
Sea salt and black pepper

**Directions** and Total Time: 10 minutes

Slice the grapefruit by cutting the ends, peeling all the white pith, and making an incise in the membrane to take out each segment. Transfer to a bowl. Stir in coleslaw, lettuce, spinach, watercress, and radishes. In a bowl, mix the lemon juice, date syrup, vinegar, salt, and pepper. Gently beat the olive oil until emulsified. Pour over the salad and toss to coat.

## Potato Salad with Artichokes & Corn

**Ingredients** for 4 servings

1 (10-oz) package frozen artichoke hearts, cooked
1/3 cup olive oil
1 ½ lb potatoes, chopped
2 cups halved cherry tomatoes
½ cup sweet corn
3 green onions, minced
1 tbsp minced fresh parsley
2 tbsp fresh lemon juice
1 garlic clove, minced
Salt and black pepper to taste

**Directions** and Total Time: 30 minutes + cooling time

Place the potatoes in a pot with salted water and boil for 15 minutes. Drain and remove to a bowl. Cut the artichokes by quarts and mix into the potato bowl. Stir in tomatoes, corn, green onions, and parsley. Set aside. Whisk the oil, lemon juice, garlic, salt, and pepper in a bowl. Pour over the potatoes and toss to coat. Let sit for 20 minutes. Serve and enjoy!

## Tomato & Cucumber Salad with Lentils

**Ingredients** for 4 servings

¾ cup olive oil
¼ cup white wine vinegar
2 tsp Dijon mustard
1 garlic clove
1 tbsp minced green onions
½ head romaine lettuce, torn
½ head iceberg lettuce, torn
1 (15.5-oz) can lentils, drained
2 ripe tomatoes, chopped
1 peeled cucumber, chopped
1 carrot, chopped
8 halved pitted kalamata olives
3 small red radishes, chopped
2 tbsp chopped fresh parsley
1 ripe avocado, chopped

**Directions** and Total Time: 15 minutes

Put the oil, vinegar, mustard, garlic, green onions, salt, and pepper in a food processor. Pulse until blended. Set aside. In a bowl, place the lettuces, lentils, tomatoes, cucumber, carrot, olives, radishes, parsley, and avocado. Pour enough dressing over the salad and toss to coat.

## Philippino Salad

**Ingredients** for 4 servings

2 cups snow peas, sliced and blanched
¼ cup olive oil
½ tsp minced garlic
½ tsp grated fresh ginger
¼ tsp crushed red pepper
3 tbsp rice vinegar
1 tbsp soy sauce
3 papaya, chopped
1 large carrot, shredded
1 cucumber, peeled and sliced
3 cups torn romaine lettuce
½ cup chopped roasted almonds
Salt to taste

**Directions** and Total Time: 15 minutes

Combine the garlic, ginger, olive oil, red pepper, vinegar, 3 tbsp of water, salt, and soy sauce in a bowl. Set aside. In another bowl, add papaya, snow peas, cucumber slices, and carrot. Drizzle with the dressing and toss to coat. Place a bed of lettuce on a plate and top with the salad. Serve topped with almonds.

## Sesame Cabbage Salad

**Ingredients** for 6 servings

2 tbsp toasted sesame oil
4 cups shredded red cabbage
2 cups sliced napa cabbage
1 cup red radishes, sliced
¼ cup fresh orange juice
2 tbsp Chinese black vinegar
1 tbsp soy sauce
1 tsp grated fresh ginger
1 tbsp black sesame seeds

**Directions** and Total Time: 15 minutes

Mix the red cabbage, napa cabbage, and radishes in a bowl. In another bowl, whisk the orange juice, vinegar, soy sauce, sesame oil, and ginger. Pour over the slaw and toss to coat. Marinate covered in the fridge for 2 hours. Serve topped with sesame seeds.

## Holiday Potato Salad

**Ingredients** for 4 servings

½ cup olive oil
1 ½ lb potatoes, chopped
4 portobello mushrooms, sliced
2 green onions, chopped
1 tbsp whole-wheat flour
2 tbsp pure date sugar
1/3 cup white wine vinegar
Salt and black pepper to taste

**Directions** and Total Time: 15 minutes

Place the potatoes in a pot with boiling salted water and cook for 20 minutes. Drain and remove to a bowl. Heat oil in a skillet over medium heat. Place the mushrooms and sauté for 5 minutes. Add the mushrooms to the potatoes. To the skillet, add in green onions and cook for 1 minute. Mix in flour, sugar, vinegar, ¼ cup of water, salt, and pepper. Bring to a boil and cook until creamy. Pour the resulting sauce over the potatoes and mushrooms and toss to coat. Serve immediately.

## Celery & Chickpea Salad

**Ingredients** for 4 servings

1 (15.5-oz) can chickpeas
1 head fennel bulb, sliced
½ cup sliced red onion
½ cup celery leaves, chopped
¼ cup mayonnaise
Salt and black pepper to taste

**Directions** and Total Time: 5 minutes

In a bowl, mash the chickpeas until chunky. Stir in fennel bulb, onion, celery, mayonnaise, salt, and pepper.

## Watercress & Eggplant Salad

**Ingredients** for 2 servings

1 lemon, half zested and juiced, half cut into wedges
1 tsp olive oil
1 eggplant, chopped
½ tsp ground cumin
½ tsp ground ginger
¼ tsp turmeric
¼ tsp ground nutmeg
Sea salt to taste
2 tbsp capers
1 tbsp chopped green olives
1 garlic clove, pressed
2 tbsp fresh mint, chopped
2 cups watercress, chopped

**Directions** and Total Time: 45 minutes

In a skillet over medium heat, warm the oil. Place the eggplant and cook for 5 minutes. Add in cumin, ginger, turmeric, nutmeg, and salt. Cook for another 10 minutes. Stir in lemon zest, lemon juice, capers, olives, garlic, and mint. Cook for 1-2 minutes more. Place some watercress on each plate and top with the eggplant mixture. Serve.

## Celery & Carrot Salad with Potatoes

**Ingredients** for 4 servings

6 potatoes, chopped
2 carrots, chopped
Salt to taste
½ cup tahini dressing
1 tsp dried dill
1 tsp Dijon mustard
4 celery stalks, chopped
2 scallions, chopped

**Directions** and Total Time: 25 minutes

Place the potatoes and carrots in a pot with salted water. Bring to a boil and cook for 20 minutes. Drain and let cool. In a bowl, mix the dressing, dill, and mustard. Toss with celery and scallions. Stir in carrots and potatoes.

## Cabbage Coleslaw with Radicchio

**Ingredients** for 2 servings

½ head white cabbage, shredded
¼ head radicchio, shredded
1 large carrot, shredded
¾ cup mayonnaise
¼ cup soy milk
1 tbsp cider vinegar
½ tsp dry mustard
¼ tsp celery seeds
Salt and black pepper to taste

**Directions** and Total Time: 10 minutes

Combine cabbage, radicchio, and carrot in a bowl. In another bowl, whisk mayonnaise, soy milk, mustard, vinegar, celery seeds, salt, and pepper. Pour over the slaw and toss to coat. Serve immediately.

## Simple Avocado Salad

**Ingredients** for 4 servings

3 tbsp sesame oil
2 medium avocados, sliced
2 tbsp soy sauce
1 tbsp mirin
2 tsp rice vinegar
2 tbsp toasted sesame seeds

**Directions** and Total Time: 15 minutes

Place the avocado in a bowl. Set aside. In another bowl, mix the oil, soy sauce, mirin, and vinegar. Pour over the avocado and toss to coat. Let sit for 10 minutes. Serve in bowls topped with sesame seeds.

## Jalapeño Veggie Relish

**Ingredients** for 6 servings

¼ cup sliced pimiento-stuffed green olives
1/3 cup olive oil
1 carrot, sliced
1 red bell pepper, sliced
1 cup cauliflower florets
2 celery stalks, chopped
½ cup chopped red onion
1 garlic clove, minced
1 jalapeño pepper, chopped
3 tbsp white wine vinegar

**Directions** and Total Time: 15 minutes

Combine the carrot, bell pepper, cauliflower, celery, and onion in a bowl. Add in salt and cold water. Cover and transfer to the fridge for 4-6 hours. Strain and wash the veggies. Remove to a bowl and mix in olives. Set aside. In another bowl, mix the garlic, jalapeño pepper, vinegar, and oil. Pour over the veggies and toss to coat. Let chill in the fridge and serve.

## Greek Olive & Potato Salad

**Ingredients** for 4 servings

¼ cup olive oil
4 potatoes, chopped
Salt and black pepper to taste
2 tbsp apple cider vinegar
2 tbsp lemon juice
1 tsp dried dill
½ cucumber, chopped
¼ red onion, diced
6 chopped kalamata olives

**Directions** and Total Time: 30 minutes

In a pot with salted water, place the potatoes. Bring to a boil and cook for 20 minutes. Drain and let cool. Mix the olive oil, vinegar, lemon juice, and dill in a bowl. Add in cucumber, red onion, and olives. Toss to coat. Stir in the potatoes. Season with salt and pepper. Serve.

# SOUPS & STEWS

## Bean & Carrot Soup

**Ingredients** for 4 servings

1 tsp olive oil
1 cup chopped onion
2 garlic cloves, minced
1 celery stalk, chopped
1 tbsp minced fresh ginger
4 carrots, peeled and chopped
1 cup cooked cannellini beans
2 cups vegetable broth
Salt and black pepper to taste
2 tbsp parsley, chopped

**Directions** and Total Time: 35 minutes

Saute olive oil, onion, garlic, celery and ginger in a large pot for 2-3 minutes. Add carrots and cook for about 3 minutes. Stir in beans, broth, 2 cups water, salt, and pepper. Reduce the heat and simmer for 20 minutes. Use an immersion blender or a regular blender to puree the soup. Ladle into bowls and garnish with parsley. Serve.

## Creamy Coconut Green Soup

**Ingredients** for 4 servings

1 tsp coconut oil
2 green onions, diced
2 cups frozen peas
4 cups vegetable stock
1 cup watercress, chopped
1 cup baby spinach
1 tbsp fresh mint, chopped
Salt and black pepper to taste
¾ cup milk
2 tbsp cilantro, chopped

**Directions** and Total Time: 20 minutes

Add coconut oil to a large pot over medium heat. When the oil is melted, add green onions and saute for 5 minutes. Stir in peas and stock. When the stock starts to boil, reduce the heat and stir in watercress, baby spinach, mint, salt, and pepper. Simmer covered for 5 minutes. Stir in milk. Use an immersion blender or a regular blender to puree the soup. Ladle into bowls and garnish with cilantro. Serve warm and enjoy.

## Split Pea & Tomato Soup

**Ingredients** for 6 servings

¼ cup white wine
1 onion, chopped
2 garlic cloves, minced
1 cup split peas
2 bay leaves
1 tbsp dried thyme
1 tbsp dried oregano
4 cups vegetable stock
1 large carrot, chopped
1 tbsp tamari
Salt and black pepper to taste
8 sun-dried tomatoes, diced
8 grape tomatoes, chopped
2 tbsp chopped chives

**Directions** and Total Time: 80 minutes

Saute wine, onion, and garlic in a large pot over medium heat. Stir occasionally for 5 minutes. Next, mix in peas, bay leaves, thyme, and oregano. Add stock and bring the soup to a boil. Reduce the heat and cover the pot. Cook for 40-50 minutes. Next, stir in the carrot and cook for another 15 minutes. When the carrot and the peas have softened, remove the bay leaves and transfer the soup to the blender jar. Puree the soup in batches if needed. Return the soup to the pot and mix in tamari, salt, pepper, and sun-dried tomatoes. Ladle the soup into bowls and garnish with grape tomatoes and chives. Serve warm.

## Garden Green Soup

**Ingredients** for 4 servings

4 tbsp butter
1 cup fresh spinach, chopped
1 cup fresh kale, chopped
1 large avocado
2 cups heavy cream
3 cups vegetable broth
3 tbsp minced mint leaves
Salt and black pepper to taste
Juice from 1 lime
1 cup collard greens, chopped
2 garlic cloves, minced
1 tsp green cardamom powder

**Directions** and Total Time: 20 minutes

Melt 2 tbsp of butter in a saucepan over medium heat and sauté spinach and kale for 5 minutes. Turn the heat off. Add the avocado, heavy cream, broth, salt, and pepper. Puree the ingredients with an immersion blender until smooth. Pour in the lime juice and set aside.

Melt the remaining butter in a pan and add the collard greens, garlic, and cardamom; sauté until the garlic is fragrant and has achieved a golden brown color, about 4 minutes. Fetch the soup into serving bowls and garnish with fried collards and mint. Serve warm.

## Twisted Goulash Soup

**Ingredients** for 4 servings

½ tbsp crushed cardamom seeds
3 tbsp butter
1 ½ cups feta, crumbled
1 white onion
2 garlic cloves
8 oz diced butternut squash
1 red bell pepper
1 tbsp paprika powder
¼ tsp red chili flakes
1 tbsp dried basil
Salt and black pepper to taste
1 ½ cups diced tomatoes
4 cups vegetable broth
1 ½ tsp red wine vinegar
2 tbsp chopped cilantro

**Directions** and Total Time: 25 minutes

Melt the butter in a pot over medium heat and sauté onion and garlic for 3 minutes. Stir in feta and cook for 3 minutes; add the butternut squash, bell pepper, paprika, red chili flakes, basil, cardamom seeds, salt, and pepper. Cook for 2 minutes. Pour in tomatoes and vegetable broth. Bring to a boil, reduce the heat and simmer for 10 minutes. Mix in red wine vinegar. Garnish with cilantro.

## Creamy Broccoli Soup

**Ingredients** for 4 servings

3 oz butter
1 fennel bulb, chopped
10 oz broccoli, cut into florets
3 cups vegetable stock
Salt and black pepper to taste
1 garlic clove
1 cup cream cheese
½ cup chopped fresh oregano

**Directions** and Total Time: 25 minutes

Put the fennel and broccoli into a pot, and cover with the vegetable stock. Bring the ingredients to a boil over medium heat until the vegetables are soft, about 10 minutes. Season the liquid with salt and black pepper, and drop in the garlic. Simmer the soup for 5 to 7 minutes and turn the heat off. Pour the cream cheese, butter, and oregano into the soup; puree the ingredients with an immersion blender until completely smooth. Adjust the taste with salt and pepper. Serve.

## Vegan Chili Sin Carne

**Ingredients** for 4 servings

1 onion, diced
2 garlic cloves, minced
2 tbsp olive oil
1 (28-oz) can tomatoes
1 tbsp tomato paste
1 (14-oz) can kidney beans
2 tbsp canned sweet corn
2 tsp chipotle chili powder
½ tsp ground cumin
Salt to taste
2 tbsp fresh cilantro, chopped

**Directions** and Total Time: 30 minutes

Heat oil in a large pot, then saute onion and garlic for 5 minutes. Next, stir in tomatoes, tomato paste, beans, chipotle powder, sweet corn, cumin, chipotle chili powder, and salt. Simmer for a minimum of 10 minutes. Ladle into bowls and garnish with cilantro. Serve warm.

## Crockpot Zuppa Toscana

**Ingredients** for 4 servings

1 cup cannellini beans, soaked
1 shallot, chopped
3 garlic cloves, minced
2 carrots, sliced
2 celery stalks, thinly sliced
6 cups vegetable broth
3 fresh rosemary sprigs
2 bay leaves
Salt and black pepper to taste
¼ tsp red pepper flakes
1 (14-oz) can diced tomatoes
10 oz spinach, chopped

**Directions** and Total Time: 8 hours 10 minutes

In a crockpot, add beans, shallot, garlic, carrots, celery, broth, rosemary, and bay leaves. Stir, cover, and cook on low for 8 hours. Remove the cover and add salt, black pepper, red pepper flakes, and tomatoes with juice. Stir, cover, and cook on high for 30 minutes. Remove the bay leaves and rosemary sprigs. Stir in spinach, cover, and let sit for 5 minutes. When it is wilted, ladle the soup into bowls. Serve warm and enjoy.

## Halloween Soup

**Ingredients** for 4 servings

2 lb pumpkin, peeled, seeded, and cubed
1 peeled potato, cubed
1 onion, chopped
3 garlic cloves, minced
4 cups vegetable broth
½ lemon, juiced
2 tbsp maple syrup
½ tsp ground nutmeg
Salt and black pepper to taste

**Directions** and Total Time: 30 minutes

Add pumpkin, potato, onion, garlic, and broth in a large pot over medium heat. Stir and cover. When it comes to a boil, reduce the heat and stir again. Cook for 15 minutes until the pumpkin is fork-tender. Add the rest of the ingredients and stir. Transfer the soup to a blender or use an immersion blender to puree until smooth. Serve.

## Thai-Spiced Coconut Soup

**Ingredients** for 4 servings

1 ½ cups vegetable broth
2 garlic cloves, minced
1 tbsp minced fresh ginger
1 celery stick, chopped
1 cup Bella mushrooms, sliced
1 (15-oz) can coconut milk
1 lemon, juiced
2 tbsp chopped Thai basil
½ tsp Thai green curry paste
1 tbsp chopped cilantro

**Directions** and Total Time: 15 minutes

In a large pot, heat ½ cup broth over medium heat. Sauté garlic and ginger for 1 minute until aromatic. Stir in celery, mushrooms, and the rest of the broth. Let it come to a boil, then reduce to low. Stir in coconut milk, lemon juice, basil, curry paste, and cilantro. Simmer for 5 minutes to heat through. Serve warm and enjoy.

## Butternut Squash Massaman Curry

**Ingredients** for 4 servings

1 ½ lb butternut squash, peeled, seeded, and cubed
1 tbsp olive oil
1 onion, chopped
1 green bell pepper, chopped
1 (15-oz) can coconut milk
4 tsp massaman curry paste
Salt to taste
½ lemon, juiced
2 tbsp chopped cilantro
4 cups cooked brown rice

**Directions** and Total Time: 30 minutes

In a large skillet, heat oil over medium heat. Sauté onion and bell pepper for 5 minutes until softened. Stir in squash, coconut milk, and curry paste. Bring to a boil, then reduce the heat to low. Simmer and cover. Cook for 10 minutes until the squash is fork-tender. Stir in salt and lime juice. Adjust the seasoning and heat with salt and curry paste as needed. Add rice to 4 plates and spoon the curry over the rice. Garnish with cilantro. Serve warm.

## Effortless Green Gazpacho

**Ingredients** for 4 servings

1 peeled avocado, cubed
2 peeled cucumbers, diced
2 tbsp chopped cilantro
1 lime, juiced
Salt to taste
½ tsp sherry vinegar
1 tbsp mint leaves

**Directions** and Total Time: 20 minutes

Place the avocado, cucumber, 1 cup of water, cilantro, lime juice, sherry vinegar, and salt in your food processor and puree until smooth. Garnish with mint leaves.

## Pumpkin Squash Cream Soup

**Ingredients** for 4 servings

2 tbsp olive oil
4 tbsp butter
2 red onions, cut into wedges
2 garlic cloves, skinned
10 oz pumpkin, cubed
10 oz pumpkin squash
Juice of 1 lime
¾ cup mayonnaise
1 tbsp toasted pumpkin seeds

**Directions** and Total Time: 55 minutes

Preheat oven to 400 F. Place the onions, garlic, and pumpkin on a baking sheet and drizzle with olive oil. Season with salt and pepper. Roast for 30 minutes or until the vegetables are golden brown and fragrant. Remove the vegetables from the oven and transfer them to a pot. Add 2 cups of water, bring the ingredients to boil over medium heat for 15 minutes. Turn the heat off. Add in butter and puree until smooth. Stir in lime juice and mayonnaise. Spoon into serving bowls and garnish with pumpkin seeds to serve.

## Winter Soup

**Ingredients** for 6 servings

2 tbsp olive oil
1 cup chopped onion
3 garlic cloves, minced
1 tbsp thyme, fresh or dried
1 tsp hot paprika
5 cups vegetable broth
2 cups peeled beets, chopped
2 peeled sweet potatoes, cubed
1 cup peeled parsnips, diced
Salt and black pepper to taste
2 tbsp fresh mint, chopped
½ avocado, chopped
2 tbsp pumpkin seeds

**Directions** and Total Time: 50 minutes

Saute olive oil, onion, and garlic in a large pot. When the onions have softened after about 5 minutes, stir in thyme, paprika, beets, sweet potato, parsnips, broth, black pepper, and salt. Cover and simmer for at least 30 minutes or until the vegetables have softened. Next, add avocado. Use an immersion blender or a regular blender to puree the soup. Ladle into bowls and garnish with mint and pumpkin seeds. Serve warm and enjoy.

## Miso Buckwheat & Bean Soup

**Ingredients** for 4 servings

½ cup buckwheat
4 cups vegetable broth
4 tbsp miso
1 cup cranberry beans, cooked
2 tbsp basil, finely chopped
2 scallions, thinly sliced

**Directions** and Total Time: 20 minutes

In a large pot of boiling water, add buckwhcat and cook for 5 minutes while stirring occasionally. In a separate pot, heat the broth until just boiling. Remove from heat and stir in miso until dissolved. Drain the buckwheat and rinse under hot water. Transfer to the pot with the miso broth along with cranberry beans, basil, and scallions.

## Holiday Jack Soup

**Ingredients** for 4 servings

1 lb butternut squash, peeled, seeded, and chopped
2 tbsp olive oil
Salt and black pepper to taste
1 onion, diced
4 cups vegetable stock
2 tsp ground sage
1 cup milk
1 tbsp butter
¼ cup toasted walnuts

**Directions** and Total Time: 45 minutes

Saute butternut squash in oil in a large saucepan over medium heat. Add salt and cook for about 10 minutes or until softened. Stir in onion and saute for another 5 minutes. Pour in stock and bring to a boil. Reduce the heat and simmer for 15 to 20 minutes. The squash will be fork-tender when ready. Stir in sage, butter, and milk. Use an immersion blender or a regular blender to puree the soup. Ladle into bowls and garnish with toasted walnuts and pepper. Serve warm and enjoy.

## Peppery Pumpkin Soup

**Ingredients** for 6 servings

1 lb pumpkin
3 tbsp olive oil
Salt to taste
2 red bell peppers
1 onion
1 head garlic
2 cups vegetable broth
Zest and juice of 1 lime
1 tbsp tahini
½ tsp cayenne pepper
½ tsp ground coriander
½ tsp ground cumin
2 tbsp toasted pumpkin seeds

**Directions** and Total Time: 60 minutes

Preheat oven to 350°F. Cut the pumpkin in half lengthwise and scoop out the seeds. Pierce the flesh with a fork, then rub the flesh and skin with some oil. Season with salt. Place the pumpkin skin-side down in a large baking dish and cook for 20 minutes. Cut the peppers in half lengthwise and scoop out the seeds. Cut the onion in half and rub with oil. Cut the top of the garlic head and rub exposed areas with the remaining oil. Transfer to the baking dish after the pumpkin has baked for 20 minutes. Bake everything for another 20 minutes or until the squash and vegetables are tender.

When the pumpkin is cool enough to handle, scoop out the flesh and transfer to a blender jar. Give the peppers and onion a rough chop before adding to the blender. Squeeze the roasted garlic into the blender. Add broth, lime zest, lime juice, and tahini. Cover and puree until smooth. Add salt, cayenne, coriander, and cumin, then pulse until just combined. Pour into bowls and garnish with pumpkin seeds. Serve warm and enjoy.

## Special Moong Dal Soup

**Ingredients** for 4 servings

1 cup red split moong dal beans
2 cups peeled and cubed sweet potatoes
1 tsp curry powder
1 tbsp coriander seeds
2 tbsp coconut oil
1 red onion, diced
1 tbsp minced fresh ginger
1 green chili, minced
1 sliced zucchini
Salt and black pepper to taste
4 cups vegetable stock
1 tsp toasted sesame oil
10 oz spinach, chopped
1 tbsp toasted sesame seeds

**Directions** and Total Time: 35 minutes

Bring beans, 2 cups water, and 1 teaspoon of curry powder to a boil in a large pot. Lower the heat and cover. Simmer for 10 minutes to soften the beans. Heat oil in another large pot over medium heat. Saute onion, ginger, and green chili for 5 minutes. When soft, add sweet potato and cook for another 10 minutes. Stir in zucchini and cook for another 5 minutes. Season with curry powder, pepper, and salt. Pour in stock and bring to a boil. Reduce the heat and cover. Simmer for 20 to 30 minutes. When the sweet potato is tender, add the beans to the soup along with salt, sesame oil, coriander seeds, and spinach. Stir and simmer to wilt the spinach. Ladle into bowls and garnish with toasted sesame seeds. Serve.

## Tomato & Spinach Soup with Quinoa

**Ingredients** for 6 servings

3 tbsp olive oil
1 onion, chopped
1 celery stalk, chopped
2 garlic cloves, minced
1 (15-oz) can diced tomatoes
3 cups vegetable broth
Salt and black pepper to taste
1 lb quinoa
1 (5-oz) package baby spinach

**Directions** and Total Time: 30 minutes

In a large stockpot, add oil over medium heat. Stir in onion and sauté for 3 minutes. When the onions are soft, stir in garlic and celery and cook for another minute. Pour in tomatoes with juice, broth, and 4 cups of water. Season with salt and pepper and bring to a boil. Cover and reduce the heat to simmer. Remove the lid and stir in quinoa. Cook for 9 minutes. Remove the pot from the heat and stir in spinach until wilted. Serve warm.

## Zuppa di Pomodoro e Ceci

**Ingredients** for 2 servings

2 cups chopped cavolo nero (curly kale)
2 tsp olive oil
½ chopped onion
2 garlic cloves, minced
1 cup mushrooms, chopped
Salt to taste
1 tbsp dried basil
½ tsp dried oregano
½ tsp dried sage
1 tbsp balsamic vinegar
1 (19-oz) can diced tomatoes
1 (14-oz) can chickpeas
2 cups water

**Directions** and Total Time: 30 minutes

Heat oil in a large pot and saute onion, garlic, mushrooms, and a pinch of salt. After 7 to 8 minutes or when the vegetables have softened, stir in basil, sage, and oregano. Pour in vinegar and scrape any browned bits from the bottom of the pan. Stir in tomatoes, chickpeas, and water. Next, add the cavolo nero and salt. Cover the pot and simmer the soup for 10 - 15 minutes. The soup is ready when the cavolo nero is soft. Serve warm.

## Red Lentil Daal

**Ingredients** for 4 servings

1 cup red lentils
1 red bell pepper, diced
1 onion, chopped
3 garlic cloves, minced
1 tsp minced fresh ginger
1 vegetable stock cube
½ lemon, juiced
1 tbsp korma curry paste
Salt to taste
¼ tsp cayenne pepper

**Directions** and Total Time: 30 minutes

Fill a large pot with 5 cups of water. Stir in all of the ingredients and cover. Over medium heat, bring to a boil. Reduce the heat to low and simmer for 15 to 20 minutes. Stir occasionally. The lentils will be soft and the daal will have thickened. Serve warm and enjoy.

## Crockpot Mexican Chili

**Ingredients** for 4 servings

1 cup black beans, soaked
1 onion, chopped
1 celery stalk, chopped
3 garlic cloves, minced
1 green bell pepper, diced
1 ½ cups frozen corn kernels
3 tbsp Tajín seasoning
4 cups vegetable broth
1 (28-oz) can diced tomatoes
Salt to taste
2 tbsp chopped cilantro
2 tbsp sour cream

**Directions** and Total Time: 8 hours 5 minutes

In a crockpot, add beans, onion, celery, garlic, bell pepper, corn, Tajin, broth, tomatoes, and salt. Stir, cover, and cook on low for 8 hours. When done, ladle into bowls and garnish with cilantro and sour cream. Serve warm.

## Golden Beet & Potato Soup

**Ingredients** for 6 servings

2 tbsp olive oil
1 onion, chopped
1 carrot, chopped
1 celery stalk, chopped
2 garlic cloves, minced
1 peeled golden beet, diced
1 yellow bell pepper, chopped
1 Yukon Gold potato, diced
6 cups vegetable broth
1 tsp dried thyme
Salt and black pepper to taste
1 tbsp lemon juice

**Directions** and Total Time: 55 minutes

Heat the oil in a pot over medium heat. Place the onion, carrot, celery, and garlic. Cook for 5 minutes or until softened. Stir in beet, bell pepper, and potato, cook uncovered for 1 minute. Pour in the broth and thyme. Season with salt and pepper. Cook for 45 minutes until the vegetables are tender. Serve sprinkled with lemon juice.

## Dilly Cauliflower Soup

**Ingredients** for 4 servings

1 head cauliflower, cut into florets
2 tbsp coconut oil
5 oz butter
½ lb celery root, trimmed
1 garlic clove
1 medium white onion
¼ cup fresh dill, chopped
1 tsp cumin powder
¼ tsp nutmeg powder
3 ½ cups vegetable stock
Juice from 1 lemon
¼ cup heavy cream

**Directions** and Total Time: 26 minutes

Set a pot over medium heat, add the coconut oil and allow heating until no longer shimmering.

Add the celery root, garlic clove, and onion; sauté the vegetables until fragrant and soft, about 5 minutes. Stir in the dill, cumin, and nutmeg, and fry further for 1 minute. Mix in the cauliflower florets and vegetable stock. Bring the soup to a boil for 12 to 15 minutes or until the cauliflower is soft. Turn the heat off. Add the butter and lemon juice. Puree the ingredients with an immersion blender until smooth. Mix in heavy whipping cream. Season the soup with salt and pepper.

## Spicy Seitan Soup with Tortilla Strips

**Ingredients** for 4 servings

2 tbsp olive oil
1 (14.5-oz) can diced tomatoes
1 (4-oz) can green chiles, minced
1 cup canned sweet corn
1 red onion, chopped
2 garlic cloves, minced
2 jalapeño peppers, sliced
4 cups vegetable broth
8 oz seitan, cut into strips
Salt and black pepper to taste
¼ cup chopped fresh cilantro
3 tbsp fresh lime juice
4 corn tortillas, cut into strips
1 ripe avocado, chopped

**Directions** and Total Time: 40 minutes

Preheat oven to 350°F. Heat the oil in a pot over medium heat. Place sweet corn, garlic, jalapeño, and onion and cook for 5 minutes. Stir in broth, seitan, tomatoes, canned chiles, salt, and pepper. Bring to a boil, then lower the heat and simmer for 20 minutes. Stir in cilantro and lime juice. Arrange the tortilla strips on a baking sheet and bake for 8 minutes until crisp. Top with tortilla strips and avocado.

## Bean & Spinach Soup

**Ingredients** for 4 servings

1 (15.5-oz) can cannellini beans, drained
2 tbsp olive oil
1 medium onion, chopped
2 large garlic cloves, minced
1 carrot, chopped
5 cups vegetable broth
¼ tsp crushed red pepper
Salt and black pepper to taste
3 cups chopped baby spinach

**Directions** and Total Time: 40 minutes

Heat oil in a pot over medium heat. Place in carrot, onion, and garlic and cook for 3 minutes. Put in beans, broth, red pepper, salt, and black pepper and stir. Bring to a boil, then lower the heat and simmer for 25 minutes. Stir in baby spinach and cook for 5 minutes until the spinach wilts. Serve warm and enjoy!

## Tomato Bean Soup

**Ingredients** for 5 servings

2 tsp olive oil
1 onion, chopped
2 garlic cloves, minced
1 cup mushrooms, chopped
Sea salt to taste
1 tbsp dried basil
½ tbsp dried oregano
1 (19-oz) can diced tomatoes
1 (14-oz) can kidney beans
2 cups chopped mustard greens

**Directions** and Total Time: 30 minutes

Heat the oil in a pot over medium heat. Place in the onion, garlic, mushrooms, and salt and cook for 5 minutes. Stir in basil and oregano, tomatoes, and beans. Pour in 5 cups of water and stir. Simmer for 20 minutes. Add in mustard greens and cook for 5 minutes until greens soften. Serve immediately.

## Vegetable Lentil Soup

**Ingredients** for 4 servings

2 tbsp olive oil
1 onion, chopped
2 garlic cloves, minced
4 cups vegetable broth
2 russet potatoes, cubed
½ tsp dried oregano
¼ tsp crushed red pepper
1 bay leaf
Salt to taste
4 cups chopped spinach
1 cup green lentils, rinsed

**Directions** and Total Time: 55 minutes

Warm the oil in a pot over medium heat. Place the onion and garlic and cook covered for 5 minutes. Stir in broth, potatoes, oregano, red pepper, bay leaf, lentils, and salt. Bring to a boil, then lower the heat and simmer uncovered for 30 minutes. Add in spinach and cook for another 5 minutes. Discard the bay leaf and serve immediately.

## Sweet Potato & White Bean Soup

**Ingredients** for 6 servings

3 tbsp olive oil
1 onion, chopped
2 carrots, chopped
1 sweet potato, chopped
1 yellow bell pepper, chopped
2 garlic cloves, minced
4 tomatoes, chopped
6 cups vegetable broth
1 bay leaf
Salt to taste
1 tsp ground cayenne pepper
1 (15.5-oz) can white beans
1/3 cup whole-wheat pasta
¼ tsp turmeric

**Directions** and Total Time: 50 minutes

Heat the oil in a pot over medium heat. Place onion, carrots, sweet potato, bell pepper, and garlic. Cook for 5 minutes. Add in tomatoes, broth, bay leaf, salt, and cayenne pepper. Stir and bring to a boil. Lower the heat and simmer for 10 minutes. Put in white beans and simmer for 15 more minutes. Cook the pasta in a pot with boiling salted water and turmeric for 8-10 minutes, until pasta is al dente. Strain and transfer to the soup. Discard the bay leaf. Spoon into a bowl and serve.

## Spicy Pumpkin Soup

**Ingredients** for 6 servings

3 tbsp olive oil
1 (2-pound) pumpkin, sliced
1 tsp salt
2 red bell peppers
1 onion, halved
1 head garlic
6 cups water
Zest and juice of 1 lime
¼ tsp cayenne pepper
½ tsp ground coriander
½ tsp ground cumin

**Directions** and Total Time: 55 minutes

Preheat oven to 350 F. Brush the pumpkin slices with oil and sprinkle with salt. Arrange the slices skin-side-down and on a greased baking dish and bake for 20 minutes. Brush the onion with oil. Cut the top of the garlic head and brush with oil. When the pumpkin is ready, add bell peppers, onion, and garlic, and bake for another 10 minutes. Allow cooling.

Take out the flesh from the pumpkin skin and transfer to a food processor. Cut the pepper roughly, peel and cut the onion, and remove the cloves from the garlic head. Transfer to the food processor and pour in the water, lime zest, and lime juice. Blend the soup until smooth. Sprinkle with salt, cayenne, coriander, and cumin. Serve.

## Mint Coconut Soup with Arugula

**Ingredients** for 4 servings

1 tsp coconut oil
1 onion, diced
2 cups green beans
4 cups water
1 cup arugula, chopped
1 tbsp fresh mint, chopped
Salt and black pepper to taste
¾ cup milk

**Directions** and Total Time: 30 minutes

Place a pot over medium heat and heat the coconut oil. Add in the onion and sauté for 5 minutes. Pour in green beans and water. Bring to a boil, lower the heat and stir in arugula, mint, salt, and pepper. Simmer for 10 minutes. Stir in milk. Transfer to a food processor and blitz the soup until smooth. Serve and enjoy!

## Herby Mushroom & Bell Pepper Soup

**Ingredients** for 6 servings

1 cup cremini mushrooms, quartered
1 cup white mushrooms, quartered
3 tbsp olive oil
1 onion, chopped
1 large carrot, chopped
1 lb mixed bell peppers, diced
6 cups vegetable broth
¼ cup chopped fresh parsley
1 tsp minced fresh thyme
Salt and black pepper to taste

**Directions** and Total Time: 45 minutes

Heat the oil in a pot over medium heat. Place onion, carrot, and mushrooms and cook for 5 minutes. Add in bell peppers and broth and stir. Bring to a boil, lower the heat, and simmer for 20 minutes. Adjust the seasoning with salt and black pepper. Serve in soup bowls topped with parsley and thyme.

## Authentic Tomato Soup

**Ingredients** for 4 servings

- 3 tbsp olive oil
- 2 lb tomatoes, halved
- 2 tsp garlic powder
- 1 tbsp balsamic vinegar
- Salt and black pepper to taste
- 4 shallots, chopped
- 2 cups vegetable broth
- ½ cup basil leaves, chopped

**Directions** and Total Time: 60 minutes

Preheat oven to 450 F. In a bowl, mix tomatoes, garlic, 2 tbsp of oil, vinegar, salt, and pepper. Arrange the tomatoes onto a baking dish. Bake for 30 minutes until the tomatoes get dark brown color. Take out from the oven. Set aside.

Heat the remaining oil in a pot over medium heat. Place the shallots and cook for 3 minutes, stirring often. Add in roasted tomatoes and broth. Bring to a boil, then lower the heat and simmer for 10 minutes. Transfer to a food processor and blitz the soup until smooth. Serve topped with basil.

## Pressure Cooker Potato Coconut Soup

**Ingredients** for 5 servings

- 1 tbsp olive oil
- 3 green onions, chopped
- 4 garlic cloves, minced
- 6 russet potatoes, chopped
- ½ (13.5-oz) can coconut milk
- 5 cups vegetable broth
- Salt and black pepper to taste

**Directions** and Total Time: 25 minutes

Set your pressure cooker to Sauté. Place in green onions, garlic, and olive oil. Cook for 3 minutes until softened. Add in potatoes, coconut milk, broth, pepper and salt. Lock the lid in place, set time to 6 minutes on High. Once ready, perform a natural pressure release for 10 minutes. Allow cooling for a few minutes. Using an immersion blender, blitz the soup until smooth. Serve and enjoy!

## Cilantro Ramen Soup

**Ingredients** for 4 servings

- 7 oz Japanese buckwheat noodles
- 4 tbsp sesame paste
- 1 cup canned pinto beans
- 2 tbsp fresh cilantro, chopped
- 2 scallions, thinly sliced

**Directions** and Total Time: 25 minutes

In boiling salted water, add in the noodles and cook for 5 minutes over low heat. Remove a cup of the noodle water to a bowl and add in the sesame paste; stir until it has dissolved. Pour the sesame mix in the pot with the noodles, add in pinto beans, and stir until everything is hot. Serve topped with cilantro and scallions in bowls.

## Eggplant & Green Pea Stew

**Ingredients** for 5 servings

- 2 tbsp canola oil
- 1 onion, chopped
- 2 garlic cloves, minced
- 2 fresh hot chilies, minced
- 1 tbsp grated fresh ginger
- 1 russet potato, chopped
- 1 medium eggplant, chopped
- 8 oz green peas
- 2 cups cauliflower florets
- 2 cups vegetable broth
- 1 (14.5-oz) can diced tomatoes
- 2 tbsp soy sauce
- ½ tsp ground turmeric
- 1 cup milk
- 1 tbsp tamarind paste
- 2 tbsp fresh lime juice
- 3 tbsp minced fresh cilantro
- 2 tbsp minced scallions

**Directions** and Total Time: 40 minutes

Warm oil in a pot over medium heat. Place onion, garlic, chilies, and ginger and cook for 5 minutes. Stir in potato, eggplant, green peas, cauliflower, broth, tomatoes, soy sauce, and turmeric. Cook for 20 minutes. Lower the heat and pour in milk, tamarind, salt, and pepper. Simmer for 5 minutes. Mix in lime juice. Top with cilantro and scallions to serve. Enjoy!

## Spicy Tamarind Bean Stew

**Ingredients** for 4 servings

- 1 (4-oz) can mild chopped green chilies
- 2 tbsp olive oil
- 1 onion, chopped
- 2 potatoes, chopped
- 2 (15-oz) cans cannellini beans
- 1 (28-oz) can diced tomatoes
- 2 tbsp tamarind paste
- ¼ cup pure agave syrup
- 1 cup vegetable broth
- 2 tbsp chili powder
- 1 tsp ground coriander
- ½ tsp ground cumin
- Salt and black pepper to taste
- 1 cup frozen peas, thawed

**Directions** and Total Time: 40 minutes

Heat the oil in a pot over medium heat. Place in the onion and sauté for 3 minutes until translucent. Stir in potatoes, beans, tomatoes, and chilies. Cook for 5 minutes more. In a bowl, whisk the tamarind paste with agave syrup and broth. Pour the mixture into the pot. Stir in chili powder, coriander, cumin, salt, and pepper. Bring to a boil, then lower the heat and simmer for 20 minutes until the potatoes are tender. Add in peas and cook for another 5 minutes. Serve warm and enjoy!

## Kale & Pea Rice Sew

**Ingredients** for 6 servings

- 2 tsp olive oil
- 1 cups bell peppers
- Salt and black pepper to taste
- 1 onion, chopped
- 2 garlic cloves, minced
- 1 tbsp dried herbs
- 1 cup brown rice
- 2 cups vegetable broth
- 4 tbsp balsamic vinegar
- 1 cup frozen peas, thawed
- 1 cup milk
- 2 cups chopped kale

**Directions** and Total Time: 30 minutes

Heat the oil in a pot over medium heat. Place in bell peppers, onion, garlic, and salt and cook for 5 minutes until tender. Put in dried herbs, brown rice, broth, vinegar, and pepper. Bring to a boil, then lower the heat and simmer for 20 minutes. Stir in peas, milk, and kale until the kale wilts. Serve warm and enjoy!

### Za´atar Chickpea Soup with Veggies

**Ingredients** for 5 servings

2 tbsp olive oil
1 onion, chopped
1 carrot, chopped
1 celery stalk, chopped
1 eggplant, chopped
1 (28-oz) can diced tomatoes
2 tbsp tomato paste
1 (15.5-oz) can chickpeas
2 tsp smoked paprika
1 tsp ground cumin
1 tsp za'atar spice
¼ tsp ground cayenne pepper
6 cups vegetable broth
4 oz whole-wheat vermicelli
2 tbsp minced cilantro

**Directions** and Total Time: 35 minutes

Heat the oil in a pot over medium heat. Place onion, carrot, and celery and cook for 5 minutes. Add the eggplant, tomatoes, tomato paste, chickpeas, paprika, cumin, za´atar spice, and cayenne pepper. Stir in broth and salt. Bring to a boil, then lower the heat and simmer for 15 minutes. Add in vermicelli and cook for another 5 minutes. Serve topped with chopped cilantro.

### Zucchini Cream Soup with Walnuts

**Ingredients** for 4 servings

2 tsp olive oil
3 zucchinis, chopped
Salt and black pepper to taste
1 onion, diced
4 cups vegetable stock
3 tsp ground sage
3 tbsp nutritional yeast
1 cup milk
¼ cup toasted walnuts

**Directions** and Total Time: 45 minutes

Heat the oil in a skillet and place zucchini, onion, salt, and pepper; cook for 5 minutes. Pour in vegetable stock and bring to a boil. Lower the heat and simmer for 15 minutes. Stir in sage, nutritional yeast, and milk. Purée the soup with a blender until smooth. Serve garnished with toasted walnuts and pepper.

### Vegetable & Black-Eyed Pea Soup

**Ingredients** for 6 servings

2 carrots, chopped
1 onion, chopped
2 cups canned black-eyed peas
1 tbsp soy sauce
3 tsp dried thyme
1 tsp onion powder
½ tsp garlic powder
Salt and black pepper to taste
9 chopped pitted black olives

**Directions** and Total Time: 45 minutes

Place carrots, onion, black-eyed peas, 3 cups of water, soy sauce, thyme, onion powder, garlic powder, salt, and pepper in a pot. Bring to a boil, then reduce the heat to low. Cook for 20 minutes. Allow cooling for a few minutes. Transfer to a food processor and blend until smooth. Stir in black olives. Serve and enjoy!

### Leek Soup with Cauliflower

**Ingredients** for 4 servings

1 head cauliflower, cut into florets
2 tbsp olive oil
3 leeks, thinly sliced
4 cups vegetable stock
Salt and black pepper to taste
3 tbsp chopped fresh chives

**Directions** and Total Time: 25 minutes

Heat the oil in a pot over medium heat. Place the leeks and sauté for 5 minutes. Add in cauliflower, vegetable stock, salt, and pepper and cook for 10 minutes. Blend the soup until purée in a food processor. Top with chives.

### Chili Lentil Soup with Collard Greens

**Ingredients** for 2 servings

1 tsp olive oil
1 onion, chopped
6 garlic cloves, minced
1 tsp chili powder
½ tsp ground cinnamon
Salt to taste
1 cup yellow lentils
1 cup canned diced tomatoes
1 celery stalk, chopped
2 cups chopped collard greens

**Directions** and Total Time: 35 minutes

Heat oil in a pot over medium heat. Place onion and garlic and cook for 5 minutes. Stir in chili powder, celery, cinnamon, and salt. Pour in lentils, tomatoes and juices, and 2 cups of water. Bring to a boil, then lower the heat and simmer for 15 minutes. Stir in collard greens. Cook for an additional 5 minutes. Serve warm and enjoy!

### Rice & Bean Soup with Spinach

**Ingredients** for 6 servings

2 tbsp olive oil
6 cups baby spinach
1 onion, chopped
2 garlic cloves, minced
1 (15.5-oz) can black-eyed peas
6 cups vegetable broth
Salt and black pepper to taste
½ cup brown rice
1 tbsp Tabasco sauce

**Directions** and Total Time: 45 minutes

Heat the olive oil in a pot over medium heat. Place the onion and garlic and sauté for 3 minutes until softened. Pour in broth and season with salt and pepper. Bring to a boil, then lower the heat and stir in rice. Simmer for 15 minutes. Stir in peas and spinach and cook for another 5 minutes. Serve topped with Tabasco sauce.

### Broccoli Soup with Ginger

**Ingredients** for 4 servings

1 head broccoli, chopped into florets
2 tsp olive oil
1 onion, chopped
1 tbsp minced fresh ginger
2 carrots, chopped
1 cup milk
3 cups vegetable broth
½ tsp turmeric
Salt and black pepper to taste

**Directions** and Total Time: 50 minutes

In a pot over medium heat, place the onion, ginger, and olive oil, cook for 4 minutes. Add in carrots, broccoli, broth, turmeric, pepper, and salt. Bring to a boil and cook for 15 minutes. Transfer the soup to a food processor and blend until smooth. Stir in milk and serve.

### Bean & Rice Noodle Soup

**Ingredients** for 6 servings

2 carrots, chopped
2 celery stalks, chopped
6 cups vegetable broth
8 oz brown rice noodles
1 (15-oz) can pinto beans
1 tsp dried herbs

**Directions** and Total Time: 10 minutes

Place a pot over medium heat and add carrots, celery, and vegetable broth. Bring to a boil. Add in noodles, beans, dried herbs, salt, and pepper. Reduce the heat and simmer for 5 minutes. Serve warm and enjoy!

## Rice Soup with Veggies

**Ingredients** for 6 servings

3 tbsp olive oil
2 carrots, chopped
1 onion, chopped
1 celery stalk, chopped
2 garlic cloves, minced
2 cups chopped cabbage
½ red bell pepper, chopped
4 unpeeled potatoes, quartered
6 cups vegetable broth
½ cup brown rice, rinsed
½ cup frozen green peas
2 tbsp chopped parsley

**Directions** and Total Time: 40 minutes

Heat the olive oil in a medium pot over medium heat. Place carrots, onion, celery, and garlic. Cook for 5 minutes. Add in cabbage, bell pepper, potatoes, and broth. Bring to a boil, lower the heat, and add the brown rice, salt, and pepper. Simmer uncovered for 25 minutes until vegetables are tender. Stir in peas and cook for 5 minutes. Top with parsley and serve warm.

## Winter Soup

**Ingredients** for 6 servings

2 tsp olive oil
6 cups water
1 chopped onion
3 garlic cloves, minced
1 tbsp thyme
2 tsp paprika
2 cups peeled daikon, cubed
2 cups red potatoes, cubed
2 peeled cups parsnips, cubed
½ tsp sea salt
1 cup fresh mint, chopped
2 tbsp balsamic vinegar
2 tbsp pumpkin seeds

**Directions** and Total Time: 40 minutes

Heat the olive oil in a pot over medium heat. Place onion and garlic. Sauté for 3 minutes. Add in thyme, paprika, daikon, red potato, parsnips, water, and salt. Bring to a boil and cook for 30 minutes. Remove the soup to a food processor and add in balsamic vinegar; purée until smooth. Top with mint and pumpkin seeds to serve.

## Traditional Ribollita

**Ingredients** for 6 servings

3 tbsp olive oil
2 celery stalks, chopped
2 carrots, chopped
3 shallots, chopped
3 garlic cloves, minced
½ cup brown rice
6 cups vegetable broth
1 (14.5-oz) can diced tomatoes
2 bay leaves
Salt and black pepper to taste
2 (15.5-oz) cans white beans
¼ cup chopped basil

**Directions** and Total Time: 1 hour 25 minutes

Heat oil in a pot over medium heat. Place celery, carrots, shallots, and garlic and cook for 5 minutes. Add in brown rice, broth, tomatoes, bay leaves, salt, and pepper. Bring to a boil, then lower the heat and simmer uncovered for 20 minutes. Stir in beans and basil and cook for 5 minutes. Discard bay leaves and spoon into bowls. Sprinkle with chopped basil. Serve warm and enjoy!

## Celery & Mushroom Stock

**Ingredients** for 6 servings

5 dried porcini mushrooms, soaked and liquid reserved
8 oz Cremini mushrooms, chopped
1 tbsp olive oil
1 onion, unpeeled and quartered
1 carrot, coarsely chopped
1 celery rib with leaves, chopped
1 onion, chopped
½ cup chopped fresh parsley
Salt and black pepper to taste
5 cups water

**Directions** and Total Time: 1 hour 15 minutes

Warm the oil in a pot over medium heat. Place in quartered onion, carrot, celery, and cremini mushrooms. Cook for 5 minutes until softened. Add in the dried mushrooms and reserved liquid, onion, salt, pepper,and water. Bring to a boil and simmer for 1 hour. Let cool for a few minutes, then pour over a strainer into a pot. Divide between glass mason jars and allow cooling completely. Seal and store in the fridge for up to 5 days or 1 month in the freezer.

## African-Style Veggie Stew

**Ingredients** for 4 servings

3 peeled russet potatoes, cubed
2 tbsp olive oil
6 carrots, sliced
1 onion, chopped
4 garlic cloves, minced
1 tbsp ground turmeric
1 tsp ground cumin
1 tsp ras el hanout seasoning
Salt to taste
1 ½ cups vegetable broth
4 cups shredded green cabbage
1 tbsp cilantro, finely chopped

**Directions** and Total Time: 20 minutes

Boil water in a pot of over medium heat. Add potatoes and cook for 10 minutes. Drain the potatoes in a colander and set to the side. While waiting for the potatoes to cook, heat a large skillet with oil over medium heat. Sauté carrots and onions for 5 minutes. Stir in garlic, turmeric, cumin, ras el hanout, and salt. Sauté for 1 minute or until aromatic. Stir in the potatoes and 1 cup of broth. Bring to a boil then reduce the heat. Top with cabbage and cover the skillet. Simmer for 3 minutes. Stir the cabbage into the potatoes. Pour the rest of the broth over the vegetables and return the lid over the skillet. Simmer for 5 minutes, stirring occasionally. When the cabbage is wilted, garnish with cilantro. Serve warm.

## Zucchini Velouté with Green Beans

**Ingredients** for 6 servings

3 tbsp olive oil
1 onion, chopped
1 garlic clove, minced
2 cups green beans
4 cups vegetable broth
3 medium zucchini, sliced
½ tsp dried marjoram
½ cup milk
2 tbsp minced jarred pimiento

**Directions** and Total Time: 30 minutes

Heat oil in a pot and sauté onion and garlic for 5 minutes. Add in green beans and broth. Cook for 10 minutes. Stir in zucchini and cook for 10 minutes. Blitz with an immersion blender until smooth. Mix in milk and cook again until hot. Top with pimiento and marjoram.

## Mushroom, Brussel Sprout & Tofu Soup

**Ingredients** for 4 servings

1 cup shredded Brussels sprouts
½-inch piece fresh ginger, minced
2 tsp olive oil
7 oz firm tofu, cubed
1 cup sliced mushrooms
1 garlic clove, minced
Salt to taste
2 tbsp apple cider vinegar
2 tbsp soy sauce
1 tsp pure date sugar
¼ tsp red pepper flakes
1 scallion, chopped

**Directions** and Total Time: 40 minutes

Heat the oil in a skillet over medium heat. Place mushrooms, Brussels sprouts, garlic, ginger, and salt. Sauté for 7-8 minutes until the veggies are soft. Pour in 4 cups of water, vinegar, soy sauce, sugar, pepper flakes, and tofu. Bring to a boil, then lower the heat and simmer for 5-10 minutes. Top with scallions and serve.

## Easy Sunday Soup

**Ingredients** for 5 servings

2 tbsp vegetable oil
1 onion, chopped
1 carrot, chopped
2 garlic cloves, minced
3 small new potatoes, sliced
1 zucchini, sliced
1 yellow summer squash, sliced
2 ripe tomatoes, diced
Salt and black pepper to taste
5 cups vegetable broth
2 cups chopped kale
¼ cup basil leaves, chopped

**Directions** and Total Time: 45 minutes

Heat the vegetable oil in a pot over medium heat. Place onion, carrot, and garlic and cook covered for 5 minutes. Add in potatoes, zucchini, yellow squash, tomatoes, salt, and pepper. Cook for 5 minutes. Stir in broth and bring to a boil. Lower the heat and simmer for 30 minutes. Stir in kale and basil. Spoon the soup into bowls. Serve.

## Country Bean Soup

**Ingredients** for 4 servings

2 tsp olive oil
1 carrot, chopped
1 onion, chopped
2 garlic cloves, minced
1 tbsp rosemary, chopped
2 tbsp apple cider vinegar
1 cup dried white beans
¼ tsp salt
2 tbsp nutritional yeast

**Directions** and Total Time: 30 minutes

Heat the oil in a pot over medium heat. Place carrots, onion, and garlic and cook for 5 minutes. Pour in vinegar to deglaze the pot. Stir in 5 cups water and beans and bring to a boil. Lower the heat and simmer for 45 minutes until the beans are soft. Add in salt and nutritional yeast and stir. Serve topped with chopped rosemary.

## Apple & Pumpkin Curry

**Ingredients** for 4 servings

1 tsp olive oil
1 onion, chopped
1-inch piece fresh ginger, diced
1 apple, cored and chopped
1 tsp curry powder
½ tsp pumpkin pie spice
½ tsp smoked paprika
¼ tsp red pepper flakes
3 cups canned pumpkin purée
Salt and black pepper to taste
½ cup milk
4 tbsp nutritional yeast

**Directions** and Total Time: 25 minutes

Warm the olive oil in a pot over medium heat. Place in the onion, ginger, and apple and cook for 5 minutes. Add in curry powder, pumpkin pie spice, paprika, and pepper flakes. Stir in 4 cups water, pumpkin, salt, and pepper. Cook for 10 minutes. Puree with an immersion blender until smooth. Pour in milk and nutritional yeast. Serve.

## Lime-Mushroom Curry Soup

**Ingredients** for 4 servings

½ cup sliced shiitake mushrooms
1 tbsp coconut oil
1 red onion, sliced
1 carrot, chopped
2 garlic cloves, minced
1 (13.5-oz) can coconut milk
4 cups vegetable stock
1 (8-oz) can tomato sauce
2 tbsp cilantro, chopped
Juice from 1 lime
Salt to taste
2 tbsp red curry paste

**Directions** and Total Time: 15 minutes

Melt coconut oil in a pot over medium heat. Place in onion, garlic, carrot, and mushrooms and sauté for 5 minutes. Pour in coconut milk, vegetable stock, tomato sauce, cilantro, lime juice, salt, and curry paste. Cook until heated through. Serve and enjoy!

## Tofu Soup with Mushrooms

**Ingredients** for 4 servings

4 cups water
2 tbsp soy sauce
4 white mushrooms, sliced
¼ cup chopped green onions
3 tbsp tahini
6 oz extra-firm tofu, diced

**Directions** and Total Time: 20 minutes

Pour the water and soy sauce into a pot over medium heat and bring the mixture to a boil. Add in mushrooms and green onions. Lower the heat and simmer for 10 minutes. In a bowl, combine ½ cup of hot soup with tahini. Pour the mixture into the pot and simmer 2 minutes more, but not boil. Stir in tofu. Serve warm.

## Autumn Squash Soup

**Ingredients** for 5 servings

1 (2-lb) butternut squash, peeled and cubed
1 red bell pepper, chopped
1 large onion, chopped
3 garlic cloves, minced
4 cups vegetable broth
1 cup heavy cream

**Directions** and Total Time: 30 minutes

Place the squash, bell pepper, onion, garlic, and broth in a pot. Bring to a boil. Lower the heat and simmer for 20 minutes. Stir in heavy cream, salt, and pepper. Transfer to a food processor purée the soup until smooth. Serve.

## Spinach Soup with Vermicelli

**Ingredients** for 6 servings

1 tbsp olive oil
1 onion, chopped
4 garlic cloves, minced
1 (14.5-oz) can diced tomatoes
6 cups vegetable broth
8 oz vermicelli
1 (5-oz) package baby spinach

**Directions** and Total Time: 20 minutes

Preparing the Ingredients

Warm the oil in a pot over medium heat. Place in onion and garlic and cook for 3 minutes. Stir in tomatoes, broth, salt, and pepper. Bring to a boil, then lower the heat and simmer for 5 minutes. Pour in vermicelli and spinach and cook for another 5 minutes. Serve warm.

## Cream of Mushroom Soup

**Ingredients** for 2 servings

2 tsp olive oil
1 onion, chopped
2 cups chopped mushrooms
Salt and black pepper to taste
2 tbsp whole-wheat flour
1 tsp dried rosemary
4 cups vegetable broth
1 cup heavy cream

**Directions** and Total Time: 20 minutes

In a pot over medium heat, warm the oil. Place the onion, mushrooms, and salt and cook for 5 minutes. Stir in the flour and cook for another 1-2 minutes. Add in rosemary, vegetable broth, heavy cream, and pepper. Lower the heat and simmer for 10 minutes. Serve.

## Cream of Pomodoro Soup

**Ingredients** for 5 servings

2 tbsp olive oil
1 (28-oz) can tomatoes
1 tsp smoked paprika
2 cups vegetable broth
2 tsp dried herbs
1 red onion, chopped
1 cup milk
Salt and black pepper to taste

**Directions** and Total Time: 15 minutes

Place the tomatoes, olive oil, paprika, broth, dried herbs, onion, milk, salt, and pepper in a pot. Bring to a boil and cook for 10 minutes. Transfer to a food processor and blend the soup until smooth.

## Sweet Potato & Mustard Green Soup

**Ingredients** for 6 servings

2 tbsp olive oil
1 red onion, chopped
1 leek, chopped
2 garlic cloves, minced
6 cups vegetable broth
1 lb red potatoes, chopped
1 lb sweet potatoes, diced
¼ tsp crushed red pepper
1 bunch mustard greens, torn

**Directions** and Total Time: 30 minutes

Heat the oil in a pot over medium heat. Place onion, leek, and garlic and sauté for 5 minutes. Pour in broth, potatoes, and red pepper. Bring to a boil, then lower the heat and season with salt and pepper. Simmer for 15 minutes. Add in mustard greens, cook for 5 minutes until the greens are tender. Serve and enjoy!

## Kale Soup with Potatoes

**Ingredients** for 4 servings

2 tbsp olive oil
1/3 cup butter
1 onion, chopped
1 ½ lb potatoes, chopped
4 cups vegetable broth
¼ tsp ground cayenne pepper
⅛ tsp ground nutmeg
Salt and black pepper to taste
4 cups kale

**Directions** and Total Time: 45 minutes

Heat the oil in a pot over medium heat. Place in the onion and sauté for 5 minutes. Pour in potatoes and broth and cook for 20 minutes. Stir in butter, cayenne pepper, nutmeg, salt, and pepper. Add in kale and cook 5 minutes until wilted. Serve and enjoy!

## Bangkok-Style Tofu Soup

**Ingredients** for 4 servings

1 cup shiitake mushrooms, sliced
1 tbsp canola oil
1 onion, chopped
2 tbsp minced fresh ginger
2 tbsp soy sauce
1 tbsp pure date sugar
1 tsp chili paste
2 cups light vegetable broth
8 oz extra-firm tofu, chopped
2 (13.5-oz) cans coconut milk
1 tbsp fresh lime juice
3 tbsp chopped fresh cilantro

**Directions** and Total Time: 30 minutes

Heat the oil in a pot over medium heat. Place in onion and ginger and sauté for 3 minutes until softened. Add in soy sauce, mushrooms, sugar, and chili paste. Stir in broth. Bring to a boil, then lower the heat and simmer for 15 minutes. Strain the liquid and discard solids. Return the broth to the pot. Stir in tofu, coconut milk, and lime juice. Cook for 5 minutes. Garnish with cilantro.

## Acorn Squash Soup with Pumpkin Seeds

**Ingredients** for 4 servings

1 tbsp canola oil
½ cup toasted pumpkin seeds
1 tbsp chopped ginger paste
1 onion, chopped
1 celery stalk, chopped
4 cups vegetable broth
1 acorn squash, chopped
1 tbsp soy sauce
¼ tsp ground allspice
Salt and black pepper to taste
1 cup milk

**Directions** and Total Time: 30 minutes

Heat the oil in a pot over medium heat. Place in onion and celery and sauté for 5 minutes until tender. Add in broth and squash, bring to a boil. Lower the heat and simmer for 20 minutes. Stir in soy sauce, ginger paste, allspice, salt, and pepper. Transfer to a food processor and blend the soup until smooth. Return to the pot. Mix in milk and cook until hot. Garnish with pumpkin seeds.

## White Bean & Carrot Soup

**Ingredients** for 4 servings

2 tsp olive oil
1 leek, chopped
4 garlic cloves, minced
2 carrots, peeled and chopped
1 tbsp dried herbs
4 cups vegetable broth
2 (15-oz) cans white beans
2 tbsp lemon juice
2 cups green beans

**Directions** and Total Time: 20 minutes

Heat the oil in a pot over medium heat. Place in leek, garlic, carrots, pepper, and salt. Cook for 5 minutes until fragrant. Season with dried herbs. Stir in broth, green beans, and white beans, reduce the heat and simmer for 10 minutes. Stir in lemon juice and serve.

## Basil Mushroom Soup

**Ingredients** for 4 servings

15 oz mixed mushrooms, chopped
5 oz shiitake mushrooms, chopped
1 vegetable stock cube, crushed
4 oz butter
1 small onion, finely chopped
1 clove garlic, minced
½ lb celery root, chopped
½ tsp dried rosemary
1 tbsp plain vinegar
1 cup heavy cream
4 leaves basil, chopped

**Directions** and Total Time: 40 minutes

Place a saucepan over medium heat, add the butter to melt, then sauté the onion, garlic, mushrooms, and celery root in the butter until golden brown and fragrant, about 6 minutes. Fetch out some mushrooms and reserve for garnishing. Add the rosemary, 3 cups of water, stock cube, and vinegar. Stir the mixture and bring it to a boil for 6 minutes. After, reduce the heat and simmer the soup for 15 minutes or until the celery is soft. Mix in the heavy cream and puree the ingredients using an immersion blender. Simmer for 2 minutes. Spoon the soup into serving bowls, garnish with the reserved mushrooms and basil. Serve and enjoy!

## Asian-Style Mushroom Soup

**Ingredients** for 4 servings

2 tbsp olive oil
4 green onions, chopped
1 carrot, chopped
8 oz shiitake mushrooms, sliced
3 tbsp rice wine
2 tbsp soy sauce
4 cups vegetable broth
Salt and black pepper to taste
2 tbsp parsley, chopped

**Directions** and Total Time: 25 minutes

Heat the oil in a pot over medium heat. Place the green onions and carrot and cook for 5 minutes. Stir in mushrooms, rice wine, soy sauce, broth, salt, and pepper. Bring to a boil, then lower the heat and simmer for 15 minutes. Top with parsley and serve warm.

## Curried Bean & Veggie Soup

**Ingredients** for 4 servings

2 tsp olive oil
1 cup canned cannellini beans
2 tsp curry powder
1 red onion, diced
1 tbsp minced fresh ginger
2 cubed sweet potatoes
1 cup sliced zucchini
Salt and black pepper to taste
4 cups vegetable stock
1 bunch spinach, chopped
Toasted sesame seeds

**Directions** and Total Time: 55 minutes

Mix the beans with 1 tsp of curry powder until well combined. Warm the oil in a pot over medium heat. Place the onion and ginger and cook for 5 minutes until soft. Add in sweet potatoes and cook for 10 minutes. Put in zucchini and cook for 5 minutes. Season with the remaining curry, pepper, and salt. Pour in the stock and bring to a boil. Lower the heat and simmer for 25 minutes. Stir in beans and spinach. Cook until the spinach wilts. Garnish with sesame seeds to serve.

## Zuppa di Pomodoro e Pasta

**Ingredients** for 4 servings

¼ cup olive oil
4 cups cubed bread
2 garlic cloves, minced
8 oz whole-wheat pasta
1 (28-oz) can diced tomatoes
4 cups vegetable broth
2 tbsp minced parsley
Salt and black pepper to taste
2 tbsp basil leaves, chopped

**Directions** and Total Time: 30 minutes

Preheat oven to 400°F. Arrange the bread cubes on a baking tray and toast for 10 minutes, shaking them once. Heat olive oil in a pot over medium heat. Place the garlic and cook for 1 minute until softened. Add in pasta, tomatoes, broth, parsley, salt, and pepper. Bring to a boil, then lower the heat and simmer for 10 minutes. Share the toasted bread into soup bowls and spoon in the soup all over. Sprinkle with basil. Serve and enjoy!

## Pinto Bean & Corn Soup

**Ingredients** for 4 servings

2 tbsp olive oil
1 red onion, chopped
1 red bell pepper, chopped
1 carrot, chopped
2 garlic cloves, minced
1 tsp ground cumin
1 tsp dried oregano
1 (14.5-oz) can diced tomatoes
1 (15.5-oz) can pinto beans
4 cups vegetable broth
2 cups corn kernels
1 tsp fresh lemon juice
Salt and black pepper to taste
2 stalks green onions, chopped
Tabasco sauce for garnish

**Directions** and Total Time: 55 minutes

Heat the oil in a pot over medium heat. Place in onion, bell pepper, carrot, and garlic. Sauté for 5 minutes. Add in cumin, oregano, tomatoes, beans, salt, pepper, and broth. Bring to a boil, then lower the heat and simmer for 15 minutes. In a food processor, transfer 1/3 of the soup and blend until smooth. Return to the pot and stir in the corn. Cook for 10 minutes. Drizzle with lemon juice and garnish with green onions and hot sauce.

## Power Green Bisque

**Ingredients** for 6 servings

3 tbsp olive oil
1 red onion, chopped
2 carrots, chopped
1 potato, peeled and chopped
1 zucchini, sliced
1 ripe tomato, quartered
2 garlic cloves, crushed
½ tsp dried rosemary
Salt and black pepper to taste
6 cups vegetable broth
1 tbsp minced fresh parsley

**Directions** and Total Time: 25 minutes

Preheat oven to 400°F. Arrange the onion, carrots, potato, zucchini, tomato, and garlic on a greased baking dish. Sprinkle with oil, rosemary, salt, and pepper. Cover with foil and roast for 30 minutes. Uncover and turn them. Roast for another 10 minutes.

Transfer the veggies into a pot and pour in the broth. Bring to a boil, lower the heat and simmer for 5 minutes. Transfer to a food processor and blend the soup until smooth. Serve topped with parsley.

### Korean-Style Bean Chili

**Ingredients** for 4 servings

2 tsp sesame oil
1 cup green onions, chopped
3 cloves garlic, minced
1 lb yellow squash, chopped
2 cups shredded napa cabbage
1 (14.5-oz) can red beans
1 (14.5-oz) can diced tomatoes
2 cups vegetable broth
2 tbsp red miso paste
2 tbsp water
1 tbsp hot sauce
2 tsp tamari sauce

**Directions** and Total Time: 35 minutes

Heat the sesame oil in a pot over medium heat. Place in green onion, garlic and yellow squash, and cook for 5 minutes. Stir in cabbage, beans, tomatoes, and broth. Bring to a boil, then lower the heat and simmer covered for 15 minutes. Mix the miso paste with hot water in a bowl. Remove the pot from heat and stir in the miso, tamari, and hot sauces. Adjust the seasoning and serve.

### Corn & Potato Chowder with Mushrooms

**Ingredients** for 4 servings

2 tbsp olive oil
1 onion, chopped
1 cup chopped fennel bulb
2 carrots, chopped
1 cup mushrooms, chopped
¼ cup whole-wheat flour
4 cups vegetable stock
2 cups canned corn
2 cups cubed red potatoes
1 cup milk
½ tsp chili paste
Salt and black pepper to taste

**Directions** and Total Time: 30 minutes

Heat the oil in a pot over medium heat. Place in onion, fennel, carrots, and mushrooms. Sauté for 5 minutes until tender. Stir in flour. Pour in vegetable stock. Lower the heat. Add in corn, potatoes, milk, and chili paste. Simmer for 20 minutes. Sprinkle with salt and pepper.

### Tomato & Celery Rice Soup

**Ingredients** for 6 servings

3 tbsp olive oil
1 onion, chopped
1 medium carrot, chopped
1 celery stalk, chopped
1 lb potatoes, chopped
½ cup long-grain brown rice
1 (14.5-oz) can diced tomatoes
2 cups tomato juice
2 bay leaves
½ tsp ground cumin
Salt and black pepper to taste
1 tbsp minced fresh parsley

**Directions** and Total Time: 40 minutes

Heat oil in a pot and sauté onion, carrot, and celery for 10 minutes. Add potatoes, rice, tomatoes, tomato juices, bay leaves, cumin, 6 cups water, salt, and pepper. Bring to a boil, then lower the heat and simmer uncovered for 20 minutes. Discard the bay leaves. Scatter with parsley.

### Italian-Style Slow-Cooked Lentil & Potato Stew

**Ingredients** for 4 servings

2 tbsp olive oil
1 carrot, cubed
2 russet potatoes, cubed
1 celery stalk, thinly sliced
1 onion, chopped
2 garlic cloves, minced
1 cup dried lentils
3 cups vegetable broth
1 cup canned tomatoes, diced
1 bay leaf
2 tsp Italian seasoning
Salt to taste
5 baby spinach

**Directions** and Total Time: 8 hours 15 minutes

Add the olive oil, carrot, potatoes, celery, onion, garlic, lentils, broth, tomatoes with liquid, bay leaf, Italian seasoning, and salt to your slow cooker pot. Stir to combine. Cover and cook on low for 8 hours. Remove the lid and take out the bay leaf. Stir in spinach and let it warm through until wilted. Serve warm and enjoy!

### Grandma´s Succotash Stew

**Ingredients** for 4 servings

1 (16-oz) package frozen succotash
2 tbsp olive oil
1 cup canned chickpeas
1 onion, chopped
2 russet potatoes, chopped
2 carrots, sliced
1 (14.5-oz) can diced tomatoes
2 cups vegetable broth
2 tbsp soy sauce
1 tsp dry mustard
½ tsp dried thyme
½ tsp ground allspice
¼ tsp ground cayenne pepper
Salt and black pepper to taste

**Directions** and Total Time: 30 minutes

Heat the olive oil in a saucepan over medium heat. Place in onion and sauté for 3 minutes. Stir in chickpeas, potatoes, carrots, tomatoes, succotash, broth, soy sauce, mustard, thyme, allspice, and cayenne pepper. Sprinkle with salt and pepper. Bring to a boil, then lower the heat and simmer for 20 minutes. Serve hot and enjoy!

### Nicaraguan Lentil Stew

**Ingredients** for 4 servings

2 tbsp olive oil
1 onion, chopped
1 carrot, sliced
2 garlic cloves, minced
1 sweet potato, chopped
¼ tsp crushed red pepper
1 cup red lentils, rinsed
1 (14.5-oz) can diced tomatoes
1 tsp hot curry powder
1 tsp chopped thyme
¼ tsp ground allspice
Salt and black pepper to taste
1 cup water
1 (13.5-oz) can coconut milk

**Directions** and Total Time: 50 minutes

Warm oil in a pot and sauté onion and carrot for 5 minutes, stirring occasionally until softened. Add in garlic, sweet potato, and crushed red pepper. Put in red lentils, tomatoes, curry powder, allspice, salt, and black pepper, stir to combine. Pour in water and simmer for 30 minutes until the vegetables are tender. Stir in coconut milk and simmer for 10 minutes. Serve topped with thyme.

### Tomato Bean Chili with Brown Rice

**Ingredients** for 6 servings

30 oz canned roasted tomatoes and peppers
3 tbsp olive oil
1 onion, chopped
4 garlic cloves, minced
1 (15-oz) can kidney beans
½ cup brown rice
2 cups vegetable stock
3 tbsp chili powder
1 tsp sea salt

**Directions** and Total Time: 30 minutes

Heat the oil in a pot over medium heat. Place onion and garlic and cook for 3 minutes until fragrant. Stir in beans, rice, tomatoes and peppers, stock, chili powder, and salt. Cook for 20 minutes. Serve and enjoy!

## Basil Soup with Rotini

**Ingredients** for 4 servings

1 tbsp olive oil
1 medium onion, chopped
1 celery rib, minced
3 garlic cloves, minced
3 cups diced fresh tomatoes
2 tbsp tomato paste
3 cups vegetable broth
2 bay leaves
½ cup rotini pasta
2 tbsp chopped fresh basil

**Directions** and Total Time: 25 minutes

Heat oil in a pot and sauté onion, celery, and garlic for 5 minutes. Add in tomatoes, tomato paste, broth, and bay leaves. Bring to a boil and add the rotini. Cook for 10 minutes. Discard bay leaves. Garnish with basil.

## Garbanzo & Pumpkin Chili with Kale

**Ingredients** for 6 servings

¾ cup garbanzo beans, soaked
1 (28-oz) can diced tomatoes
2 cups chopped pumpkin
2 tbsp chili powder
1 tsp onion powder
½ tsp garlic powder
3 cups kale, chopped
½ tsp salt

**Directions** and Total Time: 60 minutes

In a saucepan over medium heat, place garbanzo, tomatoes, pumpkin, 5 cups of water, salt, chili, onion, and garlic powders. Bring to a boil. Reduce the heat and simmer for 50 minutes. Stir in kale and cook for 5 minutes until the kale wilts. Serve warm and enjoy!

## Chickpea Chili

**Ingredients** for 4 servings

2 tsp olive oil
1 onion, chopped
1 cup vegetable broth
2 garlic cloves, minced
1 potato, cubed
1 carrot, chopped
1 (28-oz) can tomatoes
1 tbsp tomato paste
1 (14-oz) can chickpeas
1 tsp chili powder
Salt and black pepper to taste
¼ cup parsley leaves, chopped

**Directions** and Total Time: 30 minutes

Heat oil in a pot over medium heat. Place in onion and garlic and sauté for 3 minutes. Add in potato, carrot, tomatoes, broth, tomato paste, chickpeas, and chili; season. Simmer for 20 minutes. Garnish with parsley.

## Spicy Basil Gazpacho

**Ingredients** for 4 servings

2 tbsp olive oil
2 cups water
1 red onion, chopped
6 tomatoes, chopped
1 red bell pepper, diced
2 garlic cloves, minced
Juice of 1 lemon
2 tbsp chopped fresh basil
½ tsp chili pepper

**Directions** and Total Time: 15 minutes

In a food processor, place the olive oil, half of the onion, half of the tomato, half of the bell pepper, garlic, lemon juice, basil, water, and chili pepper. Season with salt and pepper. Blitz until smooth. Transfer to a bowl and add reserved onion, tomatoes, and bell pepper. Let chill in the fridge before serving.

## Turnip & Pearl Barley Stew

**Ingredients** for 6 servings

3 tbsp olive oil
1 onion, chopped
2 garlic cloves, minced
2 turnips, chopped
4 potatoes, chopped
1 cup pearl barley
1 (28-oz) can diced tomatoes
3 tsp dried mixed herbs
Salt and black pepper to taste

**Directions** and Total Time: 30 minutes

Warm the oil in a pot over medium heat. Add onion and garlic and sauté for 3 minutes until fragrant. Stir in turnips, potatoes, barley, tomatoes, 3 cups of water, salt, pepper, and herbs. Cook for 20 minutes. Serve warm.

## Potato & Kale Stew

**Ingredients** for 4 servings

2 tbsp olive oil
1/3 cup chunky butter
1 onion, diced
2 peeled potatoes, chopped
1 tsp paprika
¼ tsp red pepper flakes
Salt to taste
2 cups kale, chopped

**Directions** and Total Time: 30 minutes

Warm the olive oil in a saucepan over medium heat and cook the onion for 3 minutes. Add in potatoes, butter, paprika, pepper flakes, 4 cups water, and salt; stir. Bring to a boil and simmer 20 for minutes. Add in the kale and cook for 5 minutes. Serve warm and enjoy!

## Classic Lentil Stew

**Ingredients** for 4 servings

2 tsp olive oil
2 carrots, chopped
1 onion, chopped
Salt and black pepper to taste
1 tbsp paprika
2 garlic cloves, sliced
1 (28-oz) can diced tomatoes
1 cup lentils, rinsed

**Directions** and Total Time: 25 minutes

Heat the oil in a pot over medium heat. Place in carrots, onion, paprika, and garlic. Sauté for 5 minutes until tender. Stir in 4 cups of water, tomatoes, and lentils. Bring to a boil, then lower the heat and simmer for 20 minutes. Sprinkle with salt and pepper. Serve warm.

## Turmeric Spinach Stew

**Ingredients** for 6 servings

3 tbsp olive oil
3 potatoes, cubed
2 carrots, sliced
4 shallots, chopped
2 garlic cloves, minced
1 tbsp ground turmeric
1 tsp ground ginger
1 ½ cups vegetable broth
4 cups shredded spinach
Salt to taste

**Directions** and Total Time: 30 minutes

Cook the potatoes in salted water over medium heat, about 15 minutes. Drain and reserve. Heat the oil in a saucepan over medium heat. Place in carrots and shallots and cook for 5 minutes. Stir in garlic, turmeric, ginger, and salt. Cook for 1 minute more. Add in cooked potatoes and broth. Bring to a boil, then lower the heat. Stir in the spinach and cook for 3 minutes until wilted.

## Eggplant & Chickpea Stew with Mushrooms

**Ingredients** for 4 servings

2 tbsp olive oil
1 onion, chopped
1 eggplant, chopped
2 medium carrots, sliced
1 red potato, chopped
1 cup mushrooms, sliced
2 garlic cloves, minced
1 (15.5-oz) cans chickpeas
1 (28-oz) can diced tomatoes
1 tbsp minced parsley
½ tsp dried oregano
½ tsp dried basil
1 tbsp soy sauce
½ cup vegetable broth
Salt and black pepper to taste

**Directions** and Total Time: 30 minutes

Heat the oil in a pot over medium heat. Place in onion, garlic, eggplant, and carrots and sauté for 5 minutes. Lower the heat and stir in potato, mushrooms, chickpeas, tomatoes, oregano, basil, soy sauce, salt, pepper, and broth. Simmer for 15 minutes. Sprinkle with parsley.

## Effortless Veggie Stew

**Ingredients** for 4 servings

2 tbsp olive oil
3 shallots, chopped
1 carrot, sliced
½ cup dry white wine
3 new potatoes, cubed
1 red bell pepper, chopped
1 ½ cups vegetable broth
2 zucchini, sliced
1 yellow summer squash, sliced
1 lb plum tomatoes, chopped
Salt and black pepper to taste
3 cups fresh corn kernels
1 cup green beans
¼ cup fresh basil
¼ cup chopped fresh parsley

**Directions** and Total Time: 35 minutes

Heat oil in a pot over medium heat. Place shallots and carrot and cook for 5 minutes. Pour in white wine, potatoes, bell pepper, and broth. Bring to a boil, lower the heat, and simmer for 5 minutes. Stir in zucchini, yellow squash and tomatoes. Sprinkle with salt and pepper. Simmer for 20 more minutes. Put in corn, green beans, basil, and parsley. Simmer an additional 5 minutes.

## Spanish Veggie & Chickpea Stew

**Ingredients** for 4 servings

2 tbsp olive oil
1 onion, chopped
2 carrots, chopped
½ tsp ground cumin
½ tsp ground ginger
½ tsp paprika
½ tsp saffron
1 (14.5-oz) can diced tomatoes
½ head broccoli, cut into florets
2 cups winter squash, chopped
1 russet potato, cubed
1 ½ cups vegetable broth
1 (15.5-oz) can chickpeas
1 tsp lemon zest
Salt and black pepper to taste
½ cup pitted green olives
1 tbsp minced cilantro
½ cup toasted slivered almonds

**Directions** and Total Time: 30 minutes

Heat the olive oil in a pot over medium heat. Place onions and carrots and sauté for 5 minutes until tender. Add in cumin, ginger, paprika, salt, pepper, and saffron and cook for 30 seconds. Stir in tomatoes, broccoli, squash, potato, chickpeas, and broth. Bring to a boil, then lower the heat, and simmer for 20 minutes. Add in the olives and lemon zest, stir, and simmer for 2-3 minutes. Garnish with cilantro and almonds to serve.

## Elegant Kidney Bean Stew

**Ingredients** for 4 servings

2 tbsp olive oil
3 cups cooked red kidney beans
1 yellow onion, chopped
2 carrots, sliced
3 garlic cloves, minced
1 tsp grated fresh ginger
½ tsp ground cumin
1 tsp ras el hanout
2 russet potatoes, chopped
1 (14.5-oz) can diced tomatoes
1 (4-oz) can diced green chiles
1 ½ cups vegetable broth
Salt and black pepper to taste
3 cups eggplants, chopped
¼ cup chopped roasted peanuts

**Directions** and Total Time: 40 minutes

Heat the olive oil in a pot over medium heat. Place the onion, garlic, ginger, and carrots and sauté for 5 minutes until tender. Stir in cumin, ras el hanout, potatoes, beans, tomatoes, chiles, and broth. Season with salt and pepper. Bring to a boil, then lower the heat, and simmer for 20 minutes. Add in the eggplants, stir, and cook for 10 minutes. Serve warm garnished with peanuts.

## Italian Bean Stew

**Ingredients** for 4 servings

2 tbsp olive oil
1 onion, chopped
1 carrot, chopped
2 garlic cloves, minced
1 red bell pepper, chopped
½ cup capers
1 medium zucchini, chopped
1 (14.5-oz) can diced tomatoes
1 cup vegetable broth
Salt and black pepper to taste
8 oz porcini mushrooms, sliced
3 cups fresh baby spinach
1 (15-oz) can cannellini beans
½ tsp dried basil
2 tbsp minced fresh parsley

**Directions** and Total Time: 35 minutes

Heat the olive oil in a pot and sauté onion, carrot, garlic, mushrooms, and bell pepper for 5 minutes. Stir in capers, zucchini, tomatoes, broth, salt, and pepper. Bring to a boil, then lower the heat, and simmer for 20 minutes. Add in beans, baby spinach, and basil. Simmer an additional 2-3 minutes. Serve warm topped with parsley.

## Root-Veggie Medley Stew with Seitan

**Ingredients** for 4 servings

2 tbsp olive oil
8 oz seitan, cubed
1 leek, chopped
2 garlic cloves, minced
1 russet potato, chopped
1 carrot, chopped
1 parsnip, chopped
1 cup butternut squash, cubed
1 head savoy cabbage, chopped
1 (14.5-oz) can diced tomatoes
1 (15.5-oz) can white beans
2 cups vegetable broth
½ cup dry white wine
½ tsp dried thyme
½ cup crumbled angel hair pasta

**Directions** and Total Time: 65 minutes

Heat the olive oil in a pot over medium heat. Place in seitan and cook for 3 minutes. Sprinkle with salt and pepper. Add in the leek and garlic and cook for another 3 minutes until softened. Stir in potato, carrot, parsnip, and squash and cook for 10 minutes. Add in cabbage, tomatoes, white beans, broth, wine, thyme, salt, and pepper. Bring to a boil, lower the heat and simmer for 15 minutes. Put in pasta and cook for 5 minutes. Serve.

## Mexican Kidney Bean Chili

**Ingredients** for 4 servings

4 oz canned green chilies, minced
1 canned chipotle chili, minced
2 tbsp olive oil
1 onion, chopped
2 garlic cloves, minced
1 (16-oz) can tomato sauce
1 tsp ground cumin
½ tsp dried marjoram
1 (15.5-oz) can kidney beans
Salt and black pepper to taste
1 tbsp chili powder
½ tsp cayenne pepper

**Directions** and Total Time: 30 minutes

Heat the oil in a pot over medium heat. Sauté onion and garlic for 3 minutes. Put in tomato sauce, green chilies, chili powder, cumin, cayenne pepper, marjoram, salt, and pepper and cook for 5 minutes. Stir in kidney beans, chipotle chili, and 2 cups of water. Bring to a boil, then lower the heat and simmer for 15 minutes, stirring often.

## Gingery Black Bean Chili

**Ingredients** for 4 servings

2 tbsp olive oil
1 onion, finely chopped
2 carrots, chopped
1 tsp grated fresh ginger
1 green bell pepper, chopped
2 tbsp chili powder
1 (28-oz) can diced tomatoes
1 (15.5-oz) can black beans
3 minced green onions

**Directions** and Total Time: 25 minutes

Heat the oil in a pot over medium heat. Place onion, carrot, ginger, bell pepper, and chili powder. Sauté for 5 minutes until tender. Stir in tomatoes, 2 cups of water, black beans, salt, and pepper. Bring to a boil, then lower the heat and simmer for 15 minutes. Top with green onions.

## Garbanzo Chili with Squash & Green Peas

**Ingredients** for 4 servings

1 (15-oz) can garbanzo beans
2 tbsp olive oil
1 butternut squash, cubed
1 onion, chopped
3 cups tomato salsa
1 cup frozen green peas
1 cup corn kernels
½ tsp cayenne pepper
½ tsp ground allspice
Salt and black pepper to taste

**Directions** and Total Time: 60 minutes

Heat the oil in a saucepan over medium heat. Place in onion and squash and cook for 10 minutes until tender. Add in tomato salsa, garbanzo beans, green peas, corn, cayenne pepper, allspice, salt, and pepper. Pour in 2 cups of water. Simmer for 15 minutes. Serve warm and enjoy!.

## One-Pot Habanero Pinto Beans

**Ingredients** for 6 servings

1 tsp olive oil
2 red bell peppers, diced
1 habanero pepper, minced
2 (14.5-oz) cans pinto beans
½ cup vegetable broth
1 tsp ground cumin
1 tsp chili powder
Salt and black pepper to taste

**Directions** and Total Time: 20 minutes

Heat the oil in a pot over medium heat. Place in bell and habanero peppers, sauté for 5 minutes until tender. Add in beans, broth, cumin, chili powder, salt, and pepper. Bring to a boil, then simmer for 10 minutes. Serve.

## Rice & Bean Soup with Sun-Dried Tomatoes

**Ingredients** for 6 servings

2 tbsp olive oil
3 garlic cloves, minced
1 tbsp chili powder
1 tsp dried oregano
3 (15.5-oz) cans kidney beans
1 habanero pepper, chopped
12 sun-dried tomatoes, diced
6 cups vegetable broth
Salt and black pepper to taste
½ cup brown rice
1 tbsp chopped cilantro

**Directions** and Total Time: 40 minutes

Heat the oil in a pot over medium heat. Place in garlic and sauté for 1 minute. Add in chili powder, oregano, beans, habanero, tomatoes, broth, rice, salt, and pepper. Cook for 30 minutes. Put the rice in a pot with boiling salted water and cook for 5 minutes. Spoon the soup in individual bowls and garnish with cilantro to serve.

## Citrus Butternut Squash Soup

**Ingredients** for 6 servings

2 tbsp olive oil
1 onion, chopped
1 celery stalk, chopped
½ tsp ground allspice
1 potato, peeled and chopped
1 lb butternut squash, cubed
6 cups vegetable broth
Salt to taste
2 tbsp fresh orange juice

**Directions** and Total Time: 30 minutes

Heat the oil in a pot over medium heat. Place in onion and celery and sauté for 5 minutes until tender. Add in allspice, potato, squash, broth, and salt. Cook for 20 minutes. Stir in orange juice. Using an immersion blender, blitz the soup until purée. Return to the pot and heat.

## Parsley Rice Soup with Green Beans

**Ingredients** for 4 servings

2 tbsp olive oil
1 medium onion, minced
2 garlic cloves minced
½ cup brown rice
1 cup green beans, chopped
2 tbsp chopped parsley

**Directions** and Total Time: 50 minutes

Heat oil in a pot over medium heat. Place in onion and garlic and sauté for 3 minutes. Add in rice, 4 cups water, salt, and pepper. Bring to a boil, lower the heat, and simmer for 15 minutes. Stir in beans and cook for 10 minutes. Top with parsley. Serve warm and enjoy!

## Dilly Rice Soup with Vegetables

**Ingredients** for 6 servings

3 tbsp olive oil
1 onion, chopped
1 carrot, chopped
1 celery stalk, chopped
1 cup wild mushrooms, sliced
½ cup brown rice
7 cups vegetable broth
1 tsp dried dill weed
Salt and black pepper to taste

**Directions** and Total Time: 30 minutes

Heat olive oil in a pot over medium heat. Place in onion, carrot, and celery and sauté for 5 minutes. Add mushrooms, rice, broth, dill weed, salt, and pepper. Bring to a boil and simmer uncovered for 20 minutes. Serve.

## Home-Style Minestrone Soup

**Ingredients** for 4 servings

2 tbsp olive oil
1 onion, chopped
1 carrot, chopped
1 stalk celery, chopped
2 garlic cloves, minced
4 cups vegetable stock
1 cup green peas
½ cup orzo
1 (15-oz) can diced tomatoes
2 tsp Italian seasoning
Salt and black pepper to taste

**Directions** and Total Time: 20 minutes

Heat the oil in a pot over medium heat. Place in onion, garlic, carrot, and celery and sauté for 5 minutes until tender. Stir in vegetable stock, green peas, orzo, tomatoes, salt, pepper, and Italian seasoning. Cook for 10 minutes.

## Garbanzo & Spinach Soup

**Ingredients** for 4 servings

2 tbsp olive oil
1 onion, chopped
1 green bell pepper, diced
1 carrot, peeled and diced
4 garlic cloves, minced
1 (15-oz) can garbanzo beans
1 cup spinach, chopped
4 cups vegetable stock
¼ tsp ground cumin
Sea salt to taste
¼ cup chopped cilantro

**Directions** and Total Time: 25 minutes

Heat the oil in a pot over medium heat. Place in onion, garlic, bell pepper, and carrot and sauté for 5 minutes until tender. Stir in garbanzo beans, spinach, vegetable stock, cumin, and salt. Cook for 10 minutes. Mash the garbanzo using a potato masher, leaving some chunks. Sprinkle with cilantro. Serve and enjoy!

## Creamy Artichoke Soup with Almonds

**Ingredients** for 4 servings

2 (10-oz) packages artichoke hearts
1 tbsp olive oil
1/3 cup butter
2 medium shallots, chopped
3 cups vegetable broth
1 tsp fresh lemon juice
Salt to taste
⅛ tsp ground cayenne pepper
1 cup heavy cream
1 tbsp snipped fresh chives
2 tbsp sliced toasted almonds

**Directions** and Total Time: 30 minutes

Heat the oil in a pot over medium heat. Place in shallots and sauté until softened, about 3 minutes. Add in artichokes, broth, lemon juice, and salt. Bring to a boil, lower the heat, and simmer for 10 minutes. Stir in butter and cayenne pepper. Transfer to a food processor and blend until purée. Return to the pot. Mix in the heavy cream and simmer for 5 minutes. Serve warm topped with chives and almonds. Enjoy!

## Carrot & Spinach Gnocchi Soup

**Ingredients** for 4 servings

1 tsp olive oil
1 cup green bell peppers
Salt and black pepper to taste
2 garlic cloves, minced
2 carrots, chopped
3 cups vegetable broth
1 cup gnocchi
¾ cup milk
¼ cup nutritional yeast
2 cups chopped fresh spinach
8 pitted black olives, chopped
1 cup croutons

**Directions** and Total Time: 25 minutes

Heat the oil in a pot over medium heat. Place in bell peppers, garlic, carrots, pepper, and salt and cook for 5 minutes. Stir in broth. Bring to a boil. Put in gnocchi, cook for 10 minutes. Add in spinach and cook for another 5 minutes. Stir in milk, nutritional yeast, and olives. Serve warm in bowls topped with croutons. Enjoy!

## Cilantro Black Bean Soup

**Ingredients** for 4 servings

2 tbsp olive oil
1 onion, chopped
1 celery stalk, chopped
2 medium carrots, chopped
1 green bell pepper, chopped
2 garlic cloves, minced
2 tomatoes, chopped
4 cups vegetable broth
1 (15.5-oz) can black beans
1 tsp dried thyme
¼ tsp cayenne pepper
1 tbsp minced cilantro

**Directions** and Total Time: 50 minutes

Heat the olive oil in a pot over medium heat. Place in onion, celery, carrots, bell pepper, garlic, and tomatoes. Sauté for 5 minutes, stirring often until softened. Stir in broth, beans, thyme, salt, and cayenne. Bring to a boil, then lower the heat and simmer for 15 minutes. Transfer the soup to a food processor and pulse until smooth. Serve in soup bowls garnished with cilantro. Enjoy!

## Sopa Norteña

**Ingredients** for 4 servings

3 tbsp olive oil
1 onion, chopped
3 garlic cloves, chopped
1 cup sweet corn
1 (14.5-oz) can diced tomatoes
1 (15.5-oz) can black beans
1 (4-oz) can hot chilies
1 tsp ground cumin
½ tsp dried oregano
4 cups vegetable broth
Salt and black pepper to taste
¼ cup chopped cilantro

**Directions** and Total Time: 30 minutes

Warm the olive oil in a pot over medium heat. Place in the onion and garlic and sauté for 3 minutes. Add in sweet corn, tomatoes, beans, chilies, cumin, oregano, broth, salt, and pepper. Reduce the heat and simmer for 15 minutes. Garnish with cilantro to serve.

## Green Coconut Soup

**Ingredients** for 4 servings

2 tbsp coconut oil
1 ½ cups vegetable broth
2 garlic cloves, minced
1 onion, chopped
1 tbsp minced fresh ginger
1 green bell pepper, sliced
1 (13.5-oz) can coconut milk
Juice of ½ lime
2 tbsp chopped basil
1 tbsp chopped cilantro
4 lime wedges

**Directions** and Total Time: 15 minutes

Warm the coconut oil in a medium pot over medium heat. Place in onion, garlic, and ginger and sauté for 3 minutes. Add in bell peppers and broth. Bring to a boil, then lower the heat and simmer. Stir in coconut milk, lime juice, and chopped cilantro. Simmer for 5 minutes. Serve garnished with basil and lime. Enjoy!

# SNACKS & SIDES

## Walnut-Topped Brussels Sprout Leaves

**Ingredients** for 2 servings

1 cup Brussels sprout leaves
½ tbsp extra-virgin olive oil
Salt and black pepper to taste
½ tsp lemon zest
1 tbsp walnuts, chopped

**Directions** and Total Time: 25 minutes

Turn the oven on to 375°F. Lay parchment paper or a silicone mat on a cookie sheet and set aside. Put the Brussels sprout leaves in a bowl with the olive oil and lemon zest and toss. Add some salt and pepper and toss again. Bake in the oven for 12 minutes. Scatter with lemon zest and walnuts and serve.

## Picante Cauliflower

**Ingredients** for 2 servings

½ cauliflower head, cut into florets
1 tbsp extra-virgin olive oil
1 tsp garlic powder
Salt and black pepper to taste
1 tbsp butter
¼ cup hot sauce
1 tsp cilantro, chopped

**Directions** and Total Time: 35 minutes

Turn the oven on to 400°F. Lay a silicone mat or parchment paper on a cookie sheet and set aside. Pour some olive oil over the cauliflower, then sprinkle in the garlic powder. Add some salt and pepper, then toss. Place the cauliflower on one side of the cookie sheet and cook for 15 minutes. Use a metal spoon to flip all the pieces, then cook for an additional 10 minutes. On medium heat, put the butter and hot sauce in a pan and stir until the butter melts and is mixed into the sauce. Use a cooking brush to rub the sauce on the cauliflower, then cook for another 5 minutes. Serve hot topped with cilantro. Enjoy!

## Mediterranean Kale

**Ingredients** for 2 servings

1 tbsp extra-virgin olive oil
1 garlic clove, minced
1 shallot, thinly sliced
2 cups kale, chopped
¼ lime, juiced
1 tbsp capers, chopped
Salt and black pepper to taste

**Directions** and Total Time: 10 minutes

Pour the olive oil into a skillet and turn the burner on medium. Toss the garlic and shallot in and cook for a minute. Stir regularly. Place the kale, lime juice, and capers in the skillet and cook for another 3-4 minutes, allowing the kale to wilt. Add more salt and pepper and stir. Place in equal amounts on 2 plates. Serve.

## Thyme Roasted Asparagus

**Ingredients** for 2 servings

½ cup grated Parmesan
1 bunch of asparagus
2 tbsp extra-virgin olive oil
¼ cup bread crumbs
½ tsp garlic powder
Salt and black pepper to taste
½ tsp dried thyme

**Directions** and Total Time: 20 minutes

Turn the oven on to 425°F. Snap the ends off the asparagus and put it in a large sealable bag. Add the olive oil and shake to coat, then open the bag and toss in the bread crumbs, Parmesan cheese, and garlic powder. Last, add some thyme, salt, and pepper, then close the bag and shake until the asparagus is well-coated. Place the asparagus in one layer on the cookie sheet and cook for 8-10 minutes.

## Hot Roasted Hazelnuts

**Ingredients** for 4 servings

1 tsp ground cumin
1 tsp cayenne pepper
Salt and black pepper to taste
2 cups hazelnuts
1 tbsp extra-virgin olive oil

**Directions** and Total Time: 10 minutes

Combine the cumin, cayenne pepper, salt, and pepper in a bowl. Put a skillet on the stove and turn on medium heat. Toss the hazelnuts in the dry skillet and roast for 5 minutes. After roasting, mix with the seasoning mix, then pour in olive oil and stir, coating the nuts well. After lining a cooking sheet with parchment paper or silicone mat, put the nuts on top, and allow to chill. Serve.

## Mushroom Nori Roll Bites

**Ingredients** for 4 servings

2 tbsp butter
2 tbsp soy sauce
4 nori sheets
1 mushroom, sliced
½ chili garlic salt
1 tbsp pickled ginger
½ cup grated carrots
1 tsp chopped cilantro

**Directions** and Total Time: 25 minutes

Preheat the oven to 350°F. Whisk together butter and soy sauce until smooth. Prepare a sheet of nori with the rough side up and the long way. Smear a thin line of the peanut mixture on the far side of the nori from one side to the other. Arrange a line of mushroom slices, ginger, garlic salt, cilantro, and carrots on the closest end. Roll the vegetables inside the nori. The tahini mixture will seal the roll. Continue this process for the remaining 3 rolls. Arrange the rolls on a baking sheet and bake for 8-10 minutes. The rolls will be just browned and crispy. Cool for a few minutes until you can slice them into 3 smaller rolls. Serve warm and enjoy.

## Herb Sweet Potato Fries

**Ingredients** for 2 servings

1 medium sweet potato
1 tsp olive oil
Garlic salt to taste
¼ tsp dried basil
¼ tsp dried oregano
¼ tsp dried rosemary

**Directions** and Total Time: 55 minutes

Preheat the oven to 350°F. Peel the sweet potato then cut into fries. Use your hands to rub the oil and seasonings on the fries. Arrange in a single layer on a large baking sheet. Bake for 15-20 minutes, then flip the fries. Bake for another 15-25 minutes or until the fries are soft.

## Traditional Hummus

**Ingredients** for 6 servings

1 tbsp olive oil
1 (14-oz) can chickpeas
1 tbsp tahini
1 lemon, zested and juiced
2 garlic cloves, minced
Salt to taste
1 tsp ground cumin
1 tbsp parsley, chopped
¼ tsp paprika
Toasted pitas for serving

**Directions** and Total Time: 15 minutes

Puree olive oil, chickpeas, tahini, lemon zest, lemon juice, garlic, salt, and cumin in the food processor. Slowly pour ¼ cup water while it is blending until it reaches the desired consistency. Transfer the hummus to a serving bowl. Garnish with parsley and paprika. Serve with pitas.

## Easy-Peasy Shepherd's Pie

**Ingredients** for 6 servings

1 ½ lb cooked potatoes, mashed
1 tbsp cornstarch
1 cup vegetable broth
2 tsp olive oil
½ cup chopped onions
2 garlic cloves, minced
1 (15-oz) can lentils
1 ½ cups mushrooms, diced
1 tbsp tomato purée
1 ½ tsp dried thyme
Salt and black pepper to taste

**Directions** and Total Time: 40 minutes

Preheat the oven to 425°F. Whisk broth and cornstarch in a small bowl. Set aside. In an oven-safe skillet, heat oil over medium heat. Sauté onion for 3 minutes until softened. Sauté garlic for 1 minute until aromatic. Stir in lentils, mushrooms, tomato puree, thyme, salt, and pepper. Cook for 2 minutes, then slowly pour in the slurry. Remove from heat after 3 to 5 minutes when the mixture has thickened. Cover the lentil mixture completely with the potatoes. Bake for 18 to 20 minutes until the pie is bubbling. Serve warm and enjoy!

## Asian-Inspired Rice

**Ingredients** for 4 servings

1 tsp sesame oil
1 cup vegetable broth
1 cup jasmine rice
½ cup coconut milk
2 tsp minced fresh ginger
Salt to taste
½ lime, juiced
¾ cup shelled edamame
1 red chili, minced

**Directions** and Total Time: 20 minutes

In a saucepan, add oil, broth, rice, coconut milk, ginger, and salt over medium heat. Stir, then cover. Bring to a boil, reduce the heat. Simmer for 15 minutes until all of the liquid is absorbed. Remove and sit for 5 minutes. Fluff with a fork. Stir in lime juice, edamame, and red chili.

## Cornbread Zucchini Muffins

**Ingredients** for 6 servings

1 cup milk
1 tbsp apple cider vinegar
1 cup ground yellow cornmeal
¾ cup all-purpose flour
¼ cup sucanat
2 tsp baking soda
Salt to taste
¼ cup coconut oil
3 cups grated green zucchini

**Directions** and Total Time: 30 minutes

Preheat the oven to 400°F. Lightly spray nonstick cooking spray on a 12-cup muffin tin or use muffin liners.

Whisk milk and vinegar in a small bowl. Whisk cornmeal, flour, sucanat, baking soda, and salt in a large bowl. Stir in milk mixture and coconut oil until combined. Fold in zucchini. Add ¼ cup of the batter to each muffin cup. Bake for 20 to 22 minutes or until golden. Serve warm.

## Black Bean & Quinoa Nachos

**Ingredients** for 4 servings

½ cup shredded purple cabbage
½ cup salsa
¼ cup quinoa
1 tsp tamari sauce
½ tsp ancho chili powder
½ tsp cumin
½ tsp garlic powder
Tortilla chips
¾ cup canned black beans
½ cup cheddar shreds
½ cup chopped tomatoes
¼ cup sour cream
2 scallions, chopped

**Directions** and Total Time: 25 minutes

Over medium heat, stir together salsa, quinoa, ½ cup water, tamari sauce, ancho chili powder, cumin, and garlic powder in a medium saucepan. Cover and bring to a boil. Keep the pan covered and reduce the heat. Simmer for 15 minutes until all of the liquid is absorbed. Remove from heat and let it sit for 5 minutes. Fluff with a fork. To build the nachos, arrange a layer of chips on a platter. Top the chips with beans, quinoa, cheese shreds, tomato, and cabbage. Repeat the order for another layer. Drizzle with sour cream and garnish with scallions. Serve.

## Curry Bean Hummus

**Ingredients** for 6 servings

1 (15-oz) can cannellini beans
2 tbsp toasted sesame oil
1 tsp garlic powder
½ tsp curry powder
½ tsp dried oregano
½ tsp ground cumin
Salt and black pepper to taste
2 tbsp olive oil for drizzling

**Directions** and Total Time: 10 minutes

Add all of the ingredients except the olive oil to a blender jar. Blend until smooth, adding up to 2 tablespoons of water to adjust the consistency. To serve, pour the hummus into a bowl, then drizzle with oil. Serve.

## Cauliflower Fajitas

**Ingredients** for 4 servings

1 head cauliflower, cut into florets
½ cup corn kernels
4 garlic cloves, sliced
2 tbsp avocado oil
1 tbsp Tajín seasoning
2 scallions, thinly sliced

**Directions** and Total Time: 30 minutes

Preheat the oven to 425°F. Toss cauliflower, corn, garlic, oil, and Tajin seasoning in a large bowl. Arrange the cauliflower mixture on a parchment-lined baking sheet and bake for 15 minutes. Toss the cauliflower and bake for another 10 minutes until golden. Transfer to a serving dish and garnish with scallions. Serve warm and enjoy.

## Curried Kale & Lentil Dip

**Ingredients** for 6 servings

2 leaves kale, stemmed
1 (14-oz) can lentils
1 lemon, zested and juiced
1 tbsp tahini
1 tsp curry powder
1 tsp ground cumin
1 tsp smoked paprika
Salt to taste

**Directions** and Total Time: 30 minutes

All ingredients to a blender and blend until smooth. Adjust the seasoning and serve. Enjoy!

## Chipotle Baked Broccoli with Almonds

**Ingredients** for 2 servings

½ broccoli head, cut into florets
2 tbsp grated Parmesan cheese
2 tbsp extra-virgin olive oil
1 tsp chipotle powder
½ tsp garlic powder
Salt to taste
2 tbsp sliced almonds
2 lemon wedges

**Directions** and Total Time: 30 minutes

Turn the oven on to 400°F. Add the broccoli, olive oil, chipotle powder, and garlic powder to a bowl and toss. Add some salt and toss again. Put the broccoli in one layer on a parchment-lined cookie sheet and bake for 20 minutes. Take it out and stir the broccoli, then put the sliced almonds with the broccoli and stir again. Cook for an additional 5 minutes. Take it out, squirt the lemon wedges on top, and add Parmesan cheese on top.

## Curried Roasted Cauliflower

**Ingredients** for 2 servings

½ cauliflower head, cut into florets
1 tbsp extra-virgin olive oil
Salt and black pepper to taste
½ cup milk
2 tbsp butter
¼ tsp red curry paste
1 garlic clove, minced
1 tbsp chopped chervil

**Directions** and Total Time: 30 minutes

Turn the oven on to 400°F. Put the cauliflower on one side on a parchment-lined cookie sheet, then pour some olive oil over all of it. Add some salt and pepper as well. Cook for 20 minutes. As the cauliflower is roasting, pour the milk, butter, curry paste, and garlic in a blender, then blend until creamy. When the cauliflower is cooked, put equal amounts on 2 plates and drizzle some peanut sauce all over. Top with chervil.

## Tomatoes Provençal

**Ingredients** for 2 servings

½ cup shaved Parmesan
1 large tomato, cut into 4 slices
1 tsp herbs de Provençe
1 tsp parsley, chopped

**Directions** and Total Time: minutes

Turn the oven on to 400°F. Lay a silicone mat or parchment paper on a cookie sheet and set aside. Place the tomatoes in one layer on the cookie sheet and toss the herbs de Provençe on top. Add some Parmesan cheese and parsley, then cook for 10 minutes.

## Crispy Smoky Roasted Chickpeas

**Ingredients** for 2 servings

1 (14-oz) can chickpeas
2 tbsp shoyu soy sauce
½ tsp ginger powder
1 tsp smoked paprika
1 tsp onion powder
½ tsp garlic powder

**Directions** and Total Time: 35 minutes

Preheat the oven to 400°F. Combine all of the ingredients in a large bowl. Arrange them in a single layer on a baking sheet. Bake for 10 minutes, then stir the chickpeas with a spatula. Bake for another 10-15 minutes until the chickpeas are toasty. Serve warm and enjoy.

## Bean Tacos with Red Cabbage Slaw

**Ingredients** for 6 servings

1 cup white button mushrooms, stemmed and diced
3 cups sliced purple cabbage
¼ cup mayonnaise
½ lemon, juiced
¼ cup chopped parsley
1 (15-oz) can red beans
1 green onion, thinly sliced
1 tbsp olive oil
Salt and black pepper to taste
6 corn tortillas
3 tbsp chipotle sauce
1 tbsp sesame seeds

**Directions** and Total Time: 35 minutes

Preheat the oven to 400°F. Lightly spray a baking sheet with cooking oil. Add cabbage, mayonnaise, lemon juice, parsley, and salt in a large bowl. Toss to coat. In a separate bowl, mix beans, mushrooms, onion, oil, salt, and pepper. Transfer to the baking sheet and spread out evenly. Bake for 20 minutes, tossing with a spatula halfway through. Arrange the tortillas over the bean and mushroom mixture. Bake for 2 more minutes, then place the tortillas on a plate. To prepare the tacos, spread a spoonful of the mixture on the tortilla, then top with the slaw. Drizzle with chipotle sauce. Top with sesame seeds.

## Mexican Bean Spread

**Ingredients** for 6 servings

1 cup torn romaine lettuce
1 (15-oz) can black beans
Salt and black pepper to taste
1 cup sour cream
2 tsp taco seasoning
¼ tsp jalapeño powder
2 avocados, mashed
1 cup salsa
2 tbsp chives, chopped
Tortilla chips, for serving

**Directions** and Total Time: 25 minutes

Mash beans, salt, and pepper in a medium bowl. Spread it evenly on the bottom of a 1-quart serving dish. Combine sour cream, jalapeno powder, and taco seasoning in a small bowl. Spread that layer over the bean mixture. Next, spread on the avocado, then the salsa. Top with romaine and chives. Serve with tortilla chips and enjoy.

## Hot Butter Bean Dip

**Ingredients** for 6 servings

1 (14-oz) can butter beans
1 lime, zested and juiced
1 tbsp soy sauce
¼ cup fresh cilantro, chopped
1 tsp ground cumin
¼ tsp chili powder
1 cup tortilla chips

**Directions** and Total Time: 15 minutes

Puree the butter beans, lime zest, lime juice, and soy sauce in a food processor. Slowly add ¼ cup water while it is blending until smooth and the desired consistency. Stir in cilantro, cumin, and chili powder. Transfer to a serving bowl. Serve with tortillas and enjoy!

## Cabbage Pancakes with Hot Sauce

**Ingredients** for 4 servings

- 2 cups shredded green cabbage
- ¼ cup creamy butter
- 4 tsp tamari
- 1 tsp sriracha sauce
- 1 cup all-purpose flour
- 1 tbsp baking powder
- 1 ¼ cups vegetable broth
- 3 green onions, thinly sliced
- 2 garlic cloves, minced
- Salt and black pepper to taste
- 1 tbsp olive oil

**Directions** and Total Time: 25 minutes

Whisk butter, ¼ cup water, 2 teaspoons tamari, and sriracha in a small bowl until well blended. Set aside. Stir flour, baking powder, broth, and 2 teaspoons tamari in a large bowl. Fold in cabbage, green onions, garlic, salt, and pepper until just combined. In a medium skillet, heat olive oil over medium heat. Pour ½ cup of the batter into the skillet. Look for bubbles in the middle of the pancake. Flip the pancake, then gently press down with the spatula. Cook for another 1 to 2 minutes. Repeat the process with the rest of the batter and add more oil as needed to prevent sticking. To serve, cut the pancakes into quarters. Serve with peanut sauce for dipping.

## Rosemary Potato Wedges

**Ingredients** for 4 servings

- 3 potatoes, cut into wedges
- 8 garlic cloves, peeled
- 2 tsp olive oil
- 1 tsp nutritional yeast
- Salt to taste
- 2 tbsp chopped rosemary

**Directions** and Total Time: 35 minutes

Preheat the oven to 350°F. Toss the potato wedges in a large bowl with garlic cloves, oil, nutritional yeast, and salt. Arrange on a rectangular baking sheet and bake for 20-25 minutes. When the potatoes are soft and golden, sprinkle with rosemary. Serve warm and enjoy.

## Chili-Garlic Flatbreads

**Ingredients** for 2 servings

- 1 tsp olive oil
- ¼ tsp chili garlic salt
- 2 whole-grain round flatbreads

**Directions** and Total Time: 10 minutes

Combine oil and chili garlic salt in a small bowl. Brush the oil mixture on the flatbreads and broil on high for 5 minutes. Serve hot and enjoy.

## Kale & Beet Chips

**Ingredients** for 2 servings

- 4 cups curly kale, torn
- 1 beet, thinly sliced
- 2 tbsp apple cider vinegar
- 1 tbsp olive oil
- Sea salt to taste

**Directions** and Total Time: 15 minutes

Preheat oven to 350°F. Line a baking sheet with parchment paper. Toss kale, beet, vinegar, and olive oil in a bowl. Massage the kale with the mixture until soft and dark green. Arrange the vegetables in a single layer on the baking sheet. Bake for 20 to 25 minutes or until crisp. Season with sea salt and cool completely. Serve when cooled or store in an airtight container for up to 5 days.

## Swiss Chard & Chickpea Burritos

**Ingredients** for 6 servings

- 3 tbsp olive oil
- 1 shallot, chopped
- 2 garlic cloves, minced
- 1 (15-oz) can chickpeas
- 2 tsp paprika
- 1 tsp chipotle powder
- Salt and black pepper to taste
- 1 bunch Swiss chard, chopped
- 4 whole-wheat tortillas
- 2 cups cooked brown rice
- 2 avocados, sliced
- ½ cup sour cream
- ½ cup salsa

**Directions** and Total Time: 30 minutes

In a large skillet, heat 1 tablespoon of oil over medium heat. Stir in shallot and sauté until soft, about 3 minutes. Stir in garlic and cook for another minute or until aromatic. Next, stir in chickpeas, paprika, chipotle powder, salt, and pepper. Continue stirring for 3 minutes, then add chard and cook for another 3 minutes until wilted. To build the burrito, lay a tortilla on a flat work surface. Add ¼ cup rice, ¼ cup chard mixture, avocado slices, and 1 tablespoon sour cream on the half closest to you.

Start folding the tortilla over the mixture and roll away from you. Fold in the sides and continue until the burrito is completely rolled up. Repeat the process for the rest of the tortillas and filling. In a large skillet, heat 1 teaspoon of oil over medium-low heat. Transfer the burrito to the skillet, seam-side down. Add weight to it to keep it in place. Cook for 2 minutes, then carefully flip the burrito. Cook for another 2 minutes or until the tortilla is crisp and golden. Repeat the process for the remaining burritos. Serve with salsa and enjoy.

## Lentil Sloopy Joes

**Ingredients** for 4 servings

- 2 tsp hot sauce
- 2 tbsp olive oil
- 1 onion, chopped
- ½ green bell pepper, chopped
- 1 garlic clove, minced
- 1 (15-oz) can lentils
- 1 (7-oz) can tomato sauce
- 1 tbsp dark-brown sugar
- 1 tbsp red pepper flakes
- 1 tsp ground cumin
- ½ tsp ground fennel seeds
- 4 hamburger buns, toasted

**Directions** and Total Time: 25 minutes

In a large skillet, heat oil over medium heat. Sauté onion and bell pepper for 3 minutes until onion is softened. Reduce the heat to medium and sauté garlic for 1 minute until aromatic. Stir in lentils and heat through for 2 minutes. Stir in tomato sauce, hot sauce, sugar, red pepper flakes, cumin and fennel seeds. Cover and simmer for 10 minutes. Add salt and pepper. Portion the sloppy joes between the buns. Serve warm and enjoy.

## Tofu Muffins

**Ingredients** for 6 servings

1 cup diced white button mushrooms
1 (14-oz) block tofu
½ cup vegetable broth
2 tbsp olive oil
1 tbsp cornstarch
1 tsp onion powder
1 tsp garlic powder
½ tsp ground turmeric
Salt to taste
1 chopped shallot
½ red bell pepper, chopped
1 tsp dried rosemary

**Directions** and Total Time: 30 minutes

Preheat the oven to 425°F. Lightly spray nonstick cooking spray on a 12-cup muffin tin. Add tofu, broth, oil, cornstarch, onion powder, garlic powder, turmeric, and salt in a blender jar. Blend until smooth. Pour into a large bowl and add shallot, bell pepper, mushrooms, and rosemary. Stir to combine. Scoop ¼ cup of the mixture into each muffin cup. Bake for 20 to 25 minutes until a toothpick in the middle comes out clean. Serve warm.

## Pizza-Style Hot Avocado Tortillas

**Ingredients** for 2 servings

¼ cup thinly sliced sundried tomatoes
2 flour tortillas
1 pitted avocado, peeled
½ lime, juiced
Salt and black pepper to taste
½ tsp garlic powder
¼ cup chopped fresh basil
¼ tsp red pepper flakes

**Directions** and Total Time: 15 minutes

Preheat the oven to 370°F. Arrange the tortillas on a parchment-lined baking sheet and lightly spray with cooking oil. Bake for 5 minutes, then flip the tortillas. Lightly spray again and bake for 3 minutes until golden and just crisp. Mash avocado together with lime juice, garlic powder, salt, and pepper in a medium bowl. Spread the avocado mixture over each tortilla. Top with tomatoes, basil, and red pepper flakes. Serve and enjoy.

## Pumpkin & Cavolo Nero Hash

**Ingredients** for 4 servings

4 cups cavolo nero (kale), chopped
2 tbsp olive oil
1 onion, chopped
2 garlic cloves, minced
2 cups pumpkin cubes
1 tsp smoked paprika
1 tsp dried rosemary
½ cup vegetable broth
Salt and black pepper to taste

**Directions** and Total Time: 40 minutes

In a large skillet, heat oil over medium heat. Sauté onion for 3 minutes until soft. Stir in garlic and sauté for another minute until aromatic. Next, mix in pumpkin, smoked paprika, and rosemary. Cook for 5 minutes until the pumpkin starts to brown on the edges. Stir in broth slowly. Cover the skillet and simmer for 7 minutes. Remove the lid and top the pumpkin with cavolo nero. Return the lid and simmer until the kale is wilted, or about 2 minutes. Season with salt and pepper and simmer uncovered for 5 minutes. When the liquid has cooked off and the pumpkin is fork-tender, it is ready.

## Great Northern Bean Quesadillas with Spinach

**Ingredients** for 4 servings

1 (15-oz) can great northern beans
¼ cup vegetable broth
3 tbsp olive oil
½ lemon, juiced
2 garlic cloves, minced
½ tsp dried oregano
Salt and black pepper to taste
1 cup chopped spinach
4 whole-wheat tortillas
¼ cup barbecue sauce

**Directions** and Total Time: 25 minutes

Add beans, broth, 1 ½ tablespoons olive oil, lemon juice, garlic, oregano, salt, and pepper in a blender jar. Puree until smooth, about 1 minute. Set aside. Toss spinach and 1 tablespoon of olive oil in a bowl until coated. In a large skillet, heat ½ tablespoon olive oil over medium heat. Spread ¼ of the bean mixture over half of the tortilla, then cover with ¼ cup of spinach. Fold the tortilla in half over the mixture, then press down. Cook for 2 minutes on each side. Transfer to a plate when golden. Repeat with the remaining tortillas. To serve, cut each tortilla into quarters and plate with BBQ sauce on the side or drizzled on top. Serve warm and enjoy.

## Picante Zucchini Boats with Chickpeas & Kale

**Ingredients** for 4 servings

1 (15-oz) can chickpeas, half mashed and half left whole
½ cup cayenne-based hot sauce
2 large green zucchinis
2 cups chopped baby kale
1 tbsp butter, melted
¼ tsp garlic powder
¼ tsp shallot powder
Salt to taste
2 tbsp ranch dressing
2 tbsp chopped parsley

**Directions** and Total Time: 30 minutes

Preheat the oven to 450°F. Cut the zucchini lengthwise and scoop out some of the flesh from each half. Leave about ¼"-thick wall for the shell. Combine mashed chickpeas, whole chickpeas, kale, cayenne hot sauce, butter, garlic, shallot powder, and salt in a large bowl. Spoon the mixture into the zucchini shells, then place on a parchment-lined baking sheet. Bake for 15 to 20 minutes until the zucchini is fork-tender. Drizzle with ranch dressing and top with parsley.

## Chipotle Lentil Tortillas

**Ingredients** for 6 servings

1 ½ cups torn romaine lettuce
2 tomatoes, chopped
2 (15-oz) cans lentils
1 ½ cups chunky mild salsa
1 tbsp taco seasoning
½ tsp chipotle powder
12 corn tortillas
4 tbsp sour cream
1 cup shredded carrot
6 scallions, thinly sliced
2 tbsp hot sauce

**Directions** and Total Time: 15 minutes

Add lentils, salsa, taco seasoning, and chipotle powder to a large skillet over medium heat. Bring to a boil. Reduce the heat and simmer for 5 to 8 minutes to reduce the liquid by half. Spread a layer of the lentil mixture on each tortilla, then top with lettuce, tomatoes, and sour cream. Next, add carrots, scallions, and hot sauce. Serve.

## Primavera Spaghetti Squash

**Ingredients** for 4 servings

4 lb halved spaghetti squash, seeded
2 cups chopped broccoli florets
3 tbsp olive oil
1 onion, chopped
1 celery stalk, chopped
½ cup green olives, sliced
1 cup halved grape tomatoes
3 garlic cloves, minced
1 tsp dried oregano
Salt and black pepper to taste
1 tbsp pine nuts
2 tbsp Parmesan cheese
½ tsp red pepper flakes

**Directions** and Total Time: 50 minutes

Preheat the oven to 400°F. Line a baking sheet with parchment paper. Brush 1 tablespoon oil on the rims and inside of the squash. Place cut-side down on the baking sheet and bake for 35 to 45 minutes. When the flesh is fork-tender, set the squash aside to cool for 10 to 15 minutes. In a large skillet, heat 1 tablespoon of oil over medium heat. Sauté onion, garlic, broccoli, and celery for 3 minutes until softened. Stir in olives and tomatoes. Cook for 3 to 5 minutes until the tomatoes have shrunk and the broccoli is fork-tender. Remove from heat. Scrape the strands gently from the squash lengthwise for the longest noodles. Add the noodles to the skillet and gently stir along with 1 tablespoon oil, oregano, salt, and pepper. Portion among 4 bowls. Top with pine nuts, Parmesan cheese, and red pepper flakes. Serve warm.

## Spinach & Tofu Stuffed Portobellos

**Ingredients** for 4 servings

1 tbsp olive oil
1 leek, chopped
3 garlic cloves, minced
1(14-oz) block tofu, crumbled
5 oz baby spinach
2 tsp Italian seasoning
1 tsp onion powder
½ tsp garlic powder
½ tsp ground nutmeg
1 tomato, chopped
Salt and black pepper to taste
4 portobello mushroom caps

**Directions** and Total Time: 35 minutes

Preheat the oven to 450°F. Lightly spray a baking sheet with cooking oil. Heat oil in a large skillet over medium heat. Sauté leeks for 3 minutes until softened. Sauté garlic for 1 minute until aromatic. Add tofu and spinach to the skillet. Cook for 3 minutes to wilt the spinach. Stir in Italian seasoning, onion powder, garlic powder, nutmeg, tomato, salt, and pepper. Arrange the mushroom caps on the baking sheet with the top side down. Stuff the mushroom caps with the tofu mixture and bake for 15 to 20 minutes. The stuffing will be golden. Serve warm.

## Garam Masala Cauliflower Pakoras

**Ingredients** for 4 servings

½ cup chopped cauliflower
2/3 cup chickpea flour
1 tbsp cornstarch
Salt to taste
2 tsp cumin powder
½ tsp coriander powder
½ tsp turmeric
1 tsp garam masala
⅛ tsp baking soda
⅛ tsp cayenne powder
1 ½ cups minced onion
½ cup chopped cilantro
¼ cup lime juice

**Directions** and Total Time: 30 minutes

Preheat your air fryer to 350°F. Combine the flour, cornstarch, salt, cumin, coriander, turmeric, garam masala, baking soda, and cayenne in a bowl. Stir well. Stir in the onion, cilantro, cauliflower, and lime juice to the flour mix. Using your hands, stir the mix, massaging the flour and spices into the vegetables. Form the mixture into balls and place them in the greased frying basket. Spray the tops of the pakoras in the air fryer with oil and Air Fry for 15-18 minutes, turning once until crispy.

## Chipotle Mushroom Taquitos

**Ingredients** for 6 servings

2 portobello mushroom caps, sliced
2 tbsp soy sauce
1 tbsp olive oil
2 limes, juiced
2 tbsp chopped fresh cilantro
1 tsp ground cumin
1 tsp garlic powder
1 tsp onion powder
1 tsp chipotle powder
1 yellow bell pepper, sliced
1 red bell pepper, sliced
1 jalapeño pepper, sliced
1 onion, sliced
12 flour tortillas, warmed
½ head lettuce, torn
½ cup guacamole
3 tbsp sour cream

**Directions** and Total Time: 20 minutes

Whisk together the soy sauce, oil, lime juice, cilantro, cumin, garlic powder, onion powder, and chipotle powder in a medium bowl. Stir in the mushrooms and let sit for at least 10 minutes. After that, toss the bell peppers, jalapeño pepper, and onions with the mushroom until coated with the marinade. In a large skillet, add the vegetables and marinade over medium heat. Cook for 8 minutes stirring occasionally. When the vegetables are tender and the liquid has been absorbed, transfer to a serving dish with lettuce, guacamole, and sour cream on the side. Serve warm with tortillas and enjoy.

## No-Guilty Spring Rolls

**Ingredients** for 6 servings

2 cups shiitake mushrooms, thinly sliced
4 cups green cabbage, chopped
4 tsp sesame oil
6 garlic cloves, minced
1 tbsp grated ginger
1 cup grated carrots
Salt to taste
16 rice paper wraps
½ tsp ground cumin
½ tsp ground coriander

**Directions** and Total Time: 20 minutes

Warm the sesame oil in a pan over medium heat. Add garlic, ginger, mushrooms, cabbage, carrots, cumin, coriander, and salt and stir-fry for 3-4 minutes or until the cabbage is wilted. Remove from heat. Get a piece of rice paper, wet with water, and lay it on a flat, non-absorbent surface. Place ¼ cup of the filling in the middle, then fold the bottom over the filling and fold the sides in. Roll up to make a mini burrito. Repeat until you have the number of spring rolls you want. Preheat air fryer to 390°F. Place the spring rolls in the greased frying basket. Spray the top of each spring roll with oil and Air Fry for 8-10 minutes or until crispy and golden.

## Sundried Tomato & Bean Bruschetta

**Ingredients** for 4 servings

1 (15-oz) can cannellini beans
5 sundried tomatoes, chopped
1 garlic clove, minced
¼ cup chopped Sicilian olives
2 tbsp olive oil
¼ cup chopped fresh basil
Salt and black pepper to taste
1 sliced baguette, toasted

**Directions** and Total Time: 20 minutes

Combine all ingredients except the baguette in a large bowl until well mixed. To serve, place a heaping spoonful on top of each toasted bread slice and arrange on an appetizer plate. Serve and enjoy.

## BBQ Roasted Cauliflower

**Ingredients** for 4 servings

1 head cauliflower, cut into florets
2 tbsp olive oil
¾ cup sucanat
1/3 cup white wine vinegar
1 tbsp ketchup
¼ cup tamari sauce
2 tbsp cornstarch
4 cups cooked brown rice
2 scallions, chopped
2 tbsp white sesame seeds

**Directions** and Total Time: 30 minutes

Preheat the oven to 450°F. Line a baking sheet with parchment paper. Toss cauliflower and oil in a large bowl. Arrange in a single layer on the baking sheet and roast for 15 minutes. Toss the cauliflower and roast for another 10 minutes until golden and tender. While the cauliflower is in the oven, add sucanat, 2/3 cup water, vinegar, and ketchup in a large skillet over medium heat. Bring to a boil, then reduce the heat and simmer. Whisk tamari and cornstarch in a small bowl. Stir slowly in the skillet until combined. Cook for 2 to 4 minutes until the sauce has thickened. Mix the roasted cauliflower in the skillet with the sauce and stir until coated. Portion out rice among 4 bowls, then spoon cauliflower over the rice. Top with scallions and sesame seeds. Serve warm.

## Nutty Lentil Spread

**Ingredients** for 6 servings

1 tbsp olive oil
1 onion, chopped
1(15-oz) can lentils
½ cup chopped walnuts
1 tsp dried oregano
½ cup mayonnaise
Salt to taste
12 Kalamata olives, sliced

**Directions** and Total Time: 10 minutes

In a medium skillet, heat oil over medium heat. Sauté onion for 3 minutes to soften. In a blender jar, add onion, lentils, walnuts, mayonnaise, oregano, and salt. Puree until smooth. Be sure to scrape down the sides. Pour into a serving dish and top with olives. Serve.

## Avocado-Quinoa Collard Wraps with Coleslaw

**Ingredients** for 4 servings

4 large collard green leaves
¼ cup hummus
½ cup cooked quinoa
1 avocado, sliced
2 radishes, sliced
½ cup julienned carrots
½ cup sprouts
½ cup shredded cabbage

**Directions** and Total Time: 20 minutes

Cut the stems from each collard leaf. Lay the leaves on a flat work surface with the stem side pointing away from you. Spread 1 tablespoon of hummus down the center of each leaf, then 2 tablespoons of quinoa. Continue with some avocado slices, 2 slices of radishes, 2 tablespoons of carrots, 2 tablespoons of cabbage, and some of the sprouts. Fold the sides of the leaf toward the middle, then fold the bottom part of the leaf over the filling. Roll the leaf until completely rolled and secure with two toothpicks. Cut in half on the diagonal. Repeat the process for the rest of the leaves and filling. Serve.

## Baked Turnip Chips

**Ingredients** for 2 servings

2 peeled turnips, sliced
1 tbsp vegetable oil
1 tbsp Parmesan cheese
½ tsp garlic powder
¼ tsp salt
1 tsp paprika

**Directions** and Total Time: 30 minutes

Preheat the oven to 400°F. Line a baking sheet with parchment paper. Combine all of the ingredients in a large bowl until well coated. Arrange the slices in a single layer on the baking sheet. Bake for 15 minutes, then flip the slices. Bake for another 10 minutes until golden and the edges start to curl up. Serve and enjoy.

## Spicy Veggie Tostadas

**Ingredients** for 4 servings

½ cup diced white button mushrooms
10 oz chopped broccoli florets
1(15-oz) cannellini beans
½ cup halved grape tomatoes
2 tbsp olive oil
2 tsp soy sauce
1 tsp garlic powder
1 tsp onion powder
4 corn tortillas
Sriracha sauce
2 tbsp sour cream
2 tbsp chopped cilantro

**Directions** and Total Time: 30 minutes

Preheat the oven to 425°F. Line a baking sheet with parchment paper. Toss broccoli, beans, tomatoes, mushrooms, 1 tablespoon olive oil, soy sauce, garlic powder, and onion powder in a large bowl. Arrange the vegetable mixture in a single layer on the baking sheet. Bake for 10 minutes, toss the mixture, then bake for another 5 to 10 minutes until the broccoli is fork-tender and the beans start to split. While the vegetables are baking, add 1 tablespoon oil to a medium skillet over medium heat. Fry both sides of each tortilla until golden. Divide the tortillas among 4 plates. Scoop the broccoli mixture onto each tortilla, gently pressing the beans into the tortilla. Top with sriracha, sour cream, and cilantro. Serve warm and enjoy.

## Carrot Noodles with Spinach

**Ingredients** for 2 servings

¼ cup butter
1 chopped shallot
1 lb carrots, spiralizer
5 oz spinach, sliced
¼ cup chopped parsley
Salt and black pepper to taste

**Directions** and Total Time: 20 minutes

Melt butter in a large skillet over medium heat. Sauté shallot for 3 minutes until softened. Stir in carrot and cook for 3 minutes. When the edges start to brown, sauté the spinach for 2 minutes to wilt. Turn off the heat and stir in parsley, salt, and pepper. Serve warm and enjoy.

### Tofu Hot Dogs

**Ingredients** for 6 servings

1 (14-oz) block tofu
1 head romaine lettuce, torn
1 cup hot sauce
2 tbsp butter
1 tbsp cane sugar
½ tsp garlic powder
½ tsp shallot powder
Salt to taste
6 hot dog buns, toasted
2 tbsp ranch dressing
2 tbsp chives, thinly sliced

**Directions** and Total Time: 25 minutes

Preheat the oven to 425°F. Line a baking sheet with parchment paper. Slice the tofu horizontally into 2 thin strips. Cut each strip crosswise into 6 pieces. There will be 12 total pieces. Arrange the tofu in a single layer on the baking sheet and bake for 10 minutes. Flip the tofu and bake for another 10 minutes until golden and crisp.

While the tofu is baking, in a medium saucepan, combine hot sauce, butter, sugar, garlic powder, shallot powder, and salt over medium heat. When it just comes to a boil, reduce the heat and simmer until the butter has melted and the sugar has completely dissolved. Remove the resulting sauce from the heat. After the tofu is taken out of the oven, drizzle half of the sauce over the tofu and toss with care to coat. To make the sandwich, add romaine lettuce to a bun and add 2 pieces of tofu next to it. Drizzle with the rest of the sauce and some ranch dressing. Garnish with chives. Serve warm and enjoy.

### Meatless Lentil alla Bolognese

**Ingredients** for 4 servings

1 tbsp olive oil
1 onion, chopped
2 carrots, peeled and grated
4 garlic cloves, minced
1 (15-oz) can lentils
1 tbsp dark-brown sugar
2 tsp dried rosemary
Salt to taste
1 tsp red pepper flakes
3 cups tomato sauce
16 oz cooked fusilli pasta

**Directions** and Total Time: 25 minutes

In a large skillet, heat oil over medium heat. Sauté onion and carrots for 5 minutes until softened. Sauté garlic for 1 minute until aromatic. Stir in lentils, sugar, rosemary, salt, and red pepper flakes. Next, add tomato sauce and simmer for 5 minutes. When everything is heated through, ladle the sauce over the cooked pasta. Serve.

### Orange-Glazed Carrots

**Ingredients** for 3 servings

3 carrots, cut into spears
1 tbsp orange juice
2 tsp balsamic vinegar
1 tsp avocado oil
1 tsp maple syrup
½ tsp dried rosemary
¼ tsp salt
¼ tsp lemon zest

**Directions** and Total Time: 25 minutes

Preheat air fryer to 390°F. Put the carrots in a baking pan. Add the orange juice, balsamic vinegar, oil, maple syrup, rosemary, salt, and zest. Stir well. Roast for 15-18 minutes, shaking them once or twice until the carrots are bright orange, glazed, and tender. Serve hot and enjoy!

### Pad Thai Noodles with Tofu

**Ingredients** for 4 servings

1 cup chopped cauliflower florets
1 (14-oz) block tofu, cubed
½ cup vegetable broth
3 tbsp dark-brown sugar
3 tbsp peanut butter
2 tbsp soy sauce
1 lime, juiced and zested
2 tsp sriracha sauce
4 oz rice noodles
1 cup chopped broccoli florets
1/3 cup crushed peanuts
2 scallions, thinly sliced
2 tbsp chopped chives

**Directions** and Total Time: 25 minutes

Preheat the oven to 425°F. Arrange the tofu in a single layer on a parchment-lined baking sheet. Bake for 10 minutes and toss with a spatula. Bake for another 10 minutes until golden. While the tofu is baking, whisk broth, sugar, peanut butter, soy sauce, lime juice, lime zest, and sriracha in a small bowl. Cook the rice noodles according to the package directions. In the last 2 minutes of boiling the noodles, add the broccoli and cauliflower. Drain the pot with a colander and return the noodles and vegetables to the pot. Stir in peanut butter sauce and tofu until coated. Spoon the pad thai into 4 bowls. Garnish with crushed peanuts, chives, and scallions. Serve warm.

### Fall Squash Risotto

**Ingredients** for 4 servings

1 lb acorn squash, peeled, seeded, and cubed
1 cup brown rice
1 leek, chopped
4 garlic cloves, minced
1 tsp dried thyme
¼ tsp ground nutmeg
3 cups vegetable broth
¼ cup yellow mustard
Salt and black pepper to taste
2 tbsp olive oil
2 tbsp parsley, chopped

**Directions** and Total Time: 30 minutes

Warm the olive oil in a saucepan over medium heat. Sauté the leek and garlic for 3 minutes until softened. Add the squash, brown rice, thyme, and nutmeg and stir for 1-3 more minutes. Add the broth and cook until the liquid absorbs, stirring periodically, about 20 minutes. Stir in mustard, salt, and pepper. Top with parsley and serve.

### Home-Style Taro Chips

**Ingredients** for 2 servings

1 tbsp olive oil
1 cup thinly sliced taro
Salt to taste
½ cup hummus

**Directions** and Total Time: 20 minutes

Preheat air fryer to 325°F. Put the sliced taro in the greased frying basket, spread the pieces out, and drizzle with olive oil. Air Fry for 10-12 minutes, shaking the basket twice. Sprinkle with salt and serve with hummus.

### Pesto Brown Rice with Lima Beans

**Ingredients** for 2 servings

1 cup lima beans
1 cup pesto sauce
6 cherry tomatoes, halved
3 cups cooked brown rice

**Directions** and Total Time: 10 minutes

Heat the pesto sauce, beans and cherry tomatoes in a skillet over medium-low heat for 4-5 minutes, until heated through. Stir in the rice until well mixed and serve.

### Mouth-Watering Mushroom Noodles

**Ingredients** for 6 servings

2 cups white button mushrooms, sliced
8 oz rice noodles
3 tbsp toasted sesame oil
1 sliced red onion
1 green bell pepper, sliced
2 tbsp chili-garlic sauce
2 tbsp soy sauce
½ lime, juiced
1 cup chopped cilantro

**Directions** and Total Time: 25 minutes

Cook the pasta according to the directions. Drain in a colander and return to the pot. Toss with 1 tablespoon sesame oil, then set aside. Heat 1 tablespoon sesame oil in a large skillet over medium heat. Sauté onion and bell pepper for 5 minutes until softened. Add another tablespoon of sesame oil and sauté the mushrooms for 5 minutes. When the mushrooms have reduced in size, stir in chili garlic sauce, soy sauce, and lime juice. Cook for 2 minutes. When the mixture is heated through, toss in noodles and cilantro until well coated. Serve warm.

### Thyme Roasted Potatoes

**Ingredients** for 4 servings

1 ½ lb baby red potatoes, halved
2 tbsp olive oil
3 garlic cloves, minced
1 tbsp minced fresh thyme
Salt and black pepper to taste

**Directions** and Total Time: 35 minutes

Preheat the oven to 425°F. Combine all of the ingredients in a large bowl until well coated. Arrange the potatoes in a single layer on a parchment-lined baking sheet and bake for 15 minutes. Toss the potatoes with a spatula and bake for another 15 minutes until golden. Serve warm.

### Rosemary Potato Mash

**Ingredients** for 4 servings

3 lb Yukon gold potatoes, peeled and cubed
Salt and black pepper to taste
¼ cup milk
¼ cup butter

**Directions** and Total Time: 30 minutes

In a large stockpot, add potatoes and enough water to cover them. Salt the water and turn the heat to medium-high. Bring the water to a boil and cook the potatoes for 12-18 minutes. When the potatoes are fork-tender, drain in a colander and return to the pot. Add butter and milk to the potatoes, then mash them to the desired consistency. Season with salt and pepper. Serve warm.

### Yellow Onion Rings

**Ingredients** for 3 servings

½ sweet yellow onion
½ cup cream of tartar
¾ cup flour
1 tbsp cornstarch
Salt and black pepper to taste
¾ tsp garlic powder
½ tsp dried oregano
1 cup bread crumbs

**Directions** and Total Time: 30 minutes

Preheat air fryer to 390°F. Cut the onion into ½-inch slices. Separate the onion slices into rings. Place the cream of tartar in a bowl and set aside. In another bowl, combine the flour, cornstarch, salt, pepper, and garlic. Stir well and set aside. In a separate bowl, combine the breadcrumbs with oregano and salt. Dip the rings into the cream of tartar, dredge in flour, dip into the cream again, and then coat into the crumb mixture. Put the greased frying basket without overlapping. Spritz them with cooking oil and Air Fry for 13-16 minutes, shaking once or twice until the rings are crunchy and browned.

### Veggie & Quinoa Fajitas

**Ingredients** for 4 servings

½ cup blanched almonds
2 tbsp fajita seasoning
1 tbsp olive oil
2 green onions, chopped
1 cup Bella mushrooms, diced
1 cup cooked quinoa
5 oz baby spinach
12 corn tortillas
2 tbsp sour cream
2 tbsp salsa

**Directions** and Total Time: 45 minutes

Preheat the oven to 425°F. Line a baking sheet with parchment paper. Add almonds, ¾ cup water, and fajita seasoning to a blender jar. Blend for 2 minutes until smooth. In a large skillet, heat oil over medium heat. Sauté green onions and mushrooms for 3 to 5 minutes until mushrooms reduce in size. Stir in quinoa and spinach to wilt the spinach. After 3 minutes, reduce the heat and stir in the almond mixture. Remove from the heat. Arrange the tortillas on the baking sheet. They can overlap. Bake for 2 minutes, then transfer to a large plate. Take one of the tortillas and place on a flat work surface. Add 2 heaping tablespoons on the part of the tortilla closest to you. Tuck in the sides and roll the tortilla away from you. Transfer the fajita to the baking sheet and place seam-side down. Continue rolling the rest of the fajitas. Lightly spray with cooking oil. Bake for 18 minutes until golden. Top with sour cream and salsa. Serve warm.

### Green Chili Guacamole

**Ingredients** for 4 servings

2 avocados, diced
1 Roma tomato, chopped
1 green chili, minced
2 minced spring onions
½ lime, juiced
2 tbsp chopped cilantro
Salt and black pepper to taste
Tortilla chips for serving

**Directions** and Total Time: 20 minutes

Put the avocados, tomato, green chili, spring onions, lime juice, salt, pepper, and cilantro in a large bowl. Crush with a fork until well combined. Serve with tortilla chips.

## Tex-Mex Stuffed Avocado

**Ingredients** for 4 servings

2 halved avocados, pitted
1 (15-oz) can black beans
1 cup corn kernels
½ cup diced tomatoes
½ lime, juiced
1 garlic clove, minced
1 tsp olive oil
Salt and black pepper to taste
¼ tsp smoked paprika
1 tbsp chopped cilantro

**Directions** and Total Time: 20 minutes

Remove some flesh from the avocado, leaving about ¼ to ½-inch wall for stability. Transfer the avocado flesh to a large mixing bowl. Combine with the rest of the ingredients until thoroughly mixed. Divide the mixture among the avocado shells. Serve and enjoy.

## Savory Eggplant Fries

**Ingredients** for 4 servings

1 eggplant, sliced
2 ½ tbsp shoyu
2 tsp garlic powder
2 tsp onion powder
4 tsp olive oil
2 tbsp fresh basil, chopped

**Directions** and Total Time: 20 minutes

Preheat air fryer to 390°F. Place the eggplant slices in a bowl and sprinkle the shoyu, garlic, onion, and oil on top. Coat the eggplant evenly. Place the eggplant in a single layer in the greased frying basket and Air Fry for 5 minutes. Remove and put the eggplant in the bowl again. Toss the eggplant slices to coat evenly with the remaining liquid and put back in the fryer. Roast for another 3 minutes. Remove the basket and flip the pieces over to ensure even cooking. Roast for another 5 minutes or until the eggplant is golden and tender. Top with basil.

## Avocado-Sweet Potato Bites

**Ingredients** for 2 servings

2 sweet potatoes, cut lengthwise into slices
Salt and black pepper to taste
2 avocados, peeled and pitted
½ tsp hot sauce
1 tomato, chopped
1 tsp chopped cilantro

**Directions** and Total Time: 20 minutes

Preheat the oven to 450°F. Line a baking sheet with parchment paper. Arrange the sweet potato in a single layer on the baking sheet, spraying both sides lightly with cooking oil. Season with salt and pepper. Bake for 6 minutes and flip the slice. Bake for 6 minutes until golden. In a small bowl, mash avocado with salt and pepper. Top the sweet potatoes with the avocado mash. Drizzle with hot sauce. Top with tomatoes and cilantro.

## Spinach Fritters with Avocado Hummus

**Ingredients** for 4 servings

1 tbsp olive oil
½ cup melted butter
½ cup baby spinach
½ tsp plain vinegar
3 large avocados, chopped
¼ cup pumpkin seeds
¼ cup sesame paste
Juice from ½ lemon
1 garlic clove, minced
½ tsp coriander powder
Salt and black pepper to taste
½ cup chopped parsley

**Directions** and Total Time: 30 minutes

Preheat the oven to 300°F. Put the spinach in a bowl and toss with olive oil, vinegar, and salt. Place in a parchment paper-lined baking sheet and bake until the leaves are crispy but not burned, about 15 minutes. Place the chopped avocado into the bowl of a food processor. Add in parsley, butter, pumpkin seeds, sesame paste, lemon juice, garlic, coriander powder, salt, and black pepper. Puree until smooth. Spoon the hummus into a bowl and serve with spinach chips.

## Curried Veggie Samosas

**Ingredients** for 4 servings

4 cooked potatoes, mashed
¼ cup peas
2 tsp coconut oil
3 garlic cloves, minced
1 ½ tbsp lemon juice
1 ½ tsp cumin powder
1 tsp onion powder
1 tsp ground coriander
Salt to taste
½ tsp curry powder
¼ tsp cayenne powder
10 rice paper wrappers
1 cup cilantro chutney

**Directions** and Total Time: 30 minutes

Preheat air fryer to 390°F. In a bowl, place the mashed potatoes. Add the peas, oil, garlic, lemon juice, cumin, onion powder, coriander, salt, curry powder, and cayenne. Stir well. Fill a bowl with water. Soak a rice paper wrapper in the water for a few seconds. Lay it on a flat surface. Place ¼ cup of the potato filling in the center of the wrapper and roll like a burrito or spring roll. Repeat the process until you run out of ingredients. Place the "samosas" inside in the greased frying basket, separating them. Air Fry for 8-10 minutes or until hot and crispy around the edges. Let cool for a few minutes. Enjoy with the cilantro chutney.

## Thyme Sweet Potato Chips

**Ingredients** for 2 servings

1 sweet potato, unpeeled, thinly sliced
1 tbsp olive oil
¼ tsp dried thyme
Salt to taste

**Directions** and Total Time: 20 minutes

Preheat air fryer to 390°F. Spread the sweet potato slices in the greased basket and brush with olive oil. Air Fry for 6 minutes. Remove the basket, shake, and sprinkle with thyme and salt. Cook for 6 more minutes or until lightly browned. Serve warm and enjoy!

## Crunchy Green Beans

**Ingredients** for 4 servings

1 tbsp tahini
1 tbsp lemon juice
1 tsp allspice
1 lb green beans, trimmed

**Directions** and Total Time: 15 minutes

Preheat air fryer to 400°F. Whisk tahini, lemon juice, 1 tbsp of water, and allspice in a bowl. Put in the green beans and toss to coat. Roast for 5 minutes until golden brown and cooked. Serve immediately.

## Korean Brussels Sprouts

**Ingredients** for 4 servings

1 lb trimmed Brussels sprouts
1 ½ tbsp maple syrup
1 ½ tsp white miso
1 tsp toasted sesame oil
1 ½ tsp soy sauce
2 garlic cloves, minced
1 tsp grated fresh ginger
½ tsp Gochugaru chili flakes

**Directions** and Total Time: 20 minutes

Preheat air fryer to 390°F. Place the Brussels sprouts in the greased basket, spray with oil and Air Fry for 10-14 minutes, tossing once, until crispy, tender, and golden. In a bowl, combine maple syrup and miso. Whisk until smooth. Add the sesame oil, soy sauce, garlic, ginger, and Gochugaru flakes. Stir well. When the Brussels sprouts are done, add them to the bowl and toss with the sauce.

## Cholula Onion Rings

**Ingredients** for 4 servings

1 large Vidalia onion
½ cup chickpea flour
1/3 cup milk
2 tbsp lemon juice
2 tbsp Cholula hot sauce
1 tsp allspice
2/3 cup bread crumbs

**Directions** and Total Time: 30 minutes

Preheat air fryer to 380°F. Cut ½-inch off the top of the onion's root, then cut into ½-inch thick rings. Set aside. Combine the chickpea flour, milk, lemon juice, hot sauce, and allspice in a bowl. In another bowl, add in breadcrumbs. Submerge each ring into the flour batter until well coated, then dip into the breadcrumbs, and Air Fry for 14 minutes until brown and crispy, turning once.

## Crispy Mushrooms

**Ingredients** for 4 servings

2 portobello mushroom caps, cut into ¼-inch-thick strips
3 tbsp olive oil
2 tsp shoyu sauce
Salt and black pepper to taste
2 tbsp rosemary, chopped

**Directions** and Total Time: 30 minutes

Preheat the oven to 375°F. Line a baking sheet with parchment paper. Toss mushrooms, oil, shoyu sauce, salt, and pepper in a medium bowl until coated. Arrange on the baking sheet in a single layer. Bake for 15 minutes, then toss the mushrooms with a spatula. Bake for another 10 to 15 minutes until the mushrooms are darkened and reduced in size. Top with rosemary. Serve warm.

## Provence French Fries

**Ingredients** for 4 servings

2 russet potatoes
1 tbsp olive oil
1 tbsp herbs de Provence

**Directions** and Total Time: 25 minutes

Preheat air fryer to 400°F. Slice the potatoes lengthwise into ½-inch thick strips. In a bowl, whisk the olive oil and herbs de Provence. Toss in the potatoes to coat. Arrange them in a single and Air Fry for 18-20 minutes, shaking once, until crispy. Serve warm and enjoy!

## Garlic-Parmesan Popcorn

**Ingredients** for 2 servings

¼ cup popcorn kernels
1 tbsp lemon juice
1 tsp garlic powder
2 tsp grated Parmesan

**Directions** and Total Time: 15 minutes

Preheat air fryer to 400°F. Line the basket with aluminum foil. Put in the popcorn kernels in a single layer. Grill for 6-8 minutes until they stop popping. Remove them into a bowl. Drizzle with lemon juice and toss until well coated. Sprinkle with garlic powder and grated Parmesan cheese and toss to coat. Drizzle with more lemon juice. Serve.

## Five Spice Fries

**Ingredients** for 2 servings

1 Yukon Gold potato, cut into fries
1 tbsp coconut oil
1 tsp coconut sugar
1 tsp garlic powder
½ tsp Chinese five-spice
Salt to taste
¼ tsp turmeric
¼ tsp paprika

**Directions** and Total Time: 30 minutes

Preheat air fryer to 390°F. Toss the potato pieces with coconut oil, sugar, garlic, Chinese five-spice, salt, turmeric, and paprika in a bowl and stir well. Place in the greased frying basket and Air Fry for 18-25 minutes, tossing twice, until softened and golden. Serve warm.

## Toasted Choco-Nuts

**Ingredients** for 2 servings

2 cups almonds
2 tsp maple syrup
2 tbsp cacao powder

**Directions** and Total Time: 10 minutes

Preheat air fryer to 350°F. Distribute the almonds in a single layer in the frying basket and Bake for 3 minutes. Shake the basket and Bake for another 1 minute until golden brown. Remove them to a bowl. Drizzle with maple syrup and toss. Sprinkle with cacao powder and toss until well coated. Let cool completely. Store in a container at room temperature for up to 2 weeks or in the fridge for up to a month.

## Caraway Seed Pretzel Sticks

**Ingredients** for 4 servings

½ pizza dough
Flour, for dusting
1 tsp baking soda
2 tbsp caraway seeds

**Directions** and Total Time: 30 minutes

Preheat air fryer to 400°F. Roll out the dough, on parchment paper, into a rectangle, then cut it into 8 strips. Whisk the baking soda and 1 cup of hot water until well dissolved in a bowl. Submerge each strip, shake off any excess, and stretch another 1 to 2 inches. Scatter with caraway seeds and let rise for 10 minutes in the frying basket. Grease with cooking spray and Air Fry for 8 minutes until golden brown, turning once. Serve.

## Cheesy Potato Skins

**Ingredients** for 4 servings

2 russet potatoes, halved lengthwise
½ cup Alfredo sauce
1 tbsp grated Parmesan
2 scallions, chopped

**Directions** and Total Time: 50 minutes

Preheat air fryer to 400°F. Wrap each potato, cut-side down with parchment paper, and Roast for 30 minutes. Carefully scoop out the potato flesh, leaving ¼-inch meat, and place it in a bowl. Stir in Alfredo sauce, scallions, and Parmesan cheese until well combined. Fill each potato skin with the cheese mixture and Grill for 3-4 minutes until crispy. Serve right away.

## Rich Spinach Chips

**Ingredients** for 4 servings

10 oz spinach
2 tbsp lemon juice
2 tbsp olive oil
Salt and black pepper to taste
½ tsp garlic powder
½ tsp onion powder

**Directions** and Total Time: 20 minutes

Preheat air fryer to 350°F. Place the spinach in a bowl, and drizzle with lemon juice and olive oil and massage with your hands. Scatter with salt, pepper, garlic, and onion and gently toss to coat well. Arrange the leaves in a single layer and Bake for 3 minutes, shake and Bake for another 1-3 minutes until brown. Let cool completely.

## Spicy Roasted Cauliflower

**Ingredients** for 4 servings

½ head cauliflower, cut into florets
¼ cup chopped red onion
¾ cup chickpea flour
2 tsp allspice
3 tbsp enchilada sauce
2 tbsp lime juice
½ cup milk

**Directions** and Total Time: 30 minutes

Preheat oven to 360°F. Beat the chickpea flour, allspice, 2 tbsp of hot sauce, 1 tbsp of lime juice, and milk in a shallow bowl. Add in cauliflower florets and toss until completely coated. Bake for 15 minutes until browned and crispy, turning once. Whisk 1 tbsp of enchilada sauce, red onion, and 1 tbsp of lime juice until well combined. Drizzle over the cauliflower. Serve and enjoy!

## Turkish Mutabal (Eggplant Dip)

**Ingredients** for 2 servings

1 medium eggplant
2 tbsp tahini
2 tbsp lemon juice
1 tsp garlic powder
¼ tsp sumac
1 tsp chopped parsley

**Directions** and Total Time: 40 minutes

Preheat air fryer to 400°F. Place the eggplant in a pan and Roast for 30 minutes, turning once. Let cool for 5-10 minutes. Scoop out the flesh and place it in a bowl. Squeeze any excess water; discard the water. Mix the flesh, tahini, lemon juice, garlic, and sumac until well combined. Scatter with parsley and serve.

## Black Bean Fajitas

**Ingredients** for 2 servings

1 (15.5-oz) black beans
1 tbsp fajita seasoning
2 tbsp lime juice
2 flour tortillas
¼ cup salsa
2 scallions, thinly sliced
1 tbsp hot sauce

**Directions** and Total Time: 20 minutes

Preheat air fryer to 400°F. Using a fork, mash the beans until smooth. Stir in fajita seasoning and lime juice. Set aside. Place tortillas on a flat surface, spread half of the salsa on each tortilla, scatter with scallions, and top with the bean mixture. Drizzle with the hot sauce. For the burritos, fold in the sides of the tortilla, then fold up the bottom, and finally roll-up. Grill for 10 minutes until crispy, turning once. Serve warm and enjoy!

## Green Dip with Pine Nuts

**Ingredients** for 3 servings

10 oz canned artichokes, chopped
2 scallions, finely chopped
½ cup pine nuts
½ cup milk
3 tbsp lemon juice
2 tsp grated Parmesan
2 tsp tapioca flour
10 oz spinach, chopped
1 tsp allspice

**Directions** and Total Time: 30 minutes

Preheat air fryer to 360°F. Arrange spinach, artichokes, and scallions in a pan. Set aside. In a food processor, blitz the pine nuts, milk, lemon juice, Parmesan cheese, flour, and allspice on high until smooth. Pour it over the veggies and Bake for 20 minutes, stirring every 5 minutes.

## Original Grilled Cheese Sandwiches

**Ingredients** for 2 servings

¼ cup sliced roasted red peppers
¼ cup Alfredo sauce
4 bread slices
¼ cup mozzarella
3 tbsp sliced red onions

**Directions** and Total Time: 15 minutes

Preheat air fryer to 400°F. Lay 2 bread slices on a flat surface, spread some Alfredo sauce on one side, and place them in the frying basket. Scatter with mozzarella cheese, roasted peppers, and red onion. Drizzle with the remaining Alfredo sauce and top with the remaining bread slices. Grill for 4 minutes, turn the sandwiches, and Grill for 3 more minutes until toasted. Serve warm.

## Sweet Brussels Sprouts

**Ingredients** for 4 servings

1 lb Brussels sprouts, quartered
2 tbsp olive oil
1 tsp maple syrup
1 tbsp balsamic vinegar

**Directions** and Total Time: 20 minutes

Preheat air fryer to 400°F. Whisk the olive oil, maple syrup, and balsamic vinegar in a bowl. Put in Brussels sprouts and toss to coat. Place them, cut-side up, in a single layer, and Roast for 10 minutes until crispy. Serve.

## Sriracha Spring Rolls

**Ingredients** for 4 servings

2 tbsp butter
2 tbsp lime juice
1 tbsp sriracha hot sauce
4 scallions, sliced
16 oz coleslaw mix
8 spring roll wrappers

**Directions** and Total Time: 30 minutes

Preheat air fryer to 350°F. Whisk the butter, lime juice, and hot sauce in a bowl. Stir in scallions and coleslaw until well coated. Lay the wrappers, face-up, and fill each with 1/8 cup of filling onto the corner. Then fold up over the filling, pushing back to compact it, and finally fold the sides. Grease them with cooking spray and Bake for 17 minutes until golden brown and crispy, turning once. Serve warm and enjoy!

## Chickpea Cakes

**Ingredients** for 4 servings

1 (14-oz) can chickpeas
½ red bell pepper, chopped
3 scallions, chopped
¼ tsp garlic powder
½ tsp cayenne pepper
2 tbsp lemon juice
2 tbsp mayonnaise
1 cup chickpea flour

**Directions** and Total Time: 25 minutes

Preheat air fryer to 400°F. Using a fork, mash the chickpeas. Combine them with bell pepper, scallions, garlic, cayenne pepper, lemon juice, and mayonnaise until well mixed in a bowl. Mix in chickpea flour until fully incorporated. Make 6 equal patties out of the mixture and Air Fry for 13-15 minutes until browned and crispy, turning once. Serve immediately and enjoy!

## Healthy Seed Crackers

**Ingredients** for 6 servings

¼ cup butter, melted
1/3 cup sesame seed flour
1/3 cup pumpkin seeds
1/3 cup sunflower seeds
1/3 cup sesame seeds
1/3 cup chia seeds
1 tbsp psyllium husk powder
1 tsp salt

**Directions** and Total Time: 60 minutes

Preheat oven to 300°F. Combine the sesame seed flour with pumpkin seeds, sunflower seeds, sesame seeds, chia seeds, psyllium husk powder, and salt. Pour in the butter and 1 cup of boiling water and mix the ingredients until a dough forms with a gel-like consistency. Line a baking sheet with parchment paper and place the dough on the sheet. Cover the dough with another parchment paper and, with a rolling pin, flatten the dough into the baking sheet. Remove the parchment paper on top.

Tuck the baking sheet in the oven and bake for 45 minutes. Allow the crackers to cool and dry in the oven, about 10 minutes. After, remove the sheet and break the crackers into small pieces. Serve and enjoy!

## Cajun Sweet Potato Chips

**Ingredients** for 4 servings

2 sweet potatoes, peeled and sliced
2 tbsp melted butter
1 tbsp Cajun seasoning

**Directions** and Total Time: 55 minutes

Preheat the oven to 400°F. In a medium bowl, add the sweet potatoes, butter, and Cajun seasoning. Toss well. Spread the chips on a parchment-lined baking sheet, making sure not to overlap, and bake in the oven for 50 minutes to 1 hour or until crispy. Remove the sheet and pour the chips into a large bowl. Serve cooled.

## Fried Cauliflower with Parsnip Purée

**Ingredients** for 6 servings

½ cup grated mozzarella
1 lb peeled parsnips, quartered
½ cup milk
½ cup breadcrumbs
3 tbsp melted butter
¼ cup flour
¼ tsp cayenne pepper
30 oz cauliflower florets
A pinch of nutmeg
1 tsp cumin powder
2 tbsp sesame oil
1 cup heavy cream

**Directions** and Total Time: 35 minutes

Preheat oven to 425°F and line a baking sheet with parchment paper. In a small bowl, combine milk, flour, and cayenne pepper. In another bowl, mix salt, breadcrumbs, and mozzarella cheese. Dip each cauliflower floret into the milk mixture, coating properly, and then into the cheese mixture. Place the breaded cauliflower on the baking sheet and bake in the oven for 30 minutes, turning once after 15 minutes.

Make slightly salted water in a saucepan and add the parsnips. Bring to boil over medium heat for 15 minutes or until the parsnips are fork-tender. Drain and transfer to a bowl. Add in melted butter, cumin powder, nutmeg, and heavy cream. Puree the ingredients using an immersion blender until smooth. Spoon the parsnip mash into serving plates and drizzle with some sesame oil. Serve with the baked cauliflower when ready.

## Sticky Maple Popcorns

**Ingredients** for 4 servings

1 tsp butter, melted
½ cup popcorn kernels
¼ tsp cinnamon powder
½ tsp pure maple syrup
Salt to taste

**Directions** and Total Time: 15 minutes

Pour the popcorn kernels into a large pot and set over medium heat. Cover the lid and let the kernels pop completely. Shake the pot a few times to ensure even popping, 10 minutes. In a small bowl, mix the cinnamon powder, maple syrup, butter, and salt. When the popcorn is ready, turn the heat off, and toss in the cinnamon mixture until well distributed. Pour the popcorn into serving bowls, allow cooling, and enjoy.

## Lentil & Bean Tacos

**Ingredients** for 6 servings

¼ cup chopped red onion
1 (15-oz) can red kidney beans
1(15-oz) can red lentils
2 tbsp taco seasoning
1 tbsp hot sauce
½ cup diced tomato
¼ cup chopped cilantro
¼ cup lime juice
12 corn tortillas

**Directions** and Total Time: 35 minutes

Preheat air fryer to 360°F. Using a fork, mash the beans and lentils in a bowl. Mix in taco seasoning, hot sauce, red onion, tomato, cilantro, and lime juice. Fill each tortilla with 2 tbsp of bean mixture, keeping the filling close to one side, and roll them. Bake for 20 minutes until crispy. Serve right away.

## Lemony Pistachio Dip

**Ingredients** for 4 servings

½ cup olive oil
3 tbsp heavy cream
¼ cup water
Juice of half a lemon
½ tsp smoked paprika
½ tsp cayenne pepper
½ tsp salt
3 oz toasted pistachios

**Directions** and Total Time: 10 minutes

Pour the pistachios, heavy cream, water, lemon juice, paprika, cayenne pepper, and salt. Puree the ingredients at high speed until smooth. Add the olive oil and puree a little further. Manage the consistency of the dip by adding more oil or water. Spoon the dip into little bowls and serve with julienned celery and carrots.

## Baked Chili Eggplant with Almonds

**Ingredients** for 4 servings

2 tbsp butter
2 large eggplants
Salt and black pepper to taste
1 tsp red chili flakes
4 oz raw ground almonds

**Directions** and Total Time: 30 minutes

Preheat oven to 400°F. Cut off the head of the eggplants and slice the body into 2-inch rounds. Season with salt and black pepper and arrange on a parchment paper-lined baking sheet. Drop thin slices of the butter on each eggplant slice, sprinkle with red chili flakes, and bake in the oven for 20 minutes. Slide the baking sheet out and sprinkle with the almonds. Roast further for 5 minutes or until golden brown. Serve and enjoy!

## Broccoli & Mushroom Faux "Risotto"

**Ingredients** for 4 servings

1 cup cremini mushrooms, chopped
¾ cup grated Parmesan
1 small red onion, chopped
1 cup heavy cream
2 garlic cloves, minced
1 large head broccoli, grated
¾ cup white wine
4 oz butter
Freshly chopped thyme

**Directions** and Total Time: 25 minutes

Place a pot over medium heat, add, and melt the butter. Sauté the mushrooms in the pot until golden, about 5 minutes. Add the garlic and onions and cook for 3 minutes or until fragrant and soft. Mix in the broccoli, 1 cup water, and half of the white wine. Season with salt and black pepper and simmer the ingredients (uncovered) for 8 to 10 minutes or until the broccoli is soft.

Mix in the heavy cream and simmer until most of the cream has evaporated. Turn the heat off and stir in Parmesan cheese and thyme until well incorporated.

## Kale Carrot "Noodles"

**Ingredients** for 4 servings

4 tbsp butter
2 large carrots
¼ cup vegetable broth
1 garlic clove, minced
1 cup chopped kale
Salt and black pepper to taste

**Directions** and Total Time: 15 minutes

Peel the carrots with a slicer and run both through a spiralizer to form noodles. Pour the vegetable broth into a saucepan and add the carrot noodles. Simmer (over low heat) the carrots for 3 minutes. Strain through a colander and set the vegetables aside. Place a large skillet over medium heat and melt the butter. Add the garlic and sauté until softened and put in the kale; cook until wilted. Pour the carrots into the pan, season with salt and black pepper, and stir-fry for 3 to 4 minutes. Spoon the vegetables into a bowl and serve with pan-grilled tofu.

## Curried Mushroom Cauli "Risotto"

**Ingredients** for 4 servings

8 oz baby Bella mushrooms, stemmed and sliced
2 tbsp toasted sesame oil
1 large cauliflower head
1 onion, chopped
3 garlic cloves, minced
Salt and black pepper to taste
½ tsp curry powder
1 tsp freshly chopped parsley
2 scallions, thinly sliced

**Directions** and Total Time: 15 minutes

Use a knife to cut the entire cauliflower head into 6 pieces and transfer to a food processor. With the grater attachment, shred the cauliflower into a rice-like consistency. Heat half of the sesame oil in a large skillet over medium heat and then add the onion and mushrooms. Sauté for 5 minutes or until the mushrooms are soft. Add the garlic and sauté for 2 minutes or until fragrant. Pour in the cauliflower and cook until the rice has slightly softened, about 10 minutes.

Season with salt, black pepper, and curry powder and mix the ingredients until well combined. After, turn the heat off and stir in the parsley and scallions. Dish the cauli rice into serving plates and serve warm.

## Bell Pepper & Carrot Sushi

**Ingredients** for 4 servings rolls

2 tbsp butter
2 tbsp tamari
4 standard nori sheets
1 green bell pepper, sliced
1 tbsp pickled ginger
½ cup grated carrots

**Directions** and Total Time: 15 minutes

Preheat oven to 350°F. Whisk the butter and tamari until smooth and thick. Place a nori sheet on a flat surface with the rough side facing up. Spoon a bit of the tamari mixture at the other side of the nori sheet, and spread on all sides. Put bell pepper slices, carrots, and ginger in a layer at the other end of the sheet. Fold up in the tahini direction to seal. Repeat the process with the remaining sheets. Arrange on a baking tray and bake for about 10 minutes until browned and crispy. Allow cooling for a few minutes before slicing into 4 pieces.

## Crispy Samosa Rolls

**Ingredients** for 4 servings

2/3 cup canned peas
4 scallions, finely sliced
2 cups grated potatoes
2 tbsp lemon juice
1 tsp ground ginger
1 tsp curry powder
1 tsp Garam masala
¼ cup chickpea flour
1 tbsp tahini
8 rice paper wrappers

**Directions** and Total Time: 30 minutes

Preheat air fryer to 350°F. Mix the peas, scallions, potatoes, lemon juice, ginger, curry powder, Garam masala, and chickpea flour in a bowl. In another bowl, whisk tahini and 1/3 cup of water until combined. Set aside on a plate. Submerge the rice wrappers, one by one, into the tahini mixture until they begin to soften and set aside on a plate. Fill each wrap with 1/3 cup of the veggie mixture and wrap them into a roll. Bake for 15 minutes until golden brown and crispy, turning once.

## Balsamic Stuffed Mushrooms

**Ingredients** for 4 servings

¼ cup chopped roasted red peppers
10 oz spinach, chopped
3 scallions, chopped
¼ cup chickpea flour
1 tbsp grated Parmesan cheese
1 tsp garlic powder
1 tbsp balsamic vinegar
12 portobello mushroom caps
½ lemon

**Directions** and Total Time: 30 minutes

Preheat air fryer to 360°F. In a bowl, squeeze any excess water from the spinach; discard the water. Stir in scallions, red pepper, chickpea flour, Parmesan cheese, garlic, and balsamic vinegar until well combined. Fill each mushroom cap with spinach mixture until covering the tops, pressing down slightly. Bake for 12 minutes until crispy. Drizzle with lemon juice before serving.

## Quick-To-Make Quesadillas

**Ingredients** for 4 servings

1 ½ cups cherry tomatoes, halved
12 oz goat cheese
2 tbsp vinegar
1 tbsp taco seasoning
1 ripe avocado, pitted
4 scallions, finely sliced
2 tbsp lemon juice
4 flour tortillas
¼ cup hot sauce
½ cup Alfredo sauce

**Directions** and Total Time: 30 minutes

Preheat air fryer to 400°F. Slice goat cheese into 4 pieces. Set aside. In a bowl, whisk vinegar and taco seasoning until combined. Submerge each slice into the vinegar and Air Fry for 12 minutes until crisp, turning once. Let cool slightly before cutting into ½-inch thick strips.

Using a fork, mash the avocado in a bowl. Stir in scallions and lemon juice and set aside. Lay one tortilla on a flat surface, cut from one edge to the center, then spread ¼ of the avocado mixture on one quadrant, 1 tbsp of hot sauce on the next quadrant, and finally 2 tbsp of Alfredo sauce on the other half. Top the non-sauce half with ¼ of cherry tomatoes and ¼ of goat cheese strips. To fold, start with the avocado quadrant, folding each over the next one until you create a stacked triangle. Repeat the process with the remaining tortillas. Air Fry for 5 minutes until crispy, turning once. Serve warm.

## Easy Zucchini Lasagna Roll-Ups

**Ingredients** for 2 servings

2 medium zucchini
2 tbsp lemon juice
1 ½ cups ricotta cheese
1 tbsp allspice
2 cups marinara sauce
½ cup grated mozzarella

**Directions** and Total Time: 40 minutes

Preheat oven to 400°F. Cut the ends of each zucchini, then slice into ¼-inch thick pieces and drizzle with lemon juice. Roast for 5 minutes until slightly tender. Let cool slightly. Combine ricotta cheese and allspice in a bowl; set aside. Spread 2 tbsp of marinara sauce on the bottom of a baking pan. Spoon 1-2 tbsp of the ricotta mixture onto each slice, roll up each slice and place them spiral-side up in the pan. Scatter with the remaining ricotta mixture and drizzle with marinara sauce. Top with mozzarella and Bake at 360°F for 20 minutes until the cheese is bubbly and golden brown. Serve warm.

## Burritos Enmolados with Tofu

**Ingredients** for 2 servings

1 ½ cups shredded red cabbage
4 tbsp lime juice
2 tbsp mole hot sauce
½ tsp ground cumin
16 oz super-firm tofu
2 scallions, finely sliced
1 ½ tbsp mayonnaise
2 tbsp chopped cilantro
4 corn tortillas

**Directions** and Total Time: 30 minutes

Preheat air fryer to 400°F. Whisk 2 tbsp of lime juice, 1 tbsp of mole sauce and cumin until smooth. Set aside. Slice tofu into 4 pieces. Submerge the slices into the sauce and arrange them in a single layer. Drizzle with half of the sauce and Air Fry for 6 minutes. Turn the slices, drizzle with the remaining sauce, and Air Fry for another 6 minutes. Let cool slightly before cutting into ½-inch strips. Combine red cabbage, scallions, mayonnaise, cilantro, 2 tbsp of lime juice, and 1 tbsp of hot sauce. Set aside. Air Fry corn tortillas for 2-3 minutes in a single layer. For the tacos, fill each tortilla with ¼ of slaw and top each with ¼ of tofu strips. Serve immediately.

## Simple Pumpkin Noodles

**Ingredients** for 4 servings

¼ cup butter
½ cup chopped onion
1 lb pumpkin, spiralized
1 bunch kale, sliced
¼ cup chopped fresh parsley
Salt and black pepper to taste

**Directions** and Total Time: 15 minutes

Melt butter in a skillet over medium heat. Place the onion and cook for 3 minutes. Add in pumpkin and cook for another 7-8 minutes. Stir in kale and cook for another 2 minutes until the kale wilts. Sprinkle with parsley, salt, and pepper, and serve.

# MAIN DISHES

## Mustard Chickpea Patties

**Ingredients** for 6 servings

1 red bell pepper
1 (19-oz) can chickpeas
1 cup ground almonds
2 tsp yellow mustard
2 tsp maple syrup
1 garlic clove, pressed
Juice of ½ lemon
1 tsp dried thyme
½ tsp dried tarragon
1 cup spinach
1 ½ cups rolled oats

**Directions** and Total Time: 50 minutes

Preheat the oven to 350°F. Prep a baking sheet by lining it with parchment paper. Cut the red pepper in half lengthwise. Remove stem and seeds. Place the pepper on the baking sheet cut side up. Roast for 10 minutes. While the pepper is cooking, add chickpeas, almonds, mustard, maple syrup, garlic, lemon juice, thyme, tarragon and spinach in the food processor. Pulse to mix, but not pureed. Transfer the roasted pepper as well as oats to the food processor. Pulse to chop. Divide into 12 portions and shape into patties. Place a new sheet of parchment on the baking sheet and arrange the patties on the sheet. Bake for about 30 minutes or until the outside is golden.

## Garam Masala Chickpea Wraps

**Ingredients** for 3 servings

1 tbsp sesame oil
1 lime, juiced and zested
1 tbsp garam masala
Salt to taste
1 (14-oz) can chickpeas
1 cup diced cucumber
1 red bell pepper, diced
½ cup fresh cilantro, chopped
3 whole-grain wraps
2 cups shredded lettuce

**Directions** and Total Time: 20 minutes

Whisk the sesame oil, lime zest, lime juice, garam masala, and salt in a medium bowl to a creamy, thick consistency. Slowly add 3-4 tablespoons of water to thin out the tahini sauce. Stir in chickpeas, cucumber, bell pepper, and cilantro. Divide the chickpea salad between the three wraps. Top with lettuce. Roll it up. Serve and enjoy.

## Cilantro Sweet Potato Burgers

**Ingredients** for 4 servings

1 cup cooked brown rice
1 cup grated sweet potato
½ cup diced onion
Salt to taste
¼ cup cilantro, finely chopped
1 tsp chili powder
½ cup ground almonds
1 tsp olive oil

**Directions** and Total Time: 35 minutes

In a large bowl, combine rice, sweet potato, onion, and salt. Sit for about 5 minutes to draw out the moisture from the vegetables. Mix in cilantro, chili powder, and almonds until the batter becomes sticky. Slowly add water if necessary. Divide the mixture into 4 portions and shape into patties. In a large skillet over medium heat, add oil. When the oil starts to shimmer, place the patties in the skillet. Cook for 7-10 minutes. Flip the patties and cook for another 5-7 minutes. Serve warm

## Spinach & Tofu Benedict Florentine

**Ingredients** for 4 servings

4 English muffins, toasted
1 (14-oz) block tofu
1 tsp olive oil
10 oz baby spinach
1 cup mayonnaise
3 tbsp butter, melted
1 tsp lime juice
1 tsp Sriracha sauce
½ tsp ground turmeric
¼ tsp black pepper
2 tbsp chopped chives

**Directions** and Total Time: 30 minutes

Preheat the oven to 425°F. Line a baking sheet with parchment paper. Slice the tofu horizontally into 4 thin strips. Cut each strip crosswise into 4 pieces. There will be 16 total pieces. Arrange the tofu in a single layer on the baking sheet and bake for 10 minutes. Flip the tofu and bake for another 10 minutes until golden and crisp. While the tofu is baking, in a large skillet, heat oil over medium heat. Add spinach and sauté for 2 minutes until wilted. Add mayonnaise, butter, lime juice, sriracha sauce, turmeric, and pepper to a small saucepan. Heat on medium-low heat to warm through. Place an open, toasted English muffin on a plate. Layer some spinach, then 2 pieces of tofu. Top with the sauce and garnish with chives. Repeat for the rest of the English muffins.

## Kale & Lentils with Crispy Onions

**Ingredients** for 4 servings

2 cups cooked red lentils
1 onion, cut into rings
½ cup kale, steamed
3 garlic cloves, minced
½ lemon, juiced and zested
2 tsp cornstarch
1 tsp dried oregano
Salt and black pepper to taste

**Directions** and Total Time: 40 minutes

Preheat air fryer to 390°F. Put the onion rings in the greased frying basket; do not overlap. Spray with oil and season with salt. Air Fry for 14-16 minutes, stirring twice until crispy and crunchy. Place the kale and lentils into a pan over medium heat and stir until heated through. Remove and add the garlic, lemon juice, cornstarch, salt, zest, oregano and black pepper. Stir well and pour in bowls. Top with the crisp onion rings and serve.

## Vegetable Chickpeas & Rice

**Ingredients** for 3 servings

½ cup chopped artichoke hearts
½ cup sliced red bell peppers
4 mushrooms, thinly sliced
½ cup canned diced tomatoes
½ cup canned chickpeas
3 tbsp hot sauce
2 tbsp lemon juice
1 tbsp allspice
1 cup rice

**Directions** and Total Time: 50 minutes

Preheat air fryer to 400°F. Combine the artichokes, peppers, mushrooms, tomatoes and their juices, chickpeas, hot sauce, lemon juice, and allspice in a baking pan. Roast for 10 minutes. Pour in rice and 2 cups of boiling water, cover with aluminum foil, and Roast for 22 minutes. Discard the foil and Roast for 3 more minutes until the top is crisp. Let cool slightly before stirring.

## Couscous & Veggie Stir-Fry

**Ingredients** for 4 servings

1 cup trimmed snow peas, halved
1 head broccoli, cut into florets
1 cup couscous
Salt to taste
2 tsp olive oil
1 cup shelled edamame beans
2 cups chopped bok choy
2 scallions, chopped
1 tsp toasted sesame oil
1 tbsp soy sauce
2 tbsp sesame seeds

**Directions** and Total Time: 20 minutes

Add couscous, 2 cups water, and salt to a medium pot. Bring the water to a boil, then cover. Remove from the heat and let the couscous steep for 5 to 8 minutes. In a large skillet, saute broccoli in olive oil on high heat. Season with a pinch of salt and cook until softened. Stir in the rest of the vegetables. The bok choy needs about a minute to wilt. Add two tablespoons of water to create steam to finish off the dish. Drizzle with sesame oil and soy sauce and toss to coat. Remove the skillet from the heat. Plate a scoop of couscous, then top with the stir-fry vegetables. Garnish with sesame seeds and add extra soy sauce and sesame oil to taste. Serve warm and enjoy.

## Olive & Walnut Zoodles

**Ingredients** for 4 servings

2 tbsp olive oil
2 zucchini, sliced into noodles
1 orange, zested and juiced
1 garlic clove, minced
Salt to taste
2 tbsp parsley, chopped
10 black olives, chopped
¼ cup walnuts, chopped

**Directions** and Total Time: 15 minutes

Heat the olive oil in a large wok over high heat. Stir fry zucchini for about 2 minutes. Whisk orange zest, orange juice, garlic, and salt in a bowl. Toss the noodles in the orange sauce. Top with parsley, olives, and walnuts.

## Brussels Sprouts with Mustard-Mayo Sauce

**Ingredients** for 4 servings

1 lb Brussels sprouts, sliced
¼ cup mayonnaise
2 tbsp Dijon mustard
¼ tsp pure maple syrup
1 tsp lemon juice
2 tbsp olive oil
Salt and black pepper to taste
2 cups sliced green cabbage

**Directions** and Total Time: 20 minutes

Whisk mayonnaise, mustard, maple syrup, and lemon juice in a small bowl. Set to the side. Over medium heat, add oil to a large skillet. Sear the Brussels sprouts for two minutes on each side. Season with salt and pepper. Reduce the heat, then add the cabbage for 2-4 minutes. When the cabbage is tender, serve among 4 plates and top with maple syrup sauce. Serve hot and enjoy.

## Brown Butter Asparagus & Beans

**Ingredients** for 4 servings

¼ cup butter
3 garlic cloves, thinly sliced
1 lb asparagus, each cut into 3
1 (15-oz) can cannellini beans
Salt and black pepper to taste
2 tbsp Parmesan cheese
2 tbsp sliced almonds

**Directions** and Total Time: 15 minutes

In a large skillet, melt butter over medium heat until it begins to brown, or about 3 - 5 minutes. Reduce the heat and stir in garlic. Sauté for 30 seconds or until aromatic. Stir in asparagus and sauté for 3 minutes stirring frequently. Next, add cannellini beans and cook for 2 minutes. Season with salt and pepper. Garnish with Parmesan cheese and almonds. Serve warm and enjoy.

## Las Vegas-Inspired Burgers

**Ingredients** for 6 servings

2 eggs, beaten
2 (15-oz) cans black beans
1 cup breadcrumbs
2 tbsp tamari
1 tsp garlic powder
1 tsp ground cumin
½ tsp red pepper flakes
Salt and black pepper to taste
2 tbsp olive oil
2 ripe avocados, mashed
6 hamburger buns
1 cup salsa

**Directions** and Total Time: 25 minutes

In a large bowl, mash 1 can of beans. Stir in the second can of beans, breadcrumbs, tamari, eggs, garlic powder, cumin, red pepper flakes, salt, and pepper until well combined while keeping the second can of beans whole. On a flat surface, pour the mixture out and shape into a log. Cut into 6 equal patty portions. In a large skillet, heat olive oil over medium heat. Arrange the patties in the skillet and cook for 3 minutes. Flip the patties and cook for another 3 minutes until brown and crisp. While the patties are cooking, season the mashed avocado with salt and pepper. To build the burger, layer the burger on top of the bottom bun, then spread 2 tablespoons of salsa on the burger. Dollop ¼ cup avocado mash, then top with the bun top. Serve warm and enjoy.

## Pinto Bean & Potato Bake

**Ingredients** for 4 servings

2 russet potatoes, cubed
1 (15-oz) can pinto beans
1 red bell pepper, diced
1 onion, diced
3 tbsp olive oil
1 tsp chili garlic powder
1 tsp red pepper flakes
1 tsp ground cumin
Salt and black pepper to taste
2 tbsp sour cream
1 tbsp chopped cilantro

**Directions** and Total Time: 30 minutes

Preheat the oven to 425°F. Line a baking sheet with parchment paper. Mix potatoes, beans, bell pepper, onion, oil, chili garlic powder, red pepper flakes, cumin, salt, and black pepper in a large bowl until well combined. Arrange the mixture in a single layer on the baking sheet. Bake for 10 minutes, toss with a spatula, then bake for another 10 minutes until the potatoes are golden and fork-tender. Garnish with sour cream and cilantro. Serve.

## Amazing Parmesan Cornmeal

**Ingredients** for 6 servings

1 cup milk
1 cup yellow cornmeal
1 cup grated Parmesan cheese
2 tbsp butter
1 tsp black pepper

**Directions** and Total Time: 30 minutes

In a large saucepan, add milk and 3 cups of salted water over medium heat. Bring to a boil, then whisk in cornmeal continuously. Cook for 3 to 5 minutes, constantly whisking to avoid lumps and sticking. Reduce the heat to low and cover. Simmer for 25 minutes. Whisk every 5 minutes to prevent lumps and to stick. When the cornmeal is cooked and creamy, stir in Parmesan cheese and butter. Season with black pepper. Serve hot.

## Famous Swedish Balls

**Ingredients** for 4 servings

2 cups portobello mushrooms, diced
1 (15-oz) can chickpeas, mashed
¼ cup applesauce
1 tbsp olive oil
2 chopped green onions
3 garlic cloves, minced
1 ½ cups breadcrumbs
¼ cup chopped fresh parsley
2 tbsp soy sauce
½ tsp shallot powder
½ tsp garlic powder
¼ tsp paprika
¼ tsp caraway seeds
¼ tsp fennel seeds
Salt to taste
2 pinches cayenne pepper
2 cups mushroom gravy
2 tbsp minced parsley

**Directions** and Total Time: 45 minutes

Preheat the oven to 400°F. In a large skillet, heat oil over medium heat. Sauté mushrooms and green onions for 5 minutes until soft. Stir in garlic and sauté for 1 minute until aromatic. In a large bowl, combine chickpeas, breadcrumbs, parsley, applesauce, soy sauce, shallot powder, garlic powder, paprika, caraway seeds, fennel seeds, salt, and cayenne pepper until well mixed. Measure a heaping tablespoon of the mixture and roll into a ball in your hands. Arrange the balls on a parchment-lined baking sheet and bake for 15 minutes. Use tongs to turn the balls and bake for another 10 minutes until browned. While the Swedish balls are baking, warm the gravy in a medium saucepan. When the balls are done, transfer them to the saucepan and coat with the gravy. Garnish with parsley.

## Oven-Baked Lentil Kofta Bake

**Ingredients** for 4 servings

2 tsp olive oil
1 (15-oz) can lentils
1 egg, beaten
3 garlic cloves, minced
1 shallot, finely chopped
½ cup chopped parsley
½ lemon, juiced
1 tsp ground cumin
½ tsp tomato purée
2 tbsp parsley, chopped
Salt and black pepper to taste

**Directions** and Total Time: 40 minutes

Preheat the oven to 425°F. Line a baking sheet with parchment paper. Mix all of the ingredients in a large bowl and mash into a dough consistency. Scoop 1 heaping tablespoon of dough and shape into a ball. Arrange on the baking sheet and gently press into a disk. Repeat this process until all of the dough is used. Brush tops with olive oil and bake for 10 minutes. Flip the falafel and bake for another 10 minutes until crisp. Serve warm.

## Lentil Burritos with Cilantro Chutney

**Ingredients** for 4 servings

1 cup cilantro chutney
1 lb cooked potatoes, mashed
2 tsp sunflower oil
3 garlic cloves, minced
1 ½ tbsp fresh lime juice
1 ½ tsp cumin powder
1 tsp onion powder
1 tsp coriander powder
Salt to taste
½ tsp turmeric
¼ tsp cayenne powder
4 large flour tortillas
1 cup cooked lentils
½ cup finely chopped cabbage
¼ cup minced red onions

**Directions** and Total Time: 30 minutes

Preheat air fryer to 390°F. Place the mashed potatoes, sunflower oil, garlic, lime, cumin, onion powder, coriander, salt, turmeric, and cayenne in a large bowl. Stir well until combined. Lay the tortillas out flat on the counter. In the middle of each, distribute the potato filling. Add some of the lentils, cabbage, and red onions on top of the potatoes. Close the wraps by folding the bottom of the tortillas up and over the filling, then folding the sides in, then rolling the bottom up to form a burrito. Place the wraps in the greased frying basket, seam side down. Air Fry for 6-8 minutes, flipping once until golden and crispy. Serve topped with cilantro chutney.

## Grilled Cheese Sandwich

**Ingredients** for 1 serving

2 sprouted bread slices
1 tsp sunflower oil
2 Halloumi cheese slices
1 tsp mellow white miso
1 garlic clove, minced
2 tbsp kimchi
1 cup Iceberg lettuce, torn

**Directions** and Total Time: 15 minutes

Preheat your air fryer to 390°F. Brush the outside of the bread with sunflower oil. Put the sliced Halloumi cheese, oiled sides facing out inside and close the sandwich. Put the sandwich in the frying basket and Air Fry for 12 minutes, flipping once until golden and crispy on the outside. On a plate, open the sandwich and spread the miso and garlic clove over the inside of one slice. Top with the kimchi and lettuce. Close the sandwich and cut it in half. Serve immediately and enjoy!

## Golden Fried Tofu

**Ingredients** for 4 servings

1 (15-oz) package tofu, cubed
¼ cup flour
¼ cup cornstarch
1 tsp garlic powder
¼ tsp onion powder
Salt and black pepper to taste
2 tbsp cilantro, chopped

**Directions** and Total Time: 20 minutes

Preheat air fryer to 390°F. Combine the flour, cornstarch, salt, garlic, onion powder, and black pepper in a bowl. Stir well. Place the tofu cubes in the flour mix. Toss to coat. Spray the tofu with oil and place them in a single layer in the greased frying basket. Air Fry for 14-16 minutes, flipping the pieces once until golden and crunchy. Top with freshly chopped cilantro and serve immediately.

## Tofu Piccata

**Ingredients** for 4 servings

1 (14-oz) block tofu, drained
1 tbsp olive oil
2 shallots, chopped
3 garlic cloves, minced
Salt and black pepper to taste
1 cup vegetable broth
1 tbsp whole-wheat flour
1 ½ lemons, juiced
2 tbsp butter
2 tbsp capers
1 tbsp dry vermouth

**Directions** and Total Time: 30 minutes

Preheat the oven to 425°F. Line a baking sheet with parchment paper. Cut tofu horizontally into 3 thin strips, then cut each strip in half crosswise. Take each piece and cut on the diagonal to make 12 triangles. Arrange the tofu in a single layer on the baking sheet and bake for 10 minutes. Flip the triangles and bake for another 10 minutes until golden. While the tofu is baking, heat oil over medium heat in a large skillet. Stir in shallots and sauté for 3 minutes to soften. Sauté garlic for 1 minute until aromatic. Season with salt and pepper and slowly pour in broth. Reduce the heat and let it simmer. Whisk flour and ¼ cup water in a small bowl. Add the slurry to the skillet and stir. When the sauce starts to thicken, stir in lemon juice, butter, capers, and vermouth until the butter has completely melted. Dip the tofu in the piccata sauce until coated. Arrange on a serving platter, then drizzle with the rest of the piccata sauce. Serve warm.

## Tofu & Spinach Lasagna

**Ingredients** for 4 servings

½ cup shredded mozzarella
8 oz lasagne noodles
1 tbsp olive oil
2 cups crumbled tofu
2 cups fresh spinach
2 tbsp cornstarch
1 tsp onion powder
Salt and black pepper to taste
2 garlic cloves, minced
2 cups marinara sauce

**Directions** and Total Time: 30 minutes

Cook the noodles until a little firmer than al dente. Drain and set aside. While the noodles are cooking, make the filling. In a big pan over medium heat, add the olive oil, tofu, and spinach. Stir-fry for a minute, add the cornstarch, onion powder, salt, pepper, and garlic. Stir until the spinach wilts. Remove from heat.

Preheat oven to 390°F. Pour a thin layer of marinara sauce in a baking pan. Layer 2-3 lasagne noodles on top of the marinara sauce. Top with a little more sauce and some of the tofu mix. Add another 2-3 noodles on top, then another layer of sauce, then another layer of tofu. Finish with a layer of noodles and a final layer of sauce. Sprinkle with mozzarella on top. Bake for 15 minutes or until the noodle edges are browned and the cheese is melted. Serve.

## Black Bean Stuffed Potato Boats

**Ingredients** for 4 servings

4 russets potatoes
1 cup chipotle mayonnaise
1 cup canned black beans
2 tomatoes, chopped
1 scallion, chopped
1/3 cup chopped cilantro
1 poblano chile, minced
1 avocado, diced

**Directions** and Total Time: 55 minutes

Preheat your air fryer to 390°F. Clean the potatoes, poke with a fork, and spray with oil. Put in the air fryer basket and Bake in the air fryer for 30 minutes or until softened. Heat the beans in a pan over medium heat. Put the potatoes on a plate and cut them across the top. Open them with a fork so you can stuff them. Top each potato with chipotle mayonnaise, beans, tomatoes, scallions, cilantro, poblano chile, and avocado. Serve immediately.

## Brown Rice Stir-Fry with Vegetables

**Ingredients** for 4 servings

1 cup cremini mushrooms, chopped
¾ cup vegetable broth
2 tbsp soy sauce
1 tbsp ketchup
1 tbsp minced fresh ginger
3 garlic cloves, minced
2 tsp cornstarch
2 tbsp olive oil
¼ tsp cayenne powder
2 green onions, sliced
3 cups broccoli florets
1 red bell pepper, diced
4 cups cooked brown rice

**Directions** and Total Time: 20 minutes

Whisk broth, soy sauce, ketchup, ginger, garlic, and cornstarch in a small bowl. Set to the side. Heat oil in a large skillet over medium heat. Sauté cayenne, green onions, broccoli, bell pepper, and mushrooms for 6 to 8 minutes until softened and the broccoli is bright green. Whisk the broth mixture again and add to the vegetables. Stir, then reduce the heat to medium. Stir occasionally for 2 minutes for the sauce to thicken. Portion out the rice among 4 bowls and top with veggies. Serve warm.

## Zucchini Tamale Pie

**Ingredients** for 4 servings

1 cup canned diced tomatoes
1 zucchini, diced
3 tbsp safflower oil
1 cup cooked pinto beans
3 garlic cloves, minced
1 tbsp corn masa flour
1 tsp dried oregano
½ tsp ground cumin
1 tsp onion powder
Salt to taste
½ tsp red chili flakes
½ cup ground cornmeal
1 tsp nutritional yeast
2 tbsp chopped cilantro
½ tsp lime zest

**Directions** and Total Time: 45 minutes

Warm 2 tbsp of the oil in a skillet over medium heat and sauté the zucchini for 3 minutes or until they begin to brown. Add the beans, tomatoes, garlic, flour, oregano, cumin, onion powder, salt, and chili flakes. Cook over medium heat, stirring often, about 5 minutes until the mix is thick and no liquid remains. Remove from heat. Spray a baking pan with oil and pour the mix inside. Smooth out the top and set aside. In a pot over high heat, add the cornmeal, 1 ½ cups of water, and salt. Whisk constantly as the mix begins to boil. Once it boils, reduce the heat to low. Add the yeast and oil and continue to cook, stirring often, 10 minutes or until the mix is thick and hard to stir. Remove from heat. Preheat your air fryer to 325°F. Add the cilantro and lime zest into the cornmeal mix and thoroughly combine.

Using a rubber spatula, spread it evenly over the filling in the baking pan to form a crust topping. Put in the frying basket and Bake for 20 minutes or until the top is golden. Let it cool for 5 to 10 minutes, then cut and serve. Enjoy!

### Farfalle with White Sauce

**Ingredients** for 4 servings

4 cups cauliflower florets
1 medium onion, chopped
8 oz farfalle pasta
2 tbsp chives scallions, minced
½ cup cashew pieces
2 large garlic cloves, peeled
2 tbsp fresh lemon juice
Salt and black pepper to taste

**Directions** and Total Time: 30 minutes

Preheat your air fryer to 390°F. Put the cauliflower in the fryer basket, spray with oil, and Bake for 8 minutes. Remove the basket, stir, and add the onion. Roast for 10 minutes or until the cauliflower is golden and the onions soft. Cook the farfalle pasta according to the package directions. Set aside. Put the roasted cauliflower and onions along with the cashews, 1 ½ of cups of water, garlic, lemon juice, salt, and pepper in a blender. Blend until creamy. Pour a large portion of the sauce on top of the warm pasta and add the minced scallions. Serve.

### Pinto Bean Casserole

**Ingredients** for 2 servings

1 (15-oz) can pinto beans
¼ cup tomato sauce
2 tbsp cornstarch
2 garlic cloves, minced
½ tsp dried oregano
½ tsp cumin
1 tsp smoked paprika
Salt and black pepper to taste

**Directions** and Total Time: 15 minutes

Preheat air fryer to 390°F. Stir the beans, tomato sauce, cornstarch, garlic, oregano, cumin, smoked paprika, salt, and pepper in a bowl until combined. Spray a baking pan with oil and pour the bean mix in. Bake in the fryer for 4 minutes. Remove, stir, and Bake for 4 minutes or until the mix is thick and heated through. Serve hot.

### Bok Choy & Tofu Stir-Fry

**Ingredients** for 4 servings

2 ½ cups baby bok choy
1 tbsp sesame oil
5 oz butter
2 cups tofu, cubed
1 tsp garlic powder
1 tsp onion powder
1 tbsp plain vinegar
2 garlic cloves, minced
1 tsp chili flakes
1 tbsp fresh ginger, grated
3 green onions, sliced
1 cup mayonnaise

**Directions** and Total Time: 45 minutes

Melt half of the butter in a wok over medium heat, add the bok choy, and stir-fry until softened. Season with salt, black pepper, garlic powder, onion powder, and plain vinegar. Sauté for 2 minutes; set aside. Melt the remaining butter in the wok, add and sauté garlic, chili flakes, and ginger until fragrant. Put the tofu in the wok and cook until browned on all sides. Add the green onions and bok choy, heat for 2 minutes, and add the sesame oil. Stir in mayonnaise, cook for 1 minute, and serve.

### Baked Squash with Spicy Chimichurri

**Ingredients** for 4 servings

½ red bell pepper, chopped
1 cup olive oil
1 tbsp butter, melted
Zest and juice of 1 lemon
1 jalapeno pepper, chopped
½ cup chopped fresh parsley
2 garlic cloves, minced
1 lb butternut squash
3 tbsp toasted pine nuts

**Directions** and Total Time: 15 minutes

In a bowl, add the lemon zest and juice, red bell pepper, jalapeno, olive oil, parsley, garlic, salt, and black pepper. Use an immersion blender to grind the ingredients until your desired consistency is achieved; set aside the chimichurri.

Slice the butternut squash into rounds and remove the seeds. Drizzle with the butter and season with salt and black pepper. Preheat a grill pan over medium heat and cook the squash for 2 minutes on each side or until browned. Remove the squash to serving plates, scatter the pine nuts on top, and serve with chimichurri.

### Spicy Tofu with Sautéed Cabbage

**Ingredients** for 4 servings

1 tbsp + 3 ½ tbsp coconut oil
4 oz butter
½ cup grated coconut
2 cups tofu, cubed
1 tsp yellow curry powder
½ tsp onion powder
2 cups Napa cabbage, grated
Salt and black pepper to taste
Lemon wedges for serving

**Directions** and Total Time: 55 minutes

Drizzle 1 tablespoon of coconut oil on the tofu. In a bowl, mix the shredded coconut, yellow curry powder, salt, and onion powder. Toss the tofu cubes in the spice mixture. Heat the remaining coconut oil in a non-stick skillet and fry the coated tofu until golden brown on all sides. Transfer to a plate. In another skillet, melt half of the butter, add, and sauté the cabbage until slightly caramelized. Then, season with salt and black pepper. Dish the cabbage into serving plates with tofu and lemon wedges. Melt the remaining butter in the skillet and drizzle over the cabbage and tofu. Serve.

### Sweet & Spicy Vegetable Stir-Fry

**Ingredients** for 2 servings

½ pineapple, cut into chunks
¼ cup Tabasco sauce
¼ cup lime juice
2 tsp allspice
5 oz cauliflower florets
1 carrot, thinly sliced
1 cup frozen peas, thawed
2 scallions, chopped

**Directions** and Total Time: 45 minutes

Preheat air fryer to 400°F. Whisk Tabasco sauce, lime juice, and allspice in a bowl. Then toss in cauliflower, pineapple, and carrots until coated. Strain the remaining sauce; reserve it. Air Fry the veggies for 12 minutes, shake, and Air Fry for 10-12 more minutes until cooked. Once the veggies are ready, remove to a bowl. Meanwhile, combine peas, scallions, and reserved sauce until coated. Transfer to a pan and Air Fry them for 3 minutes. Remove them to the bowl and serve right away.

## Kale Stuffed Zucchini Boats

**Ingredients** for 2 servings

1 cup grated mozzarella
2 tbsp tomato sauce
1 tsp olive oi
4 tbsp butter
2 garlic cloves, minced
1 zucchini
1 ½ oz baby kale
Salt and black pepper to taste

**Directions** and Total Time: 40 minutes

Preheat oven to 375°F. Use a knife to slice the zucchini in halves and scoop out the pulp with a spoon into a plate. Keep the flesh. Grease a baking sheet with olive oil and place the zucchini boats on top.

Put the butter in a skillet and melt over medium heat. Sauté the garlic for 1 minute. Add in kale and zucchini pulp. Cook until the kale wilts; season with salt and black pepper. Spoon tomato sauce into the boats and spread to coat the bottom evenly. Then, spoon the kale mixture into the zucchinis and sprinkle with the mozzarella cheese. Bake for 20-25 minutes. Serve.

## Veggie & Tofu Scramble Bowls

**Ingredients** for 2 servings

1 russet potato, cubed
1 bell pepper, cut into strips
½ tofu, cubed
1 tbsp nutritional yeast
½ tsp garlic powder
½ tsp onion powder
¼ tsp ground turmeric
1 tbsp apple cider vinegar

**Directions** and Total Time: 25 minutes

Preheat your air fryer to 400°F. Put in potato cubes and bell pepper strips and Air Fry for 10 minutes. Combine the tofu, nutritional yeast, garlic, onion, turmeric, and apple vinegar in a small pan. Fit a trivet in the fryer, lay the pan on top, and Air Fry for 5 more minutes until potatoes are tender. Share the potatoes and bell peppers into 2 bowls and top each with the tofu scramble. Serve.

## Pizza Margherita with Spinach

**Ingredients** for 4 servings

½ cup pizza sauce
1 tsp dried oregano
1 tsp garlic powder
1 pizza dough
1 cup baby spinach
½ cup grated mozzarella

**Directions** and Total Time: 50 minutes

Preheat air fryer to 400°F. Whisk pizza sauce, oregano, and garlic in a bowl. Set aside. Form 4 balls with the pizza dough and roll out each into a 6-inch round pizza. Lay one crust in the basket, spread ¼ of the sauce, then scatter with ¼ of spinach and finally top with mozzarella cheese. Grill for 8 minutes until golden brown and the crust is crispy. Repeat the process with the remaining crusts. Serve immediately and enjoy!

## Mushroom Bolognese Casserole

**Ingredients** for 4 servings

1 cup canned diced tomatoes
2 garlic cloves, minced
1 tsp onion powder
¾ tsp dried basil
¾ tsp dried oregano
1 cup chopped mushrooms
16 oz cooked spaghetti

**Directions** and Total Time: 20 minutes

Preheat air fryer to 400°F. Whisk the tomatoes and their juices, garlic, onion powder, basil, oregano, and mushrooms in a baking pan. Cover with aluminum foil and Bake for 6 minutes. Slide out the pan and add the cooked spaghetti; stir to coat. Cover with aluminum foil and Bake for 3 minutes until heated through and bubbly.

## Thyme Meatless Patties

**Ingredients** for 3 servings

½ cup oat flour
1 tsp allspice
½ tsp ground thyme
1 tsp maple syrup
½ tsp liquid smoke
1 tsp balsamic vinegar

**Directions** and Total Time: 25 minutes

Preheat air fryer to 400°F. Mix the oat flour, allspice, thyme, maple syrup, liquid smoke, balsamic vinegar, and water in a medium bowl. Make 6 patties out of the mixture. Place them onto a parchment paper and flatten them to ½-inch thick. Grease the patties with cooking spray and Grill for 12 minutes until crispy, turning once.

## Quinoa Green Pizza

**Ingredients** for 2 servings

¾ cup quinoa flour
½ tsp dried basil
½ tsp dried oregano
1 tbsp apple cider vinegar
1/3 cup ricotta cheese
2/3 cup broccoli florets
½ tsp garlic powder

**Directions** and Total Time: 25 minutes

Preheat air fryer to 350°F. Whisk quinoa flour, basil, oregano, apple cider vinegar, and ½ cup of water until smooth. Set aside. Cut 2 pieces of parchment paper. Place the quinoa mixture on one paper, top with another piece, and flatten to create a crust. Discard the top piece of paper. Bake for 5 minutes, turn and discard the other piece of paper. Spread the ricotta cheese over the crust, scatter with broccoli, and sprinkle with garlic. Grill at 400°F for 5 minutes until golden brown. Serve warm.

## Coconut Mini Tarts

**Ingredients** for 2 servings

¼ cup butter
1 tbsp coconut sugar
2 tbsp Greek yogurt
½ cup oat flour
2 tbsp strawberry jam

**Directions** and Total Time: 25 minutes

Preheat air fryer to 350°F. Use 2 pieces of parchment paper, each 8-inches long. Draw a rectangle on one piece. Beat the butter, coconut sugar, and Greek yogurt in a shallow bowl until well combined. Mix in oat flour until you get a dough. Put the dough onto the undrawing paper and cover it with the other one, rectangle-side up. Using a rolling pin, roll out until you get a rectangle. Discard top paper. Cut it into 4 equal rectangles. Spread on 2 rectangles, 1 tbsp of strawberry jam each, then top with the remaining rectangles. Using a fork, press all edges to seal them. Bake for 8 minutes.

### Effortless Mac `n´ Cheese

**Ingredients** for 4 servings

1 cup cream cheese
1 cup milk
½ cup grated mozzarella
1 tbsp grated Parmesan
16 oz cooked elbow macaroni

**Directions** and Total Time: 15 minutes

Preheat your air fryer to 400°F. Whisk the cream cheese, milk, mozzarella cheese, and Parmesan cheese until smooth in a bowl. Stir in the macaroni and pour into a baking dish. Cover with foil and bake in the air fryer for 6 minutes. Remove foil and Bake until cooked through and bubbly, 3-5 minutes. Serve warm and enjoy!

### Pineapple & Veggie Souvlaki

**Ingredients** for 4 servings

1 (15-oz) can pineapple rings in pineapple juice
8 whole mushrooms, quartered
1 red bell pepper, seeded
2 tbsp apple cider vinegar
2 tbsp hot sauce
1 tbsp allspice
1 tsp ground nutmeg
14 oz tofu cheese
1/3 cup butter, softened
1 red onion, peeled

**Directions** and Total Time: 35 minutes

Preheat your grill to 400°F. Whisk the butter, pineapple juice, apple vinegar, hot sauce, allspice, and nutmeg until smooth. Slice the tofu into 16 cubes, then the bell pepper into 16 chunks, and finally red onion into 8 wedges, separating each wedge into 2 pieces. Cut pineapple ring into quarters. Place veggie cubes and tofu into the butter bowl and toss to coat. Thread the veggies, tofu, and pineapple onto 8 skewers, alternating 16 pieces on each skewer. Grill for 15 minutes until golden brown.

### Curried Cauliflower

**Ingredients** for 2 servings

12 oz cauliflower florets
1 cup canned diced tomatoes
2 cups milk
2 tbsp lime juice
1 tbsp allspice
1 tbsp curry powder
1 tsp ground ginger
½ tsp ground cumin
16 oz cheddar, cubed
¼ cup chopped cilantro

**Directions** and Total Time: 30 minutes

Preheat your air fryer to 375°F. Combine the tomatoes and their juices, milk, lime juice, allspice, curry powder, ginger, and cumin in a baking pan. Toss in cauliflower and cheddar cheese until coated. Roast for 15 minutes, stir well, and Roast for another 10 minutes until bubbly. Scatter with cilantro. Serve and enjoy!

### Spicy Spaghetti Squash Bake

**Ingredients** for 4 servings

2 oz grated Parmesan cheese
1 tbsp coconut oil
2 tbsp melted butter
Olive oil for drizzling
2 lb spaghetti squash
Salt and black pepper to taste
½ tbsp garlic powder
1/5 tsp chili powder
1 cup heavy cream
2 oz cream cheese
1 cup mozzarella
2 tbsp fresh cilantro, chopped

**Directions** and Total Time: 40 minutes

Preheat oven to 350°F. Cut the squash in halves lengthwise and spoon out the seeds and fiber. Place on a baking dish, brush with coconut oil, and season with salt and pepper. Bake for 30 minutes. Remove and use two forks to shred the flesh into strands.

Empty the spaghetti strands into a bowl and mix with butter, garlic and chili powders, heavy cream, cream cheese, half of the mozzarella and Parmesan cheeses. Spoon the mixture into the squash cups and sprinkle with the remaining mozzarella cheese. Bake further for 5 minutes. Sprinkle with cilantro and drizzle with oil. Serve.

### Tempeh & Grilled Zucchini with Spinach Pesto

**Ingredients** for 4 servings

¾ cup olive oil
2 tbsp melted butter
3 oz spinach, chopped
1 ripe avocado, chopped
Juice of 1 lemon
1 garlic clove, minced
2 oz pecans
Salt and black pepper to taste
2 zucchini, sliced
1 tbsp fresh lemon juice
1 ½ lb tempeh slices

**Directions** and Total Time: 20 minutes

Place the spinach in a food processor along with the avocado, lemon juice, garlic, and pecans. Blend until smooth and then season with salt and black pepper. Add the olive oil and process a little more. Pour the pesto into a bowl and set aside. Place zucchini in a bowl. Season with 1 tbsp of lemon juice, salt, black pepper, and butter. Also, season the tempeh with salt and black pepper, and brush with olive oil. Preheat a grill pan and cook both the tempeh and zucchini slices until browned on both sides. Plate the tempeh and zucchini, spoon some pesto to the side, and serve immediately.

### Vegetable Biryani

**Ingredients** for 4 servings

1 cup chopped cremini mushrooms
3 white onions, chopped
1 tbsp turmeric powder
6 garlic cloves, minced
1 tsp ginger puree
3 tbsp butter
1 cup brown rice
¼ tsp cinnamon powder
2 tsp garam masala
½ tsp cardamom powder
½ tsp cayenne powder
½ tsp cumin powder
1 tsp smoked paprika
3 large tomatoes, diced
2 green chilies, minced
1 tbsp tomato puree
1 cup chopped mustard greens
1 cup yogurt
2 tbsp parsley, chopped

**Directions** and Total Time: 50 minutes

Melt the butter in a pot over medium heat. Sauté the onions until softened, 3 minutes. Mix in garlic, ginger, turmeric, cinnamon powder, garam masala, cardamom powder, cayenne pepper, cumin powder, paprika, and salt. Stir-fry for 1-2 minutes. Stir in tomatoes, green chili, tomato puree, and mushrooms. Once boiling, mix in the rice and cover it with water. Cook until the liquid absorbs and the rice is tender, 15-20 minutes. Fluff in the mustard greens. Top with yogurt and parsley.

## Dijon Burgers

**Ingredients** for 6 servings

1 tbsp soy sauce
1 tbsp white wine vinegar
2 tsp Dijon mustard
2 garlic cloves, minced
1 tsp dried thyme
½ tsp dried oregano
½ tsp dried sage
½ tsp smoked paprika
¼ tsp cayenne pepper
2 tbsp cilantro, chopped
Salt and black pepper to taste
1 cup millet
2 carrots, grated
2 tbsp parsley, chopped
3 tbsp olive oil
1 cup arugula

**Directions** and Total Time: 45 minutes

Mix together soy sauce, white wine vinegar, and mustard in a medium bowl until it comes together in a thick consistency. Slowly add 1 to 2 tablespoons of water to thin out the dressing. Whisk until smooth, then add the garlic, thyme, oregano, sage, smoked paprika, cayenne pepper, cilantro, salt, and black pepper. Stir well. Set the resulting dressing aside. Add the millet, 2 cups of water, and salt in a medium pot over high heat. Bring to a boil and cook for 2-3 minutes. Reduce the heat, cover, and simmer the millet for 15 minutes. Do not stir. Millet should be soft with no more liquid in the pan when it is done. Add cooked millet to a large bowl along with carrots, parsley, and the dressing that was made. Combine until it comes together. Measure ¼-cup portions and shape into patties. Add 1 teaspoon olive oil to a large skillet. Cook each patty for 5 minutes on one side, then flip. Cook for 5 more minutes. Serve warm with arugula.

## Cumin Lentil Patties

**Ingredients** for 6 servings

1 cup lentils
3 carrots, grated
1 shallot, diced
¾ cup almond flour
½ tsp smoked paprika
½ tsp ground cumin
½ tsp garlic powder
½ tsp tabasco sauce
Salt and black pepper to taste

**Directions** and Total Time: 45 minutes

In a medium pot, add lentils and 3 cups of water. When the water comes to a boil, reduce the heat and simmer for 15 minutes. Toss carrots and shallots in a large bowl along with flour, paprika, cumin, garlic, tabasco, salt, and pepper. When the lentils are cooked and soft, drain extra water then transfer to the bowl. Mash the ingredients slightly. Divide into 12 portions and shape into patties. Add oil to a large skillet over medium heat. Pan-fry the patties for 15 minutes, flipping once. Serve warm.

## Tofu Scramble with Mushrooms & Kale

**Ingredients** for 4 servings

1 cup sliced white button mushrooms
1 (14-oz) block tofu
2 tbsp butter, melted
¼ cup vegetable broth
1 tsp garlic powder
½ tsp ground turmeric
Salt and black pepper to taste
1 tbsp olive oil
½ cup diced onion
½ cup diced red bell pepper
1 cup kale, chopped
5 oz baby spinach
2 scallions, thinly sliced

**Directions** and Total Time: 25 minutes

Divide tofu into 4 equal portions. Crumble one piece of tofu into a blender jar and set the other 3 to the side. Put butter, broth, salt, garlic powder, turmeric, and pepper in the blender jar. Puree until smooth. In a medium skillet, heat oil over medium heat. Sauté onion, bell pepper, and mushrooms for 3 to 5 minutes until softened. Crumble the rest of the tofu into the skillet and stir to combine. Sauté for 2 minutes, stirring occasionally. Pour in the sauce from the blender and stir to combine. Stir in spinach and kale and cook for 3 minutes or until wilted. Simmer for 5 minutes stirring halfway through. Sprinkle with sliced scallions. Serve warm and enjoy.

## Chili Black Bean Burritos

**Ingredients** for 6 servings

1 tsp olive oil
1 red onion, diced
2 garlic cloves, minced
1 zucchini, chopped
1 bell pepper, diced
1 tomato, diced
2 tsp chili powder
1 tsp ground cumin
Salt to taste
1 (14-oz) can black beans
6 corn tortillas

**Directions** and Total Time: 55 minutes

Preheat the oven to 325°F. Heat the olive oil in a large skillet over medium heat. Saute onion for about 5 minutes until soft. Next, add garlic and saute until fragrant. Stir in zucchini and bell pepper for another 5 minutes. Then add the tomato and heat through for about 1-2 minutes. Mix in chili powder, cumin, salt, and black beans. Scoop some of the black bean mixture in the middle of each tortilla. Fold in the sides and roll into the burrito. Place each roll seam side down in a baking dish. Cover the burritos with any excess juices from the skillet. Bake in the oven for 20-30 minutes. Serve warm and enjoy.

## Sicilian-Style Vegan Pasta

**Ingredients** for 1 serving

½ cup cooked cannellini beans
½ cup whole-grain pasta
Salt to taste
1 tsp olive oil
¼ cup sliced mushrooms
¼ cup thinly sliced zucchini
½ cup spinach
1 tbsp balsamic vinegar
3 black Sicilian olives, chopped

**Directions** and Total Time: 30 minutes

Cook pasta in a pot of boiling water and salt according to the package directions. While the pasta is cooking, heat oil in a large skillet and saute mushrooms and zucchini for about 7 to 8 minutes. Stir in beans and heat for 2 minutes. Next, add the spinach and cook until it just wilts. Drizzle with vinegar. Mix the pasta with the bean mixture. Garnish with olives. Serve warm and enjoy.

## Sesame Soy Roasted Broccoli

**Ingredients** for 4 servings

1 head broccoli, cut into florets
1 tbsp soy sauce
1 tbsp sesame seeds
2 tbsp sesame oil

**Directions** and Total Time: 20 minutes

Preheat the oven to 425°F. Line a baking sheet with parchment paper. Toss broccoli, oil, and soy sauce in a large bowl until well coated. Arrange the florets on the baking sheet and roast for 10 minutes. Toss the florets with a spatula and roast for another 5 minutes until just browning on the edges. Transfer to a serving bowl and sprinkle with sesame seeds. Serve warm and enjoy.

## Spaghetti Squash in Lemon-Mint Sauce

**Ingredients** for 3 servings

1 cup cherry tomatoes, diced
3 tbsp olive oil
1 lemon, zested and juiced
2 tbsp mint, minced
1 garlic clove, pressed
1 spaghetti squash
Salt and to taste
1 cup chopped bell pepper
½ tsp dried basil
½ tsp ground fennel

**Directions** and Total Time: 50 minutes

Whisk olive oil and lemon juice, then mix in the mint, lemon zest, and garlic. Reserve until ready to use. Bring a large pot of water to a boil. Cut the squash in half lengthwise and remove seeds. Carefully place the squash in the boiling water along with salt. Boil for 30 minutes. Remove the squash carefully from the hot water and let cool. Reserve half of the squash for another dish. Scrape out the flesh and transfer the "noodles" to a strainer. Let drain for about 10 minutes, tossing about halfway through. In a large bowl, add cooked spaghetti squash and mint-lime dressing. Toss to coat. Add cherry tomatoes and bell pepper. Garnish with basil and fennel.

are softened, add peas, thyme, coriander, and white wine. Stir to combine. Transfer to the dish with the lentils. Stir in pepper, salt, and flour. Add ½ cup of water and continue stirring until the flour is dissolved. Cover the lentil mixture with the mashed potatoes. Bake for 20-30 minutes until the top of the shepard's pie is golden. Serve warm and enjoy.

## Spanish Vegetarian Paella

**Ingredients** for 4 servings

1 cup canned artichokes, quartered
1 lemon, cut into wedges for garnish
2 tbsp olive oil
1 onion, chopped
1 red bell pepper, 2 sliced
3 garlic cloves, minced
1 tomato, diced
1 cup frozen peas, thawed
½ cup green beans, chopped
1 tbsp Spanish paprika
1 tsp ground turmeric
Salt to taste
2 cups cooked brown rice
2 tbsp chopped parsley

**Directions** and Total Time: 25 minutes

In a large skillet, heat oil over medium heat. Sauté onion and bell pepper for 3 to 5 minutes until softened. Sauté garlic for 1 minute until aromatic. Stir in tomato, peas, green beans, artichokes, paprika, turmeric, and salt. Heat through for 4 minutes, stirring occasionally. Stir in rice until completely mixed. Transfer to a serving dish and garnish with parsley and lemon wedges. Serve warm.

## Picante Tomato Seitan with Brown Rice

**Ingredients** for 4 servings

2 tbsp olive oil
1 lb seitan, cut into cubes
Salt and black pepper to taste
1 tsp chili powder
1 tsp onion powder
1 tsp cumin powder
1 tsp garlic powder
1 yellow onion, chopped
2 celery stalks, chopped
2 carrots diced
4-5 cloves garlic
1 cup vegetable broth
1 tsp oregano
1 cup chopped tomatoes
3 green chilies, chopped
1 lime, juiced
1 cup brown rice

**Directions** and Total Time: 50 minutes

Add brown rice, 2 cups of water, and salt to a pot. Cook for 15-20 minutes. Heat the olive oil in a large pot, season the seitan with salt, pepper, and cook in the oil until brown, 10 minutes. Stir in the chili powder, onion powder, cumin powder, garlic powder, and cook until fragrant, 1 minute. Mix in the onion, celery, carrots, garlic, and cook until softened. Pour in the vegetable broth, 1 cup of water, oregano, tomatoes, and green chilies.

Cover the pot and cook until the tomatoes soften and the liquid reduces by half, 10 to 15 minutes. Open the lid, adjust the taste with salt, black pepper, and mix in the lime juice. Dish and serve warm with brown rice.

## Chili Quinoa a la Puttanesca

**Ingredients** for 4 servings

4 Kalamata olives, sliced
1 ½ tbsp capers
4 cups plum tomatoes, diced
1 tbsp olive oil
1 cup brown quinoa
2 cups water
1/8 tsp salt
4 pitted green olives, sliced
2 garlic cloves, minced
1 tbsp chopped fresh parsley
¼ cup chopped fresh basil
1/8 tsp red chili flakes

**Directions** and Total Time: 30 minutes

Add the quinoa, water, and salt to a medium pot over medium heat. Cook for 15 minutes. In a bowl, mix tomatoes, green olives, Kalamata olives, capers, garlic, olive oil, parsley, basil, and red chili flakes. Allow sitting for 5 minutes. Serve the puttanesca with the quinoa.

## Basil Fettucine with Peas

**Ingredients** for 4 servings

½ cup butter, softened
1 tbsp olive oil
16 oz whole-wheat fettuccine
Salt and black pepper to taste
¾ cup milk
2 garlic cloves, minced
1 ½ cups frozen peas
½ cup chopped fresh basil

**Directions** and Total Time: 25 minutes

Cook the fettuccine in a large pot over medium heat until al dente, 8-10 minutes. Drain the pasta through a colander and set aside. In a bowl, whisk the milk, butter, and salt until smooth. Set aside.

Heat the olive oil in a large skillet and sauté the garlic until fragrant, 30 seconds. Mix in peas, fettuccine, and basil. Toss well until the pasta is well-coated in the sauce and season with black pepper. Dish the food and serve.

## Cheesy Eggplant Lasagna

**Ingredients** for 4 servings

¾ cup chickpea flour
½ cup milk
3 tbsp lemon juice
1 tbsp chili sauce
2 tsp allspice
1 ½ cups panko bread crumbs
1 eggplant, sliced
2 cups jarred tomato sauce
½ cup ricotta cheese
1/3 cup grated mozzarella

**Directions** and Total Time: 40 minutes

Preheat air fryer to 400°F. Whisk chickpea flour, milk, lemon juice, chili sauce, and allspice until smooth. Set aside. On a plate, put the breadcrumbs. Submerge each eggplant slice into the batter, shaking off any excess, and dip into the breadcrumbs until well coated. Bake for 10 minutes, turning once. Let cool slightly. Spread 2 tbsp of tomato sauce at the bottom of a baking pan. Lay a single layer of eggplant slices, scatter with ricotta and top with tomato sauce. Repeat the process until no ingredients are left. Scatter with mozzarella cheese on top and Bake at 350ºF for 10 minutes until the eggplants are cooked and the cheese golden brown. Serve immediately.

## Creamy Cauliflower Alfredo Rigatoni

**Ingredients** for 6 servings

4 cups cauliflower florets
1 ½ cups milk
¼ cup silken tofu
½ lemon, juiced
2 tbsp Dijon mustard
1 ½ tsp shallot powder
Salt and black pepper to taste
1 tsp garlic powder
1 lb cooked rigatoni pasta
3 tbsp Parmesan cheese
2 tbsp chopped parsley
2 tsp truffle oil

**Directions** and Total Time: 20 minutes

Steam cauliflower for 10 to 12 minutes. When it is fork-tender, place in a blender jar. Add milk, tofu, lemon juice, mustard, shallot powder, salt, garlic powder, and pepper. Puree for 1 to 2 minutes until smooth. In a large bowl, add pasta and pour over the sauce. Toss to coat. Portion out the pasta among 6 bowls. Top with Parmesan cheese, parsley, and truffle oil. Serve warm and enjoy.

## Tortilla Pizza Margherita

**Ingredients** for 1 serving

1/3 cup grated mozzarella
1 flour tortilla
¼ cup tomato sauce
3 basil leaves

**Directions** and Total Time: 15 minutes

Preheat oven to 350°F. Put the tortilla in a greased baking sheet and pour the sauce in the center. Spread across the whole tortilla. Sprinkle with cheese and bake for 8-10 minutes or until crisp. Remove and top with basil leaves.

## Vegetarian Stuffed Bell Peppers

**Ingredients** for 3 servings

1 cup mushrooms, chopped
1 tbsp allspice
¾ cup Alfredo sauce
½ cup canned diced tomatoes
1 cup cooked rice
2 tbsp dried parsley
2 tbsp hot sauce
Salt and black pepper to taste
3 large bell peppers

**Directions** and Total Time: 40 minutes

Preheat oven to 375°F. Whisk mushrooms, allspice and 1 cup of boiling water until smooth. Stir in Alfredo sauce, tomatoes, rice, parsley, hot sauce, salt, and black pepper. Set aside. Cut the top of each bell pepper, take out the core and seeds without breaking the pepper. Fill each pepper with the rice mixture and cover them with aluminum foil, folding the edges. Roast for 30 minutes until tender. Let cool before unwrapping. Serve warm.

## Bagels with Avocado & Tomatoes

**Ingredients** for 2 servings

2/3 cup all-purpose flour
½ tsp active dry yeast
1/3 cup Greek yogurt
8 cherry tomatoes
1 ripe avocado
1 tbsp lemon juice
2 tbsp chopped red onions
Black pepper to taste

**Directions** and Total Time: 35 minutes

Preheat your air fryer to 400°F. Beat the flour, dry yeast, and Greek yogurt until you get a smooth dough, adding more flour if necessary. Make 2 equal balls out of the mixture. Using a rolling pin, roll each ball into a 9-inch long strip. Form a ring with each strip and press the ends together to create 2 bagels. In a bowl with hot water, soak the bagels for 1 minute. Shake excess water and let rise for 15 minutes in the fryer. After, Bake for 5 minutes, turn the bagels, top with tomatoes, and Bake for another 5 minutes. Cut avocado in half, discard the pit and remove the flesh into a bowl. Mash with a fork and stir in lemon juice and onions. Once the bagels are ready, let cool slightly and cut them in half. Spread on each half some guacamole, top with 2 slices of Baked tomatoes, and sprinkle with pepper. Serve immediately.

## Cheddar-Bean Flautas

**Ingredients** for 4 servings

1 cup shredded cheddar
8 corn tortillas
1 (15-oz) can refried beans
1 cup guacamole

**Directions** and Total Time: 15 minutes

Preheat air fryer to 390°F. Wet the tortillas with water. Spray the frying basket with oil and stack the tortillas inside. Air Fry for 1 minute. Remove to a flat surface, laying them out individually. Scoop an equal amount of beans in a line down the center of each tortilla. Top with cheddar cheese. Roll the tortilla sides over the filling and put seam-side down in the greased frying basket. Air Fry for 7 minutes or until the tortillas are golden and crispy. Serve immediately topped with guacamole.

## Vegan Buddha Bowls

**Ingredients** for 2 servings

12 oz broccoli florets
½ cup quinoa
1 peeled sweet potato, cubed
¾ cup bread crumbs
¼ cup chickpea flour
¼ cup hot sauce
16 oz super-firm tofu, cubed
1 tsp lemon juice
2 tsp olive oil
Salt to taste
2 scallions, thinly sliced
1 tbsp sesame seeds

**Directions** and Total Time: 45 minutes

Preheat your air fryer to 400°F. Add quinoa and 1 cup of boiling water in a baking pan, cover it with aluminum foil, and Air Fry for 10 minutes. Set aside covered. Put the sweet potatoes in the air fryer basket and Air Fry for 2 minutes. Add in broccoli and Air Fry for 5 more minutes. Shake up and cook for another 3 minutes. Set the veggies aside. On a plate, put the breadcrumbs.

In a bowl, whisk chickpea flour and hot sauce. Toss in tofu cubes until coated and dip them in the breadcrumbs. Air Fry for 10 minutes until crispy. Share quinoa and fried veggies into 2 bowls. Top with crispy tofu and drizzle with lemon juice, olive oil and salt to taste. Scatter with scallions and sesame seeds before serving. Enjoy!

## Baked Meat-Free Burgers

**Ingredients** for 3 servings

¾ cup canned red kidney beans
¼ cup roasted red peppers
1 tbsp hot sauce
1 tbsp balsamic vinegar
½ tsp ground coriander
3 tbsp aquafaba

**Directions** and Total Time: 30 minutes

Preheat oven to 360°F. In a food processor, blitz the beans, red peppers, hot sauce, balsamic vinegar, and ¼ cup of water until smooth. Remove to a bowl. Add ground coriander and aquafaba and toss until well combined. Make 3 patties out of the mixture and bake for 16 minutes until golden brown, turning once. Serve.

## Balsamic Lentil Patties

**Ingredients** for 4 servings

1 (15.5-oz) can lentils
¼ cup canned diced tomatoes
2 tbsp balsamic vinegar
2 tbsp hot sauce
1 tbsp allspice
1 tsp liquid smoke
2 tbsp aquafaba

**Directions** and Total Time: 25 minutes

Preheat air fryer to 360°F. Using a fork, mash the lentils in a bowl. Stir in tomatoes and their juice, balsamic vinegar, hot sauce, allspice, liquid smoke, and aquafaba with hands. Make 4 patties out of the mixture. Bake them for 15 minutes until crispy, turning once. Serve.

## Tex-Mex Stuffed Sweet Potatoes

**Ingredients** for 2 servings

2 medium sweet potatoes
1 (15.5-oz) can black beans
2 scallions, finely sliced
1 tbsp hot sauce
1 tsp taco seasoning
2 tbsp lime juice
¼ cup Ranch dressing

**Directions** and Total Time: 40 minutes

Preheat your air fryer to 400°F. Add the sweet potatoes to the fryer basket and Roast for 30 minutes. Toss the beans, scallions, hot sauce, taco seasoning, and lime juice. Set aside. Once the potatoes are ready, cut them lengthwise, 2/3 through. Spoon ¼ of the bean mixture into each half and drizzle Ranch dressing before serving.

## Green Pea & Potato Stir-Fry

**Ingredients** for 4 servings

2 tbsp olive oil
4 medium potatoes, diced
1 medium onion, chopped
1 tsp red chili powder
1 tsp fresh ginger-garlic paste
1 tsp cumin powder
¼ tsp turmeric powder
Salt and black pepper to taste
1 cup fresh green peas

**Directions** and Total Time: 21 minutes

Steam potatoes in a safe microwave bowl in the microwave for 8-10 minutes or until softened. Heat the olive oil in a wok and sauté the onion until softened, 3 minutes. Mix in the chili powder, ginger-garlic paste, cumin powder, turmeric powder, salt, and black pepper and cook until fragrant, about 1 minute. Stir in the green peas, potatoes, and cook until softened, 2-3 minutes. Serve.

## California-Style Veggie Bowls

**Ingredients** for 4 servings

1 yellow onion, finely diced
1 avocado, sliced
1 cup grated cheddar
1 tbsp olive oil
1 lb extra firm tofu, cubed
Salt and black pepper to taste
½ cup cauliflower florets
1 jalapeño pepper, minced
2 garlic cloves, minced
1 tbsp red chili powder
1 tsp cumin powder
1 (8 oz) can sweet corn kernels
1 (8 oz) can lima beans, rinsed
1 cup quick-cooking quinoa
1 (14 oz) can diced tomatoes
2 ½ cups vegetable broth
2 tbsp chopped fresh cilantro
2 limes, cut into wedges

**Directions** and Total Time: 30 minutes

Heat olive oil in a pot and cook the tofu until golden brown, 5 minutes. Season with salt, pepper, and mix in onion, cauliflower, and jalapeño pepper. Cook until the vegetables soften, 3 minutes. Stir in garlic, chili powder, and cumin powder; cook for 1 minute. Mix in sweet corn kernels, lima beans, quinoa, tomatoes, and vegetable broth. Simmer until the quinoa absorbs all the liquid, 10 minutes. Fluff quinoa. Top with the cheddar cheese, cilantro, lime wedges, and avocado. Serve.

## Rice Bowls with Soy Chorizo

**Ingredients** for 4 servings

1 (8 oz) can pinto beans
2 tbsp olive oil
2 cups chopped soy chorizo
1 tsp taco seasoning
2 green bell peppers, sliced
1 cup brown rice
2 cups vegetable broth
¼ cup salsa
1 lemon, zested and juiced
1 (7 oz) can sweet corn kernels
2 green onions, chopped
2 tbsp freshly chopped parsley

**Directions** and Total Time: 50 minutes

Heat the olive oil in a medium pot and cook the soy chorizo until golden brown, 5 minutes. Season with the taco seasoning and stir in bell peppers; cook until the peppers slightly soften, 3 minutes. Stir in the brown rice, vegetable broth, salt, salsa, and lemon zest. Cook the food until the rice is tender and all the liquid is absorbed, 15 to 25 minutes. Mix in the lemon juice, pinto beans, corn kernels, and green onions. Allow warming for 3-5 minutes. Garnish with parsley and serve.

## BBQ Tofu Kabobs with Squash Purée

**Ingredients** for 4 servings

3 cups butternut squash, cubed
2 oz grated Parmesan
4 tbsp basil, chopped
2/3 cup olive oil
½ cup cold butter
1 tbsp melted butter
2 garlic cloves
Juice of ½ lemon
4 tbsp capers
1 lb extra firm tofu, cubed
½ tbsp BBQ sauce

**Directions** and Total Time: 20 minutes

In your blender, add basil, garlic, lemon juice, capers, olive oil, salt, and pepper. Process until smooth; set aside the resulting salsa verde. Thread the tofu cubes on wooden skewers. Season with salt and brush with BBQ sauce. Melt butter in a grill pan and fry the tofu until browned. Remove to a plate. Pour the squash into a pot, add some lightly salted water, and bring the vegetable to a boil until soft, about 6 minutes. Drain and pour into a bowl. Add the cold butter, Parmesan cheese, salt, and black pepper. Mash the vegetable with an immersion blender until the consistency of mashed potatoes is achieved. Serve the tofu skewers with the mashed squash and salsa verde.

## Seitan Panini with Basil Pesto

**Ingredients** for 4 servings

**For the seitan:**
2/3 cup basil pesto
½ lemon, juiced
1 garlic clove, minced
1/8 tsp salt
1 cup chopped seitan

**For the panini:**
¼ cup grated Parmesan
8 thick ciabatta slices
3 tbsp basil pesto
Olive oil for brushing
8 mozzarella slices
1 yellow bell pepper, chopped

**Directions** and Total Time: 15 minutes+ cooling time

In a medium bowl, mix the pesto, lemon juice, garlic, and salt. Add the seitan and coat well with the marinade. Cover with plastic wrap and marinate in the refrigerator for 30 minutes. Preheat a large skillet over medium heat and remove the seitan from the fridge. Cook the seitan in the skillet until brown and cooked through, 2-3 minutes.

Preheat a panini press to medium heat. In a small bowl, mix the pesto in the inner parts of two slices of bread. On the outer parts, apply some olive oil and place a slice with (the olive oil side down) in the press. Lay 2 slices of mozzarella cheese on the bread, spoon some seitan on top. Sprinkle with some bell pepper and some Parmesan cheese. Cover with another bread slice. Close the press and grill the bread for 1 to 2 minutes. Flip the bread, and grill further for 1 minute or until the cheese melts and golden brown on both sides.

## Tomato & Mushroom Lettuce Wraps

**Ingredients** for 4 servings

4 oz baby Bella mushrooms, sliced
1 iceberg lettuce, leaves extracted
1 cup grated cheddar
1 ½ lb tofu, crumbled
2 tbsp butter
1 large tomato, sliced

**Directions** and Total Time: 25 minutes

Melt the butter in a skillet, add mushrooms, and sauté until browned and tender, about 6 minutes. Transfer to a plate. Add the tofu to the skillet and cook until brown, about 10 minutes. Spoon the tofu and mushrooms into the lettuce leaves, sprinkle with the cheddar cheese, and share the tomato slices on top. Serve immediately.

## Rice & Bean Tortillas

**Ingredients** for 4 servings

1 (15 oz) can black beans
4 flour tortillas, warmed
1 cup heavy cream
1 cup grated cheddar
1 tbsp olive oil
1 cups brown rice
Salt and black pepper to taste
1 medium red onion, chopped
1 green bell pepper, diced
2 garlic cloves, minced
1 tbsp chili powder
1 tsp cumin powder
1/8 tsp red chili flakes
1 cup salsa

**Directions** and Total Time: 50 minutes

Add 2 cups of water and brown rice to a medium pot, season with some salt, and cook over medium heat until the water absorbs and the rice is tender, 15 to 20 minutes.

Heat the olive oil in a medium skillet over medium heat and sauté the onion, bell pepper, and garlic until softened and fragrant, 3 minutes.

Mix in the chili powder, cumin powder, red chili flakes, and season with salt and black pepper. Cook for 1 minute or until the food releases fragrance. Stir in the brown rice, black beans, and allow warming through, 3 minutes. Lay the tortillas on a clean, flat surface and divide the rice mixture in the center of each. Top with salsa, heavy cream, and cheddar cheese. Fold the sides and ends of the tortillas over the filling to secure.

## Pepper & Tofu Bake

**Ingredients** for 4 servings

1 tbsp melted butter
3 oz cream cheese
¾ cup mayonnaise
2 oz cucumber, diced
1 large tomato, chopped
2 tsp dried parsley
4 orange bell peppers
2 ½ cups cubed tofu
1 tsp dried basil

**Directions** and Total Time: 20 minutes

Preheat the oven's broiler to 450°F and line a baking sheet with parchment paper. In a salad bowl, combine cream cheese, mayonnaise, cucumber, tomato, salt, pepper, and parsley. Refrigerate. Arrange the bell peppers and tofu on the baking sheet, drizzle with melted butter, and season with basil, salt, and pepper. Bake for 10-15 minutes or until the peppers have charred lightly and the tofu browned. Remove and serve with the salad.

## Mouth-Watering Vegetable Casserole

**Ingredients** for 3 servings

1 red bell pepper, chopped
½ lb okra, trimmed
1 red onion, chopped
1 (28-oz) can diced tomatoes
2 tbsp balsamic vinegar
1 tbsp allspice
1 tsp ground cumin
1 cup baby spinach

**Directions** and Total Time: 45 minutes

Preheat your air fryer to 400°F. Combine the bell pepper, red onion, okra, tomatoes and juices, balsamic vinegar, allspice, and cumin in a baking pan and Roast for 25 minutes, stirring every 10 minutes. Stir in spinach and Roast for another 5 minutes. Serve warm and enjoy!

## Indian-Style Tempeh Bake

**Ingredients** for 4 servings

1 green bell pepper, diced
3 tbsp butter
3 cups tempeh slices
2 tbsp garam masala
1 ¼ cups coconut cream
1 tbsp cilantro, finely chopped

**Directions** and Total Time: 30 minutes

Preheat oven to 400°F. Place a skillet over medium heat, add, and melt the butter. Meanwhile, season the tempeh with some salt. Fry the tempeh in the butter until browned on both sides, about 4 minutes. Stir half of the garam masala into the tempeh until evenly mixed. Transfer the tempeh and spice to a baking dish.

Then, mix green bell pepper, coconut cream, cilantro, and remaining garam masala in a small bowl. Pour the mixture over the tempeh and bake in the oven for 20 minutes until golden brown on top. Garnish with cilantro.

## Grilled Vegetable Steaks with Greek Salad

**Ingredients** for 2 servings

5 oz cheddar, cubed
¼ cup coconut oil
1 eggplant, sliced
1 zucchini, sliced
Juice of ½ a lemon
10 Kalamata olives
2 tbsp pecans
1 oz mixed salad greens
½ cup mayonnaise
Salt to taste
½ tsp cayenne pepper

**Directions** and Total Time: 35 minutes

Set oven to broil. Arrange eggplant and zucchini on a parchment-lined baking sheet. Brush with coconut oil and sprinkle with cayenne pepper and salt. Broil for 15-20 minutes. Remove to a serving platter and drizzle with the lemon juice. Arrange the cheddar cheese, Kalamata olives, pecans, and mixed greens with the grilled veggies. Top with mayonnaise and serve.

## Bell Pepper & Cauliflower Gratin

**Ingredients** for 4 servings

4 oz grated Parmesan cheese
½ cup celery stalks, chopped
1 head cauliflower, chopped
1 green bell pepper, chopped
Salt and black pepper to taste
2 oz butter
1 white onion, finely chopped
1 cup mayonnaise
1 tsp red chili flakes

**Directions** and Total Time: 35 minutes

Preheat oven to 400°F. Season onion, celery, and bell pepper with salt and black pepper. In a bowl, mix cauliflower, mayonnaise, Parmesan cheese, and red chili flakes. Pour the mixture into a greased baking dish and add the vegetables; mix to distribute. Bake for 20 minutes. Remove and serve warm.

## BBQ Bean-Oat Burgers

**Ingredients** for 4 servings

3 (15 oz) cans black beans
4 hamburger buns, split
2 tbsp whole-wheat flour
2 tbsp quick-cooking oats
¼ cup chopped fresh basil
2 tbsp pure barbecue sauce
1 garlic clove, minced
Salt and black pepper to taste

**For topping:**

Red onion slices
Tomato slices
Fresh basil leaves
Additional barbecue sauce

**Directions** and Total Time: 20 minutes

In a medium bowl, mash the black beans and mix in the flour, oats, basil, barbecue sauce, garlic salt, and black pepper until well combined. Mold 4 patties out of the mixture and set aside.

Heat a grill pan to medium heat and lightly grease with cooking spray. Cook the bean patties on both sides until light brown and cooked through, 10 minutes. Place the patties between the burger buns and top with the onions, tomatoes, basil, and barbecue sauce. Serve warm.

## Hot Chili Brussel Sprout Sauté

**Ingredients** for 4 servings

4 oz butter
4 shallots, chopped
1 tbsp apple cider vinegar
Salt and black pepper to taste
1 lb Brussels sprouts, halved
½ cup hot chili sauce

**Directions** and Total Time: 15 minutes

Put the butter in a saucepan and melt over medium heat. Pour in the shallots and sauté for 2 minutes, to caramelize and slightly soften. Add the apple cider vinegar, salt, and black pepper. Stir and reduce the heat to cook the shallots further with continuous stirring, about 5 minutes. Transfer to a plate after.

Pour the Brussel sprouts into the saucepan and stir-fry with more butter until softened but al dente. Season with salt and black pepper, stir in the onions and hot chili sauce, and heat for a few seconds. Serve immediately.

## Mixed Mushroom Pizza with Pesto

**Ingredients** for 4 servings

¾ cup grated Parmesan cheese
2 tbsp olive oil
2 eggs, beaten
½ cup mayonnaise
¾ cup whole-wheat flour
1 tsp baking powder
1 cup sliced mixed mushrooms
1 tbsp basil pesto
½ cup red pizza sauce

**Directions** and Total Time: 40 minutes

Preheat the oven to 350°F. In a bowl, mix the beaten eggs, mayonnaise, whole-wheat flour, baking powder, and salt until dough forms. Spread the dough on a pizza pan and bake in the oven for 10 minutes or until the dough sets. In a medium bowl, mix the mushrooms, olive oil, basil pesto, salt, and black pepper. Remove the pizza crust spread the pizza sauce on top. Scatter mushroom mixture on the crust and top with Parmesan cheese. Bake further until the cheese melts and the mushrooms soften, 10-15 minutes. Remove the pizza, slice, and serve.

## Basil Mushroom Pizza

**Ingredients** for 4 servings

1 cup chopped button mushrooms
½ cup sliced mixed bell peppers
1 cup Parmesan cheese
2 tsp butter
Salt and black pepper to taste
1 pizza crust
1 cup tomato sauce
5-6 basil leaves

**Directions** and Total Time: 35 minutes

Melt the butter in a skillet over medium heat. Sauté mushrooms and bell peppers for 10 minutes until softened. Season with salt and black pepper. Put the pizza crust on a pizza pan, spread the tomato sauce all over, and scatter vegetables evenly on top. Sprinkle with Parmesan cheese. Bake for 20 minutes until the cheese has melted. Garnish with basil and serve.

## Original Caprese Bake

**Ingredients** for 4 servings

1 cup mozzarella, cut into pieces
1 cup cherry tomatoes, halved
2 tbsp basil pesto
4 tbsp olive oil
1 cup mayonnaise
2 tbsp grated Parmesan
1 cup arugula

**Directions** and Total Time: 25 minutes

Preheat oven to 350°F. In a baking dish, mix the cherry tomatoes, mozzarella, pesto, mayonnaise, half of the Parmesan cheese, salt, and black pepper. Level the ingredients with a spatula and sprinkle the remaining Parmesan cheese on top. Bake for 20 minutes or until the top of the casserole is golden brown. Remove and allow cooling for a few minutes. Top with arugula and drizzle with olive oil. Serve.

## Grilled Tempeh with Green Beans

**Ingredients** for 4 servings

1 lb tempeh, sliced into 4 pieces
1 lb green beans, trimmed
1 tbsp butter, melted
2 tbsp olive oil
Salt and black pepper to taste
2 sprigs thyme
1 tbsp pure corn syrup
1 lemon, juiced

**Directions** and Total Time: 15 minutes

Preheat a grill pan over medium heat and brush with the butter. Season the tempeh and green beans with salt, black pepper, and place the thyme in the pan. Grill the tempeh and green beans on both sides until golden brown and tender, 10 minutes. Transfer to serving plates. In a small bowl, whisk the olive oil, corn syrup, lemon juice, and drizzle all over the food. Serve warm.

## Tofu Balls with Jalapeño Mayo

**Ingredients** for 4 servings

4 oz grated cheddar
2 tbsp butter
1/3 cup mayonnaise
¼ cup pickled jalapenos
1 tsp paprika powder
1 tbsp mustard powder
1 pinch cayenne pepper
1 egg, beaten
2 ½ cup crumbled tofu

**Directions** and Total Time: 40 minutes

In a bowl, mix mayonnaise, jalapeños, paprika, mustard powder, cayenne powder, and cheddar cheese; set aside. Add the beaten egg to the cheese mixture, crumbled tofu, salt, and pepper and combine well. Form meatballs out of the mix. Melt butter in a skillet and fry the tofu balls until browned. Serve and enjoy!

## Baked Tempeh with Garden Peas

**Ingredients** for 4 servings

½ cup grated Parmesan cheese
16 oz bow-tie pasta
2/3 lb tempeh, cubed
Salt and black pepper to taste
1 yellow onion, chopped
2 tbsp olive oil, divided
½ cup sliced white mushrooms
2 tbsp whole-wheat flour
¼ cup white wine
¾ cup vegetable stock
¼ cup milk
2 tsp chopped fresh thyme
¼ cup chopped cauliflower
3 tbsp breadcrumbs

**Directions** and Total Time: 50 minutes

Cook the pasta in 8 cups of slightly salted water for 10 minutes or until al dente. Drain and set aside. Preheat the oven to 375°F. Heat the 1 tbsp of olive oil in a skillet, season the tempeh with salt and pepper, and cook until golden brown all around. Mix in onion, mushrooms, and cook for 5 minutes. Stir in flour and cook for 1 more minute. Mix in wine and add two-thirds of the vegetable stock. Cook for 2 minutes while occasionally stirring and then add milk; continue cooking until the sauce thickens, 4 minutes. Season with thyme, salt, black pepper, and half of the Parmesan cheese. Once the cheese melts, turn the heat off and allow cooling.

Add the rest of the vegetable stock and cauliflower to a food processor and blend until smooth. Pour the mixture into a bowl, add in the sauce, and mix in pasta until combined. Grease a baking dish with cooking spray and spread in the mixture. Drizzle the remaining olive oil on top, breadcrumbs, some more thyme, and remaining cheese. Bake until the cheese melts and is golden brown on top, 30 minutes. Allow cooling for 3 minutes. Enjoy!

## Buckwheat-Tofu Stuffed Cabbage Rolls

**Ingredients** for 4 servings

1 head Savoy cabbage, leaves separated (scraps kept)
1 (23-oz) cand diced tomatoes
2 cups tofu, crumbled
½ sweet onion, chopped
2 garlic cloves, minced
Salt and black pepper to taste
1 cup buckwheat groats
2 tbsp butter
1 ¾ cups vegetable stock
1 bay leaf
2 tbsp chopped cilantro

**Directions** and Total Time: 30 minutes

Melt the butter in a large bowl and cook the tofu until golden brown, 8 minutes. Stir in the onion and garlic until softened and fragrant, 3 minutes. Season with salt and black pepper and mix in the buckwheat, bay leaf, and vegetable stock. Close the lid, allow boiling, and then simmer until all the liquid is absorbed. Open the lid, remove the bay leaf, and adjust the taste.

Lay the cabbage leaves on a flat surface and add 3 to 4 tablespoons of the cooked buckwheat onto each leaf. Roll the leaves to firmly secure the filling. Pour the tomatoes with juices into a medium pot, season with a little salt, black pepper, and lay the cabbage rolls in the sauce. Cook over medium heat until the cabbage softens, 5 to 8 minutes. Turn the heat off and dish the food onto serving plates. Garnish with more cilantro and serve.

### Artichoke-Broccoli Pizza

**Ingredients** for 4 servings

6 ¼ oz grated Parmesan cheese
2 eggs, beaten
4 ¼ oz grated broccoli
2 tbsp tomato sauce
2 oz mozzarella
2 oz canned artichoke wedges
1 garlic clove, thinly sliced
1 tbsp dried oregano
Green olives for garnish

**Directions** and Total Time: 40 minutes

Preheat oven to 350°F. In a bowl, add the beaten eggs, broccoli, 4 ½ oz of Parmesan cheese, salt, and stir to combine. Pour the mixture into the baking sheet and spread out with a spatula. Bake until the crust is lightly browned, about 20 minutes. Remove from the oven and spread the tomato sauce on top, sprinkle with the remaining Parmesan cheese and mozzarella cheese. Add the artichokes and garlic. Sprinkle with oregano. Bake the pizza further for 5-10 minutes at 420°F. When ready, slice the pizza, garnish with olives, and serve.

### Tempeh & Bean Brown Rice

**Ingredients** for 4 servings

1 (8 oz) can black beans, drained
2 tbsp olive oil
1 ½ cups crumbled tempeh
1 tsp Creole seasoning
2 red bell peppers, sliced
1 cup brown rice
2 cups vegetable broth
Salt to taste
1 lemon, zested and juiced
2 chives, chopped
2 tbsp freshly chopped parsley

**Directions** and Total Time: 50 minutes

Heat the olive oil in a medium pot and cook in the tempeh until golden brown, 5 minutes. Season with the Creole seasoning and stir in the bell peppers. Cook until the peppers slightly soften, 3 minutes. Stir in the brown rice, vegetable broth, salt, and lemon zest. Cover and cook until the rice is tender and all the liquid is absorbed, 15 to 25 minutes. Mix in the lemon juice, beans, and chives. Allow warming for 3 to 5 minutes and dish the food. Garnish with the parsley and serve warm.

### Arugula & White Bean Pitas

**Ingredients** for 6 servings

4 tsp olive oil
1 (14-oz) can white beans
2 scallions, minced
¼ cup fresh parsley, chopped
2 Kalamata olives, chopped
1 tbsp tahini
1 tbsp lemon juice
½ tsp ground cumin
¼ tsp paprika
6 whole-grain wraps, warm
1 cup hummus
1 cup arugula, chopped
2 tomatoes, chopped
1 cucumber, chopped
¼ cup chopped avocado

**Directions** and Total Time: 60 minutes

In a blender, place the white beans, scallions, parsley, and olives. Pulse until finely chopped. In a bowl, beat the tahini with lemon juice. Add in cumin, paprika, and salt. Transfer into beans mixture and mix well to combine. Shape the mixture into balls; flatten to make 6 patties.

In a skillet over medium heat, warm the oil and cook the patties for 8-10 minutes on both sides. Spread each wrap with hummus and top with patties, tomatoes, cucumber, arugula, and avocado. Roll the wraps up. Serve.

### Basil Bean & Quinoa Burgers

**Ingredients** for 4 servings

4 hamburger buns, split
4 small lettuce leaves
½ cup mayonnaise
1 (15-oz) can pinto beans
1 tbsp olive oil
1 cup quick-cooking quinoa
1 shallot, chopped
2 tbsp chopped fresh celery
1 garlic clove, minced
2 tbsp whole-wheat flour
¼ cup chopped fresh basil
2 tbsp pure maple syrup

**Directions** and Total Time: 35 minutes

Cook the quinoa with 2 cups of water in a medium pot until the liquid absorbs, 10 to 15 minutes. Heat the olive oil in a medium skillet over medium heat and sauté the shallot, celery, and garlic until softened and fragrant, 3 minutes. Transfer the quinoa and shallot mixture to a medium bowl and add the pinto beans, flour, basil, maple syrup, salt, and black pepper. Mash and mold 4 patties out of the mixture and set aside.

Heat a grill pan to medium heat and lightly grease with cooking spray. Cook the patties on both sides until light brown, compacted, and cooked through, 10 minutes. Place the patties between the burger buns and top with the lettuce and mayonnaise. Serve and enjoy!

### Nutty Tofu Loaf

**Ingredients** for 4 servings

1 lb firm tofu, crumbled
2 tbsp olive oil
1 cup diced mixed bell peppers
2 white onions, finely chopped
4 garlic cloves, minced
2 tbsp soy sauce
¾ cup chopped mixed nuts
1 egg, beaten
1 tbsp sesame seeds
Salt and black pepper to taste
1 tbsp Italian seasoning
½ tsp pure date syrup
½ cup tomato sauce

**Directions** and Total Time: 65 minutes

Preheat the oven to 350°F and grease a loaf pan with olive oil. Heat 1 tbsp of olive oil in a small skillet and sauté the onion and garlic until softened and fragrant, 2 minutes. Pour the onion mixture into a large bowl and mix with the tofu, soy sauce, nuts, egg, sesame seeds, bell peppers, salt, black pepper, Italian seasoning, and date syrup until well combined. Spoon the mixture into the loaf pan, press to fit, and spread the tomato sauce on top. Bake the tofu loaf in the oven for 45 minutes to 1 hour or until well compacted. Remove the loaf pan from the oven, invert the tofu loaf onto a chopping board, and cool for 5 minutes. Slice and serve.

## Hush Puppies with Sriracha Mayo

**Ingredients** for 6 servings

1 (15-oz) can chickpeas
2 chopped spring onions
2 garlic cloves, minced
6 tbsp milk
¾ cup yellow cornmeal
½ cup all-purpose flour
2 tsp baking powder
Salt to taste
4 tbsp canola oil
1 cup sriracha mayo

**Directions** and Total Time: 20 minutes

Mash chickpeas in a large bowl along with spring onions, garlic, milk, cornmeal, flour, baking powder, and salt. In a heavy, deep skillet or saucepan, add 2 inches of oil. Heat to 350°F. Test with a drop of batter. If the batter sizzles when it hits the oil, it is ready. Roll out a heaping teaspoon of batter to make a hush puppy. Set aside until the oil is hot enough. Use a slotted spoon to carefully add hush puppies to the oil. Do not overfill the pot. Fry for 1 to 2 minutes or until golden. Transfer to a plate lined with paper towel. Continue frying the rest of the hush puppies. Serve warm with sriracha mayo.

## Caribbean Roasted Kabocha Squash

**Ingredients** for 4 servings

2 lb kabocha squash, sliced
½ cup dark rum
1/3 cup maple syrup
¼ cup butter
¼ tsp ground cinnamon
Salt to taste

**Directions** and Total Time: 40 minutes

Preheat the oven to 425°F. Arrange the squash in a single layer on a parchment-lined baking sheet. Roast for 20 minutes. While the squash is roasting, heat rum, maple syrup, and butter in a small saucepan over low heat. Stir until combined. Flip the squash and spoon over rum sauce. Season with cinnamon and salt. Bake for 8 to 10 minutes until the squash is fork-tender and caramelized. Serve warm.

## Cauliflower Governator

**Ingredients** for 4 servings

1 head cauliflower, cut into florets
1 cup milk
1 tbsp apple cider vinegar
1 cup all-purpose flour
1 tbsp chili powder
Salt and black pepper to taste
1 tsp dried oregano
1 tsp dried coriander
½ tsp dried thyme
½ tsp shallot powder
½ tsp garlic powder

**Directions** and Total Time: 40 minutes

Preheat oven to 450°F. Whisk milk and vinegar in a small bowl. Whisk flour, chili powder, salt, pepper, oregano, coriander, thyme, shallot powder, and garlic powder in a medium bowl. Dip cauliflower first in the milk mixture, then dredge it in the flour mixture. Arrange on a parchment-lined baking sheet. Repeat the process for the rest of the cauliflower. Lightly spray the cauliflower with nonstick cooking spray. Bake the cauliflower for 15 minutes, then flip the cauliflower. Spray again with nonstick cooking spray and bake for another 15 minutes until golden and crunchy. Serve warm and enjoy.

## Fettuccine Alfredo with Cherry Tomatoes

**Ingredients** for 4 servings

¾ cup grated Parmesan cheese
3 tbsp butter
2 cups milk
1 ½ cups vegetable broth
1 large garlic clove, minced
16 oz whole-wheat fettuccine
½ cup heavy cream
¼ cup halved cherry tomatoes
2 tbsp chopped parsley

**Directions** and Total Time: 20 minutes

Bring milk, vegetable broth, butter, and garlic to a boil in a large pot, 5 minutes. Mix in the fettuccine and cook until tender while frequently tossing for about 10 minutes. Mix in heavy cream, tomatoes, Parmesan cheese, salt, and pepper. Cook for 3 minutes or until the cheese melts. Garnish with parsley and serve.

## Hot Chickpea Burgers with Avocado Spread

**Ingredients** for 4 servings

1 avocado, pitted and peeled
4 hamburger buns, split
3 (15 oz) cans chickpeas
2 tbsp almond flour
1 tomato, chopped
1 small red onion, chopped
2 tbsp quick-cooking oats
¼ cup chopped fresh parsley
1 tbsp hot sauce
1 garlic clove, minced
¼ tsp garlic salt
1/8 tsp black pepper

**Directions** and Total Time: 20 minutes

In a medium bowl, mash avocados and mix in the tomato and onion. Set aside the dip. In another bowl, mash the chickpeas and mix in the almond flour, oats, parsley, hot sauce, garlic, garlic salt, and black pepper. Mold 4 patties out of the mixture and set aside.

Heat a grill pan over medium heat and lightly grease with cooking spray. Cook the patties on both sides until light brown and cooked through, 10 minutes. Place each patty between each burger bun and top with avocado dip.

## Basil Fidelini Primavera

**Ingredients** for 4 servings

8 oz fidelini pasta
12 cherry tomatoes, halved
½ tsp paprika
1 small red onion, sliced
2 tbsp olive oil
3 tbsp butter, cubed
2 garlic cloves, minced
1 cup dry white wine
Salt and black pepper to taste
1 lemon, zested and juiced
1 cup packed fresh basil leaves

**Directions** and Total Time: 25 minutes

Heat the olive oil in a pot over medium heat. Mix in fidelini, paprika, onion, garlic, and stir-fry for 2-3 minutes. Pour white wine and season with salt and pepper. Cover with water. Cook until the water absorbs and the fidelini is al dente, 5 minutes. Mix in the cherry tomatoes, butter, lemon zest, lemon juice, and basil. Serve warm.

## Cumin Black Beans

**Ingredients** for 4 servings

2 tsp olive oil
4 shallots, chopped
1 tsp ground cumin
1 (14.5-oz) cans black beans
1 cup vegetable broth
2 tbsp sherry vinegar

**Directions** and Total Time: 25 minutes

Heat the oil in a pot over medium heat. Place in shallots and cumin and cook for 3 minutes until soft. Stir in beans and broth. Bring to a boil, then lower the heat and simmer for 10 minutes. Add in sherry vinegar, increase the heat and cook for an additional 3 minutes. Serve.

## Tempeh Filled Zucchini Rolls

**Ingredients** for 4 servings

1/3 cup grated Parmesan
2 cups grated mozzarella cheese
¼ cup chopped basil leaves
1 ½ cups marinara sauce
1 tbsp olive oil
2 garlic cloves, minced
3 zucchinis, sliced lengthwise
¾ lb crumbled tempeh
1 cup crumbled tofu cheese

**Directions** and Total Time: 60 minutes

Line a baking sheet with paper towels and lay the zucchini slices in a single layer. Sprinkle each side with some salt and allow releasing of liquid for 15 minutes. Heat the olive oil in a skillet and cook tempeh for 10 minutes; set aside. In a bowl, mix tempeh, tofu cheese, Parmesan cheese, basil, and garlic.

Preheat the oven to 400°F. Spread 1 cup of marinara sauce onto the bottom of a baking pan and set aside. Spread 1 tbsp of the cheese mixture evenly along with each zucchini slice; sprinkle with 1 tbsp of mozzarella cheese. Roll up the zucchini slices over the filling and arrange in the baking pan. Top with the remaining marinara sauce and sprinkle with the remaining mozzarella cheese. Bake for 25-30 minutes or until the cheese begins to brown.

## Cajun-Style Stuffed Mushrooms

**Ingredients** for 4 servings

½ head broccoli, cut into florets
1 lb cremini mushroom caps
1 onion, finely chopped
1 tsp garlic, minced
2 tbsp olive oil
1 bell pepper, chopped
1 tsp Cajun seasoning mix
Salt and black pepper, to taste
¼ cup mozzarella

**Directions** and Total Time: 35 minutes

Preheat oven to 360°F. Bake mushroom caps in a greased baking dish for 10-12 minutes. In a food processor, place broccoli and pulse until it becomes like small rice-like granules. In a heavy-bottomed skillet, warm olive oil; stir in bell pepper, garlic, and onion and sauté until fragrant. Place in pepper, salt, and Cajun seasoning mix. Fold in broccoli rice. Divide the filling mixture among mushroom caps. Top with mozzarella cheese and bake for 17 more minutes. Serve warm and enjoy!

## Oat & Black-Eyed Pea Casserole

**Ingredients** for 4 servings

1 (15-oz) can black-eyed peas
1 carrot, shredded
1 onion, chopped
2 garlic cloves, minced
¾ cup whole-wheat flour
¾ cup quick-cooking oats
½ cup breadcrumbs
¼ cup minced fresh parsley
1 tbsp soy sauce
½ tsp dried sage

**Directions** and Total Time: 25 minutes

Preheat oven to 360°F. Combine the carrot, onion, garlic, and peas and pulse until creamy and smooth in a blender. Add in flour, oats, breadcrumbs, parsley, soy sauce, and sage. Blend until ingredients are evenly mixed. Spoon the mixture into a greased loaf pan. Bake for 40 minutes until golden. Allow it to cool down for a few minutes before slicing. Serve immediately. Enjoy!

## Sherry Tofu with Mushrooms

**Ingredients** for 4 servings

2 cups baby Bella mushrooms, sliced
1 (14-oz) block tofu, drained
1 tbsp sesame oil
1 onion, chopped
3 garlic cloves, minced
½ cup dry sherry
1 tsp soy sauce
1 cup vegetable broth
1 tbsp tomato paste
1 tbsp corn starch
Salt and black pepper to taste
2 tbsp chopped parsley

**Directions** and Total Time: 30 minutes

Preheat oven to 425°F. Cut tofu horizontally into 3 thin strips, then cut each strip in half crosswise. Take each piece and cut on the diagonal to make 12 triangles. Arrange the tofu in a single layer on a parchment-lined baking sheet and bake for 10 minutes. Flip the triangles and bake for another 10 minutes until golden. Heat oil over medium heat in a skillet. Sauté onion for 3 minutes. Sauté garlic for 1 minute until aromatic. Stir in sherry and mushrooms and cook for 5-7 minutes to reduce the wine. Make a slurry by whisking soy sauce, broth, tomato paste, and corn starch in a small bowl. Add the slurry to the skillet and continue stirring for 3 minutes until the sauce has thickened. Add salt and pepper. Dip the tofu in the sauce until coated. Remove to a serving platter. Drizzle with the remaining mushroom sauce. Top with parsley.

## Hot Mushroom Fried Cauli Rice

**Ingredients** for 4 servings

1 cup white button mushrooms, sliced
1 cup grated purple cabbage
1 large head cauliflower
3 garlic cloves, minced
1 cup frozen peas
1 cup sliced carrots
2 tbsp olive oil
1 onion, chopped
3 tbsp tamari
Salt and black pepper to taste
2 tbsp chives, sliced
2 tbsp hot sauce

**Directions** and Total Time: 30 minutes

Grate the cauliflower in either a food processor or box grater to make about 4 cups of cauliflower rice. In a large skillet, heat 1 tablespoon oil over medium heat. Sauté onion and mushrooms for 5 minutes until softened. Sauté garlic for 1 minute until aromatic. Add another tablespoon of oil along with the cauliflower rice. Cook for 2 minutes stirring often. Then stir in peas, carrot, cabbage, and tamari sauce. Cook for another 4 minutes, stirring occasionally. When the rice starts to get tender, season with salt and pepper and stir. Transfer to a serving dish and top with chives and hot sauce. Serve.

### Curried Lentil Burgers with Walnuts

**Ingredients** for 4 servings

2 tbsp olive oil
1 cup dry lentils, rinsed
2 carrots, grated
1 onion, diced
½ cup walnuts
1 tbsp tomato puree
¾ cup almond flour
2 tsp curry powder
4 whole-grain buns

**Directions** and Total Time: 70 minutes

Place lentils in a pot and cover with water. Bring to a boil and simmer for 15-20 minutes. Meanwhile, combine the carrots, walnuts, onion, tomato puree, flour, curry powder, salt, and pepper in a bowl. Toss to coat. Once the lentils are ready, drain and transfer into the veggie bowl. Mash the mixture until sticky. Shape the mixture into balls; flatten to make patties. Heat the oil in a skillet over medium heat. Brown the patties for 8 minutes on both sides. To assemble, put the cakes on the buns and top with your desired toppings.

### Piri Piri Mushroom Burgers

**Ingredients** for 4 servings

4 large portobello mushroom caps, stemmed
Salt and black pepper to taste
1 cup Piri Piri spicy sauce
¼ cup butter, melted
4 Boston lettuce leaves
4 hamburger buns
4 tomato slices
¼ red onion, thinly sliced
2 tbsp ranch dressing

**Directions** and Total Time: 25 minutes

Preheat the oven to 425°F. Whisk piri piri sauce and butter in a small bowl. Set aside. Season mushroom caps with salt and pepper and place on a parchment-lined baking sheet. Drizzle with 2 tablespoons of the piri piri mixture. Bake for 10 minutes, flip the mushroom caps and drizzle another tablespoon of piri piri sauce. Bake for another 10 minutes until the mushrooms have reduced in size. Serve in buns garnished with lettuce, tomatoes, onion, and dressing.

### Dijon Black Bean Sandwiches with Pecans

**Ingredients** for 4 servings

2 tbsp olive oil
1 onion, chopped
1 garlic clove, crushed
¾ cup pecans, chopped
¾ cup canned black beans
¾ cup almond flour
2 tbsp minced fresh parsley
1 tbsp soy sauce
Salt and black pepper to taste
½ tsp ground sage
½ tsp sweet paprika
Bread slices
1 tsp Dijon mustard
4 lettuce leaves
4 tomato slices

**Directions** and Total Time: 20 minutes

Put the onion, garlic, and pecans in a blender. Pulse until roughly ground. Add in the beans and pulse until everything is well combined. Transfer to a large bowl and stir in the flour, parsley, soy sauce, mustard, salt, sage, paprika, and pepper. Mold patties out of the mixture. Heat the oil in a skillet over medium heat. Brown the patties for 10 minutes on both sides. To assemble, lay patties on the bread slices. Top with mustard, lettuce, and tomato.

### Kale & Tofu Filled Mushrooms

**Ingredients** for 4 servings

4 large portobello mushrooms, stems removed
Garlic salt and pepper to taste
1 small onion, chopped
1 cup chopped fresh kale
½ tsp olive oil
¼ cup crumbled tofu cheese
1 tbsp chopped fresh basil

**Directions** and Total Time: 25 minutes

Preheat the oven to 350°F and grease a baking sheet with cooking spray. Lightly oil the mushrooms with some cooking spray and season with black pepper and garlic salt. Arrange the mushrooms on the baking sheet and bake in the oven until tender, 10 to 15 minutes.

Heat the olive oil in a skillet over medium heat and sauté the onion until tender, 3 minutes. Stir in kale until wilted, 3 minutes. Spoon the mixture into the mushrooms and top with tofu cheese and basil. Serve and enjoy!

### Andalusian Spinach & Chickpeas

**Ingredients** for 4 servings

1 tbsp olive oil
1 onion, chopped
2 garlic cloves, minced
2 tsp ground cumin
½ tsp sherry vinegar
2 tsp Spanish paprika
1 (15-oz) can chickpeas
1 (14-oz) can diced tomatoes
1/3 cup raisins
Salt and black pepper to taste
5 oz baby spinach

**Directions** and Total Time: 15 minutes

In a large skillet, heat oil over medium heat. Sauté onion for 3 minutes until soft, then stir in garlic, cumin, vinegar, and paprika. Sauté for another minute until aromatic. Stir in chickpeas, tomatoes and the juice, raisins, salt, and pepper. Combine to coat and stir occasionally for 3 minutes. Stir in spinach and cook for another 3 minutes until it is wilted. Serve warm and enjoy.

### Potato Wedges with Mushroom Gravy

**Ingredients** for 2 servings

2 large russet potatoes, cut into wedges
Salt and black pepper to taste
½ tsp Italian seasoning
½ tsp garlic powder
½ tsp chili powder
½ cup mushroom gravy

**Directions** and Total Time: 30 minutes

Preheat the oven to 475°F. Line a baking sheet with parchment paper. In a large bowl, toss potatoes, Italian seasoning, garlic powder, and chili powder. Arrange the potatoes on the baking sheet and lightly spray them with cooking oil. Bake for 10 minutes, then flip the wedges. Bake for another 5 to 10 minutes until fork-tender. Serve warm with mushroom gravy. Enjoy!

### Instant Pot Green Lentil Stew

**Ingredients** for 6 servings

3 tbsp coconut oil
2 tbsp curry powder
1 tsp ground ginger
1 onion, chopped
2 garlic cloves, sliced
1 cup green lentils
Salt and black pepper to taste

**Directions** and Total Time: 30 minutes

Set your IP to Sauté. Add coconut oil, curry powder, ginger, onion, and garlic. Cook for 3 minutes. Stir in green lentils. Pour in 3 cups of water. Lock the lid and set the time to 10 minutes on High. Once ready, perform a natural pressure release for 10 minutes. Unlock the lid and season with salt and pepper. Serve and enjoy!

### Barbecued Mushroom Sandwiches

**Ingredients** for 4 servings

1 cup white button mushrooms, stemmed and sliced
2 garlic cloves, minced
1 tbsp avocado oil
1 onion, chopped
½ cup barbecue sauce
1 tsp smoked paprika
½ tsp ground cinnamon
4 hamburger buns
¼ red onion, thinly sliced

**Directions** and Total Time: 30 minutes

Heat oil in a large skillet over medium heat. Sauté onion for 3 minutes until softened. Sauté mushrooms for 5 minutes. When reduced in size, sauté garlic for 1 minute until aromatic.Stir in barbecue sauce, paprika, and cinnamon. Reduce heat and simmer for 10 minutes for the sauce to reduce. Scoop ¼ of the mixture onto a bun and top with red onion. Repeat for the rest of the buns and mixture. Serve warm and enjoy.

### Balsamic Quinoa & Couscous Burgers

**Ingredients** for 4 servings

2 tbsp olive oil
¼ cup couscous
¼ cup boiling water
2 cups cooked quinoa
2 tbsp balsamic vinegar
3 tbsp chopped olives
½ tsp garlic powder
Salt to taste
4 burger buns
Lettuce leaves, for serving
Tomato slices, for serving

**Directions** and Total Time: 20 minutes

Preheat oven to 350°F. In a bowl, place the couscous with boiling water. Let sit covered for 5 minutes. Once the liquid is absorbed, fluff with a fork. Add in quinoa and mash them to form a chunky texture. Stir in vinegar, olive oil, olives, garlic powder, and salt. Shape the mixture into 4 patties. Arrange them on a greased tray and bake for 25-30 minutes. To assemble, place the patties on the buns and top with lettuce and tomato slices. Serve.

### White Bean & Bulgur with Green Onions

**Ingredients** for 4 servings

2 tbsp olive oil
3 green onions, chopped
1 cup bulgur
1 tbsp soy sauce
Salt to taste
1 ½ cups cooked white beans
1 tbsp nutritional yeast
1 tbsp dried parsley

**Directions** and Total Time: 55 minutes

Heat the oil in a pot over medium heat. Place in green onions and sauté for 3 minutes. Stir in bulgur, 1 cup of water, soy sauce, and salt. Bring to a boil, then lower the heat and simmer for 20-22 minutes. Mix in beans and yeast. Cook for 5 minutes. Serve topped with parsley.

### Green Bean & Rice

**Ingredients** for 4 servings

3 hot green chilies, chopped
3 tbsp canola oil
1 roasted bell pepper, chopped
2 ½ cups vegetable broth
½ cup chopped fresh parsley
1 onion, chopped
2 garlic cloves, chopped
Salt and black pepper to taste
½ tsp dried oregano
1 cup long-grain brown rice
1 ½ cups cooked black beans
2 tbsp minced fresh cilantro

**Directions** and Total Time: 35 minutes

In a food processor, place bell pepper, chilies, 1 cup of broth, parsley, onion, garlic, pepper, oregano, salt, and pepper and blend until smooth. Heat oil in a skillet over medium heat. Add in rice and veggie mixture. Cook for 5 minutes, stirring often. Add in the remaining broth and and simmer for 15 minutes. Mix in beans and cook for another 5 minutes. Serve topped with cilantro.

### Cauliflower & Quinoa Sauté with Swiss Chard

**Ingredients** for 4 servings

1 head cauliflower, break into florets
2 tsp untoasted sesame oil
1 tsp toasted sesame oil
1 cup quinoa
Salt to taste
1 cup snow peas, cut in half
2 cups chopped Swiss chard
2 scallions, chopped
2 tbsp water
1 tbsp soy sauce
2 tbsp sesame seeds

**Directions** and Total Time: 30 minutes

Place quinoa with 2 cups of salted water in a pot over medium heat. Bring to a boil, lower the heat and simmer for 15 minutes. Do not stir. Heat the oil in a skillet over medium heat and sauté the cauliflower for 4-5 minutes. Add in snow peas and salt and stir well. Mix in Swiss chard, scallions, and 2 tbsp of water; cook until wilted. Drizzle with sesame oil and soy sauce and cook for 1 minute. Divide the quinoa between bowls and top with the cauliflower mixture. Garnish with sesame seeds.

### Rich Kitchari

**Ingredients** for 5 servings

4 cups chopped cauliflower and broccoli florets
½ cup split peas
½ cup brown rice
1 red onion, chopped
1 (14.5-oz) can diced tomatoes
3 garlic cloves, minced
1 jalapeño pepper, seeded
½ tsp ground ginger
1 tsp ground turmeric
1 tsp fennel seeds
Juice of 1 large lemon
1 tsp olive oil
Salt and black pepper to taste

**Directions** and Total Time: 40 minutes

In a food processor, place onion, tomatoes with juices, garlic, jalapeño pepper, ginger, turmeric, and 2 tbsp of water. Pulse until ingredients are evenly mixed. Heat the oil in a pot over medium heat. Cook the fennel seeds for 2-3 minutes, stirring often. Pour in the puréed mixture, split peas, rice, and 3 cups of water. Bring to a boil, then lower the heat and simmer for 10 minutes. Stir in cauliflower, broccoli, and cook for another 10 minutes. Mix in lemon juice and adjust seasoning. Serve.

### Japanese-Style Rice

**Ingredients** for 4 servings

2 cups snow peas, cut diagonally
2 tbsp canola oil
4 matcha tea bags
1 ½ cups brown rice
8 oz extra-firm tofu, chopped
3 green onions, minced
1 tbsp fresh lemon juice
1 tsp grated lemon zest
Salt and black pepper to taste

**Directions** and Total Time: 35 minutes

Boil 3 cups of water in a pot. Place in the tea bags and turn the heat off. Let sit for 7 minutes. Discard the bags. Wash the rice and put it into the tea. Cook for 20 minutes over medium heat. Drain and set aside.

Heat the oil in a skillet over medium heat. Fry the tofu for 5 minutes until golden. Stir in green onions and snow peas and cook for another 3 minutes. Mix in lemon juice and lemon zest. Place the rice in a serving bowl and mix it in the tofu mixture. Adjust the seasoning with salt and pepper. Serve right away and enjoy!

### Italian Seasoned Summer Squash Skillet

**Ingredients** for 4 servings

2 zucchinis, sliced into half-moons
1 yellow summer squashes, sliced into half-moons
2 tbsp olive oil
1 red onion, sliced
3 garlic cloves, sliced
10 cherry tomatoes, halved
1 tsp Italian seasoning
¼ tsp ground nutmeg
Salt and black pepper to taste

**Directions** and Total Time: 20 minutes

In a large skillet over medium heat, heat the olive oil. Sauté red onion for 5 minutes until softened. Sauté garlic for another minute until aromatic. Stir in zucchini, squash, tomato, Italian seasoning, nutmeg, salt, and pepper until combined. Cook for 4 to 6 minutes stirring occasionally. Adjust the seasoning with salt and pepper if needed. Cook until the zucchini and squash become golden and fork-tender. Serve warm and enjoy.

### Tangy Chickpeas

**Ingredients** for 6 servings

1 onion, cut into half-moon slices
2 (14.5-oz) cans chickpeas
3 tbsp olive oil
½ cup vegetable broth
2 tsp dried oregano
Salt and black pepper to taste

**Directions** and Total Time: 5 minutes

Heat the olive oil in a skillet over medium heat. Cook the onion for 3 minutes. Stir in chickpeas, broth, oregano, salt, and pepper. Bring to a boil, then lower the heat and simmer for 10 minutes. Serve and enjoy!

### Navy Bean Fussili with Chimichurri Salsa

**Ingredients** for 4 servings

½ cup chopped pitted black olives
8 oz whole-wheat fusilli
1 ½ cups canned navy beans
½ cup chimichurri salsa
1 cup chopped tomatoes
1 red onion, chopped

**Directions** and Total Time: 25 minutes

In a large pot over medium heat, pour 8 cups of salted water. Bring to a boil and add in the pasta. Cook for 8-10 minutes, drain and let cool. Combine the pasta, beans, and chimichurri in a bowl. Toss to coat. Stir in tomato, red onion, and olives. Serve right away and enjoy!

### Buckwheat & Rice Croquettes

**Ingredients** for 6 servings

¾ cup cooked buckwheat groats
½ cup cooked brown rice
¼ cup minced onion
1 celery stalk, chopped
¼ cup shredded carrots
1/3 cup whole-wheat flour
¼ cup chopped fresh parsley
3 tbsp olive oil
Salt and black pepper to taste

**Directions** and Total Time: 25 minutes

Combine the groats and rice in a bowl. Set aside. Heat 1 tbsp of oil in a skillet over medium heat. Place in onion, celery, and carrot and cook for 5 minutes. Transfer to the rice bowl. Mix in flour, parsley, salt, and pepper. Place in the fridge for 20 minutes. Mold the mixture into cylinder-shaped balls. Heat the remaining oil in a skillet over medium heat. Fry the croquettes for 8 minutes, turning occasionally until golden. Serve and enjoy!

### Smoked Bean Burgers

**Ingredients** for 4 servings

4 tbsp olive oil
1 minced onion
1 garlic clove, minced
1 (15.5-oz) can fava beans
1 tbsp minced fresh parsley
½ cup breadcrumbs
¼ cup almond flour
1 tsp smoked paprika
½ tsp dried thyme
4 burger buns, toasted
4 lettuce leaves
1 ripe tomato, sliced

**Directions** and Total Time: 15 minutes

In a blender, add onion, garlic, beans, parsley, breadcrumbs, flour, paprika, thyme, salt, and pepper. Pulse until uniform but not smooth. Shape 4 patties out of the mixture. Refrigerate for 15 minutes. Heat olive oil in a skillet over medium heat. Fry the patties for 10 minutes on both sides until golden brown. Serve in toasted buns with lettuce and tomato slices.

### Cilantro Bean & Millet Pot

**Ingredients** for 4 servings

1 (15.5-oz) can black-eyed peas
2 tbsp olive oil
1 onion, chopped
2 zucchinis, chopped
2 garlic cloves, minced
1 tsp dried thyme
½ tsp ground cumin
1 cup millet
2 tbsp chopped fresh cilantro

**Directions** and Total Time: 40 minutes

Heat the oil in a pot over medium heat. Place in onion and sauté for 3 minutes until translucent. Add in zucchinis, garlic, thyme, and cumin and cook for 10 minutes. Put in peas, millet, and 2 ½ cups of hot water. Bring to a boil, then lower the heat and simmer for 20 minutes. Fluff the millet using a fork. Serve garnished with cilantro.

### Gingery Mushroom Red Lentils

**Ingredients** for 4 servings

2 tsp olive oil
2 cloves garlic, minced
2 tsp grated fresh ginger
½ tsp ground cumin
½ tsp fennel seeds
1 cup mushrooms, chopped
1 large tomato, chopped
1 cup dried red lentils
2 tbsp lemon juice

**Directions** and Total Time: 25 minutes

Heat the oil in a pot over medium heat. Place in the garlic and ginger and cook for 3 minutes. Stir in cumin, fennel, mushrooms, tomato, lentils, and 2 ¼ cups of water. Bring to a boil, then lower the heat and simmer for 15 minutes. Mix in lemon juice. Serve and enjoy!

### Thyme Mushroom Stroganoff

**Ingredients** for 6 servings

1 onion, sliced into half-moons
1 cup baby Bella mushrooms, sliced
1 cup shiitake mushrooms, sliced
4 garlic cloves, minced
¼ cup vegetable broth
1 tsp paprika
1 tbsp olive oil
Salt and black pepper to taste
¼ cup sour cream
½ tsp Dijon mustard
4 tbsp chopped thyme
1 lb tagliatelle, cooked

**Directions** and Total Time: 25 minutes

In a large skillet, heat oil over medium heat. Sauté onion and mushrooms for 5 to 8 minutes until softened. Sauté garlic for 1 minute until aromatic. Next, add broth, paprika, salt, and pepper. Cook for 5 minutes, stirring occasionally. Remove from heat, then stir in sour cream, mustard, and 2 tablespoons of thyme. Combine with pasta and garnish with the rest of the thyme. Serve warm.

### Black Bean & Faro Loaf

**Ingredients** for 6 servings

2 (15.5-oz) cans black beans, mashed
3 tbsp olive oil
1 onion, minced
1 cup faro
½ cup quick-cooking oats
1/3 cup whole-wheat flour
2 tbsp nutritional yeast
1 ½ tsp dried thyme
½ tsp dried oregano

**Directions** and Total Time: 50 minutes

Heat the oil in a pot over medium heat. Place in onion and sauté for 3 minutes. Add in faro, 2 cups of water, salt, and pepper. Bring to a boil, lower the heat and simmer for 20 minutes. Remove to a bowl.

Preheat oven to 350°F. Add the mashed beans, oats, flour, yeast, thyme, and oregano to the faro bowl. Toss to combine. Adjust the seasoning. Shape the mixture into a greased loaf. Bake for 20 minutes. Slice and serve.

### Vegetable Fried Rice

**Ingredients** for 4 servings

1 head broccoli, cut into florets
2 tbsp canola oil
1 tbsp toasted sesame oil
1 onion, chopped
1 large carrot, chopped
2 garlic cloves, minced
2 tsp grated fresh ginger
3 green onions, minced
3 ½ cups cooked brown rice
1 cup frozen peas, thawed
3 tbsp soy sauce
2 tsp dry white wine

**Directions** and Total Time: 20 minutes

Heat the canola oil in a skillet over medium heat. Place in onion, carrot, and broccoli, sauté for 5 minutes until tender. Add in garlic, ginger, and green onions and sauté for another 3 minutes. Stir in rice, peas, soy sauce, and white wine and cook for 5 minutes. Add in sesame oil, toss to combine. Serve right away and enjoy!

### Cilantro Wild Rice Pilaf

**Ingredients** for 6 servings

3 tbsp olive oil
1 onion, minced
1 carrot, chopped
2 garlic cloves, minced
1 cup wild rice
1 ½ tsp ground fennel seeds
½ tsp ground cumin
Salt and black pepper to taste
3 tbsp minced fresh cilantro

**Directions** and Total Time: 30 minutes

Heat the olive oil in a pot over medium heat. Place in onion, carrot, and garlic and sauté for 5 minutes. Stir in rice, fennel seeds, cumin, and 2 cups water. Bring to a boil, then lower the heat and simmer for 20 minutes. Remove to a bowl and fluff using a fork. Serve topped with cilantro and black pepper. Enjoy!

### Bell Pepper & Seitan Rice

**Ingredients** for 4 servings

2 tbsp olive oil
2 cups water
1 cup long-grain brown rice
1 onion, chopped
8 oz seitan, chopped
1 green bell pepper, chopped
1 tsp dried basil
½ tsp ground fennel seeds
¼ tsp crushed red pepper
Salt and black pepper to taste

**Directions** and Total Time: 35 minutes

Bring water to a boil in a pot. Place in rice and lower the heat. Simmer for 20 minutes. Heat the oil in a skillet over medium heat. Sauté the onion for 3 minutes until translucent. Add in the seitan and bell pepper and cook for another 5 minutes. Stir in basil, fennel, red pepper, salt, and black pepper. Once the rice is ready, remove it to a bowl. Add in seitan mixture and toss to combine.

### Olive & Endive Salad

**Ingredients** for 6 servings

1 lb curly endive, chopped
1/3 cup mayonnaise
¼ cup rice vinegar
2 tbsp yogurt
1 tbsp pure date sugar
10 black olives for garnish
¼ tsp ground black pepper
¼ tsp smoked paprika
¼ tsp chipotle powder
Salt to taste

**Directions** and Total Time: 10 minutes

In a bowl, mix the mayonnaise, vinegar, yogurt, sugar, salt, pepper, paprika, and chipotle powder. Gently add the curly endive and mix with a wooden spatula to coat. Top with black olives. Serve and enjoy!

## Pistachio-Mushroom Bulgur with Dried Cherries

**Ingredients** for 4 servings

1 cup chopped dried cherries, soaked
1 tbsp butter
1 white onion, chopped
1 carrot, chopped
1 celery stalk, chopped
1 cup chopped mushrooms
1 ½ cups bulgur
4 cups vegetable broth
½ cup chopped pistachios

**Directions** and Total Time: 45 minutes

Preheat oven to 375°F. Melt butter in a skillet over medium heat. Sauté the onion, carrot, and celery for 5 minutes until tender. Add in mushrooms and cook for 3 more minutes. Pour in bulgur and broth. Transfer to a casserole and bake covered for 30 minutes. Once ready, uncover and stir in cherries. Top with pistachios to serve.

## Mushrooms & Asparagus & with Potato Mash

**Ingredients** for 4 servings

5 large portobello mushrooms, stems removed
2 tsp olive oil
3 tsp coconut oil
6 potatoes, chopped
4 garlic cloves, minced
½ cup milk
2 tbsp nutritional yeast
Sea salt to taste
7 cups asparagus, chopped
Cooking spray

**Directions** and Total Time: 60 minutes

Place the chopped potatoes in a pot and cover with salted water. Cook for 20 minutes. Heat the olive oil in a skillet and sauté the garlic for 1 minute. Once the potatoes are ready, drain them and reserve the water. Transfer to a bowl and mash them with some hot water, garlic, milk, nutritional yeast, and salt.

Preheat your grill to medium. Grease the mushrooms with cooking spray and season with salt. Arrange the mushrooms face down on the grill and cook for 10 minutes. After, grill the asparagus for about 10 minutes, turning often. Arrange the veggies in a serving platter. Add in the potato mash. Serve and enjoy!

## Lemon Couscous with Green Peas

**Ingredients** for 6 servings

1 cup green peas
2 ¾ cups vegetable stock
Juice and zest of 1 lemon
2 tbsp chopped fresh thyme
1 ½ cups couscous
¼ cup chopped fresh parsley

**Directions** and Total Time: 15 minutes

Pour the vegetable stock, lemon juice, thyme, salt, and pepper into a pot. Bring to a boil, then add in green peas and couscous. Turn the heat off and let sit covered for 5 minutes until the liquid has absorbed. Fluff the couscous using a fork and mix in the lemon zest and parsley. Serve.

## One-Skillet Chickpeas with Kale

**Ingredients** for 4 servings

4 tbsp olive oil
1 (15-oz) can chickpeas
Juice and zest of 1 lemon
1 onion, chopped
2 garlic cloves, minced
1 tbsp Italian seasoning
2 cups kale, chopped
Salt and black pepper to taste

**Directions** and Total Time: 20 minutes

Heat the olive oil in a skillet over medium heat. Place in the chickpeas and cook for 5 minutes. Add in onion, garlic, Italian seasoning, and kale and cook for 5 minutes until the kale wilts. Stir in salt, lemon juice, lemon zest, and pepper. Serve warm and enjoy!

## Chickpea & Quinoa Pot

**Ingredients** for 2 servings

2 tsp olive oil
1 cup cooked quinoa
1 (15-oz) can chickpeas
1 bunch arugula chopped
1 tbsp soy sauce
Salt and black pepper to taste

**Directions** and Total Time: 15 minutes

Heat the olive oil in a skillet over medium heat. Stir in quinoa, chickpeas, and arugula and cook for 3-5 minutes until the arugula wilts. Pour in soy sauce, salt, and black pepper. Toss to coat. Serve immediately and enjoy!

## Parsley Buckwheat with Pine Nuts

**Ingredients** for 4 servings

2 tbsp olive oil
1 cup buckwheat groats
2 cups vegetable stock
¼ cup pine nuts
½ onion, chopped
1/3 cup chopped fresh parsley

**Directions** and Total Time: 25 minutes

Put the groats and vegetable stock in a pot over medium heat. Bring to a boil, then lower the heat and simmer for 15 minutes. Heat a skillet over medium heat. Place in the pine nuts and toast for 2-3 minutes, shaking often. Heat the oil in the same skillet and sauté the onion for 3 minutes until translucent. Once the groats are ready, fluff them using a fork. Mix in pine nuts, onion, and parsley. Sprinkle with salt and pepper. Serve and enjoy!

## Festive Mushroom & Quinoa Stuffing

**Ingredients** for 4 servings

1 cup button mushrooms, sliced
3 garlic cloves, minced
¼ cup butter
1 onion, chopped
2 celery stalks, sliced
½ cup vegetable broth
½ cup raisins
½ cup chopped walnuts
2 cups cooked quinoa
1 tsp Italian seasoning
Sea salt to taste
2 tbsp chopped fresh parsley

**Directions** and Total Time: 25 minutes

In a skillet over medium heat, melt the butter. Sauté the onion, garlic, celery, and mushrooms for 5 minutes until tender, stirring occasionally. Pour in broth, raisins, and walnuts. Bring to a boil, then lower the heat and simmer for 5 minutes. Stir in quinoa, Italian seasoning, and salt. Cook for another 4 minutes. Serve topped with parsley.

## Cherry Tomato & Potato Bake

**Ingredients** for 5 servings

10 cherry tomatoes, halved
2 tbsp olive oil
5 russet potatoes, sliced
2 tbsp rosemary
Salt and black pepper to taste

**Directions** and Total Time: 55 minutes

Preheat oven to 390°F. Make several incisions with a fork in each potato. Rub each potato and cherry tomato with olive oil and sprinkle with salt, rosemary, and pepper. Arrange on a baking dish and bake for 40-45 minutes. Once ready, transfer to a rack and allow cooling. Serve.

## Okra & Mushroom Fried Rice

**Ingredients** for 6 servings

1 cup sliced shiitake mushrooms
2 tbsp sesame oil
1 onion, chopped
1 carrot, chopped
1 cup okra, chopped
2 garlic cloves, minced
¼ cup soy sauce
1 cups cooked brown rice
2 green onions, chopped

**Directions** and Total Time: 25 minutes

Heat the oil in a skillet over medium heat. Place in onion and carrot and cook for 3 minutes. Add in okra and mushrooms, cook for 5-7 minutes. Stir in garlic and cook for 30 seconds. Put in soy sauce and rice. Cook until hot. Add in green onions and stir. Serve warm and enjoy!

## Mango & Cauliflower Tacos

**Ingredients** for 6 servings

1 head cauliflower, cut into pieces
16 cherry tomatoes, halved
2 tbsp whole-wheat flour
2 tbsp nutritional yeast
2 tsp paprika
1 tsp cayenne pepper
2 tbsp olive oil
Salt to taste
1 cups shredded watercress
2 carrots, grated
½ cup mango salsa
½ cup guacamole
8 small corn tortillas, warm

**Directions** and Total Time: 40 minutes

Preheat oven to 350°F. Brush the cauliflower with oil in a bowl.Mix the flour, yeast, paprika, cayenne pepper, and salt in another bowl. Pour into the cauliflower bowl and toss to coat. Spread the cauliflower on a greased baking sheet. Bake for 20-30 minutes. Combine the watercress, cherry tomatoes, carrots, mango salsa, and guacamole in a bowl. Once the cauliflower is ready, divide it between the tortillas, add the mango mixture, roll up and serve.

## Instant Pot Green Chickpeas

**Ingredients** for 5 servings

1 cup chickpeas, soaked
1 onion, chopped
2 garlic cloves, minced
2 tbsp olive oil
1 tbsp coconut oil
1 celery stalk, chopped
3 tsp ground cinnamon
½ tsp ground nutmeg
1 cup spinach, chopped

**Directions** and Total Time: 50 minutes

Place chickpeas in your IP with the onion, garlic, celery, olive oil, 2 cups of water, cinnamon, and nutmeg.

Lock the lid in place; set the time to 30 minutes on High. Once ready, perform a natural pressure release for 10 minutes. Unlock the lid and drain the excess water. Put back the chickpeas and stir in coconut oil and spinach. Set the pot to Sauté and cook for another 5 minutes.

## Artichoke Rice & Beans

**Ingredients** for 4 servings

1 cup artichoke hearts, diced
2 grape tomatoes, quartered
1 ½ cups brown rice
1 tsp dried basil
1 ½ cups cooked navy beans
2 tbsp olive oil
3 garlic cloves, minced
3 cups vegetable broth
Salt and black pepper to taste
2 tbsp minced fresh parsley

**Directions** and Total Time: 35 minutes

Heat the olive oil in a pot over medium heat. Sauté the garlic for 1 minute. Stir in artichokes, basil, navy beans, rice, and vegetable broth. Sprinkle with salt and black pepper. Lower the heat and simmer for 20-25 minutes. Remove to a bowl and mix in tomatoes and parsley. Using a fork, fluff the rice. Serve right away and enjoy!

## Green Bean & Rice Alfredo

**Ingredients** for 3 servings

1 cup Alfredo arugula pesto
1 cup green beans
2 cups brown rice

**Directions** and Total Time: 25 minutes

Cook the rice in salted water in a pot over medium heat for 20 minutes. Drain and let it cool completely. Place the Alfredo sauce and beans in a skillet. Cook over low heat for 3-5 minutes. Stir in the rice to coat. Serve warm.

## Lentil Paella

**Ingredients** for 4 servings

1 ½ cups cooked lentils
¼ cup sliced black olives
1 ½ cups brown rice
2 tbsp olive oil
1 onion, chopped
1 (14.5-oz) can diced tomatoes
1 tbsp capers
¼ tsp crushed red pepper
1 green bell pepper, chopped
2 garlic cloves, minced
2 tbsp minced fresh parsley
3 cups vegetable broth

**Directions** and Total Time: 50 minutes

Heat oil in a pot over medium heat and sauté onion, bell pepper, and garlic for 5 minutes. Stir in tomatoes, capers, red pepper, and salt. Cook for 5 minutes. Pour in the rice and broth. Bring to a boil, then lower the heat. Simmer for 20 minutes. Turn the heat off and mix in lentils. Serve garnished with olives and parsley. Enjoy!

## Turkish-Style Pizza

**Ingredients** for 2 servings

1 tbsp olive oil
½ eggplant, sliced
½ red onion, sliced
1 cup cherry tomatoes, halved
3 tbsp chopped black olives
Salt to taste
2 prebaked pizza crusts
½ cup hummus
2 tbsp oregano

**Directions** and Total Time: 25 minutes

Preheat oven to 390°F. Combine the eggplant, onion, tomatoes, olives, and salt in a bowl. Toss to coat. Sprinkle with olive oil. Arrange the crusts on a baking sheet and spread the hummus on each pizza. Top with the eggplant mixture. Bake for 20-30 minutes. Top with oregano.

## Tomato Lentils with Brown Rice

**Ingredients** for 4 servings

2 tbsp olive oil
4 scallions, chopped
1 carrot, diced
1 celery stalk, chopped
2 (15-oz) cans lentils, drained
1 (15-oz) can diced tomatoes
1 tbsp dried rosemary
1 tsp ground coriander
1 tbsp garlic powder
2 cups cooked brown rice
Salt and black pepper to taste

**Directions** and Total Time: 25 minutes

Heat the oil in a pot over medium heat. Place in scallions, carrot, and celery and cook for 5 minutes until tender. Stir in lentils, tomatoes, rosemary, coriander, and garlic powder. Lower the heat and simmer for 5-7 minutes. Mix in rice, salt, and pepper. Cook for another 2-3 minutes.

## Gochugaru Millet

**Ingredients** for 4 servings

1 cup dried millet, drained
1 tsp gochugaru flakes
Salt and black pepper to taste

**Directions** and Total Time: 30 minutes

Place the millet and gochugaru flakes in a pot. Cover with enough water and bring to a boil. Lower the heat and simmer for 20 minutes. Drain and let cool. Transfer to a serving bowl and season with salt and pepper. Serve.

## Barbecued Pinto Beans

**Ingredients** for 6 servings

1 green bell pepper, cut into strips
1 serrano pepper, cut into strips
1 red bell pepper, cut into strips
1 (18-oz) bottle barbecue sauce
1 onion, chopped
2 carrots, chopped
2 garlic cloves, minced
3 (15-oz) cans pinto beans
½ tsp chipotle powder

**Directions** and Total Time: 30 minutes

In a blender, place the serrano and bell peppers, onion, carrot, and garlic. Pulse until well mixed. Place the mixture in a pot over medium heat. Add the pinto beans, BBQ sauce, and chipotle powder. Cook for 15 minutes. Season with salt and pepper. Serve warm and enjoy!

## Edamame, Zucchini & Rice Sauté

**Ingredients** for 4 servings

1 red bell pepper, chopped
2 cups cooked shelled edamame
1 medium zucchini, chopped
2 cups corn kernels
2 tbsp olive oil
1 ½ cups brown rice, rinsed
4 shallots, chopped
2 tomatoes, chopped
3 tbsp chopped parsley

**Directions** and Total Time: 40 minutes

Boil 3 cups of salted water in a pot over high heat. Place in rice, lower the heat, and cook for 20 minutes. Set aside.

Heat the oil in a skillet over medium heat. Add in shallots, zucchini, and bell pepper and sauté for 5 minutes until tender. Mix in edamame, corn, tomatoes, salt, and pepper. Cook for 5 minutes, stirring often. Put in cooked rice and parsley, toss to combine. Serve warm and enjoy!

## Mushroom & Broccoli Skillet with Hazelnuts

**Ingredients** for 4 servings

½ cup slivered toasted hazelnuts
2 tbsp olive oil
1 lb broccoli, cut into florets
3 garlic cloves, minced
1 cup sliced white mushrooms
¼ cup dry white wine
2 tbsp minced fresh parsley
Salt and black pepper to taste

**Directions** and Total Time: 20 minutes

Steam the broccoli for 8 minutes or until tender. Remove and set aside. Heat 1 tbsp of olive oil in a skillet over medium heat. Add in garlic and mushrooms and sauté for 5 minutes until tender. Pour in the white wine and cook for 1 minute. Stir in broccoli florets, parsley, salt, and pepper. Cook for 3 minutes until the liquid has reduced. Remove to a bowl and add in the remaining oil and hazelnuts and toss to coat. Serve warm and enjoy!

## Smoked Chipotle Black-Eyed Peas

**Ingredients** for 4 servings

1 cup black-eyed peas, soaked
8 sun-dried tomatoes, diced
2 tsp ground chipotle pepper
1 ½ tsp ground cumin
2 tbsp olive oil
1 ½ tsp onion powder
1 tsp dried oregano
¾ tsp garlic powder
½ tsp smoked paprika
Salt to taste

**Directions** and Total Time: 35 minutes

Place the black-eyed peas, 2 cups of water, olive oil, chipotle pepper, cumin, onion powder, oregano, garlic powder, salt, and paprika in a pot over medium heat. Cook for 20 minutes. Mix in sun-dried tomatoes. Let sit for a few minutes. Serve and enjoy!

## Spinach Quinoa Curry

**Ingredients** for 4 servings

4 tsp olive oil
1 onion, chopped
2 tbsp curry powder
1 tsp ginger powder
1 ½ cups quinoa
1 cup canned diced tomatoes
4 cups chopped spinach
½ cup milk
2 tbsp soy sauce
Salt to taste

**Directions** and Total Time: 35 minutes

Heat the oil in a pot over medium heat. Sauté the onion, curry powder, and ginger powder for 3 minutes until tender. Pour in quinoa, and 3 cups of water. Bring to a boil, then lower the heat and simmer for 15-20 minutes. Mix in tomatoes, spinach, milk, soy sauce, and salt. Simmer for an additional 3 minutes. Serve and enjoy!

## Basil Pesto Millet

**Ingredients** for 4 servings

1 cup millet
2 ½ cups vegetable broth
½ cup basil pesto

**Directions** and Total Time: 50 minutes

Place the millet and broth in a pot. Bring to a boil, then lower the heat and simmer for 25 minutes. Let cool for 5 minutes and fluff the millet. Mix in the pesto and serve.

## Red Pepper Steamed Broccoli

**Ingredients** for 6 servings

1 head broccoli, cut into florets
Salt to taste
1 tsp red pepper flakes

**Directions** and Total Time: 15 minutes

Boil 1 cup water in a pot over medium heat. Place in a steamer basket and put in the broccoli florets. Steam covered for 5-7 minutes. In a bowl, toss the broccoli with red pepper flakes and salt. Serve and enjoy!

## Asian Kale Slaw

**Ingredients** for 4 servings

1 tbsp toasted sesame oil
¼ cup tahini
2 tbsp white miso paste
1 tbsp rice vinegar
2 tsp soy sauce
1 (12-oz) bag kale slaw
2 scallions, minced
¼ cup toasted sesame seeds

**Directions** and Total Time: 15 minutes

Combine the tahini, miso, vinegar, oil, and soy sauce in a bowl. Stir in kale slaw, scallions, and sesame seeds. Let sit for 20 minutes. Serve immediately and enjoy!

## Baked Chili Carrots

**Ingredients** for 4 servings

2 lb carrots, chopped into ¾ inch cubes
½ tsp chili powder
½ tsp smoked paprika
½ tsp dried oregano
½ tsp dried thyme
2 tsp olive oil
½ tsp garlic powder
Salt to taste

**Directions** and Total Time: 35 minutes

Preheat oven to 400°F. Line with parchment paper a baking sheet. Rinse the carrots and pat dry. Chop into ¾ inch cubes. Place in a bowl and toss with olive oil. Mix the chili powder, paprika, oregano, thyme, salt, and garlic powder in a bowl. Pour over the carrots and toss to coat. Transfer to a greased baking sheet and bake for 30 minutes, turn once by half. Serve and enjoy!

## Tofu & Haricot Vert Pilaf with Mushrooms

**Ingredients** for 4 servings

5 shiitake mushroom caps, sliced
1 tbsp grapeseed oil
1 tbsp toasted sesame oil
1 cup haricots vert
1 onion, minced
1 tsp grated fresh ginger
3 green onions, minced
8 oz firm tofu, crumbled
2 tbsp soy sauce
3 cups hot cooked rice
1 tbsp toasted sesame seeds

**Directions** and Total Time: 25 minutes

Place the haricots in boiled salted water and cook for 10 minutes until tender. Drain and set aside. Heat the grapeseed oil in a skillet over medium heat. Place in the onion and cook for 3 minutes until translucent. Add in mushrooms, ginger, green onions, tofu, and soy sauce. Cook for 10 minutes. Share cooked rice into 4 bowls and top with haricot and tofu mixture. Sprinkle with sesame oil. Garnish with sesame seeds. Serve warm and enjoy!

## Herby Green Cabbage

**Ingredients** for 4 servings

1 lb green cabbage, halved
2 tsp olive
3 tsp miso paste
1 tsp dried oregano
½ tsp dried rosemary
1 tbsp balsamic vinegar

**Directions** and Total Time: 50 minutes

Preheat oven to 390°F. Line with parchment paper a baking sheet. Put the green cabbage in a bowl. Coat with olive oil, miso, oregano, rosemary, salt, and pepper. Remove to the baking sheet and bake for 35-40 minutes, shaking every 5 minutes until tender. Remove from the oven to a plate. Drizzle with balsamic vinegar and serve.

## Tamari Eggplants

**Ingredients** for 4 servings

2 unpeeled eggplants, sliced
1 tbsp canola oil
1 tsp toasted sesame oil
1 garlic cloves, minced
2 tbsp tamari sauce
1 tbsp dry sherry
½ tsp pure date sugar
2 green onions, minced
10 pitted black olives, chopped

**Directions** and Total Time: 20 minutes

Combine the garlic, tamari, sherry, sesame oil, and sugar in a bowl. Set aside. Heat the oil in a skillet over medium heat. Place in the eggplant slices, fry for 4 minutes per side. Spread the tamari sauce on the eggplants. Pour in ¼ cup water and cook for 15 minutes. Remove to a plate and sprinkle with green onions and black olives. Serve.

## Sautéd Okra

**Ingredients** for 4 servings

Salt and black pepper to taste
2 tbsp olive oil
4 cups okra, halved
3 tbsp chopped fresh cilantro

**Directions** and Total Time: 10 minutes

Heat the oil in a skillet over medium heat. Place in the okra, cook for 5 minutes. Turn the heat off and mix in salt, pepper, and cilantro. Serve immediately and enjoy!

## Orzo Stuffed Tomatoes

**Ingredients** for 4 servings

2 tsp olive oil
2 cups cooked orzo
Salt and black pepper to taste
3 green onions, minced
1/3 cup golden raisins
1 tsp orange zest
4 large ripe tomatoes
1/3 cup toasted pine nuts
¼ cup minced fresh parsley

**Directions** and Total Time: 40 minutes

Preheat oven to 380°F. Mix orzo, green onions, raisins, and orange zest in a bowl. Set aside. Slice the top of the tomato by ½-inch and take out the pulp. Cut the pulp and place it in a bowl. Stir in orzo mixture, pine nuts, parsley, salt, and pepper. Spoon the mixture into the tomatoes and arrange on a greased baking tray. Sprinkle with oil and cover with foil. Bake for 15 minutes. Uncover and bake for another 5 minutes until golden. Serve and enjoy!

## Tasty Zucchini "Pasta" a la Bolognese

**Ingredients** for 4 servings

1 tbsp Worcestershire sauce
2 tbsp olive oil
2 tbsp butter
1 white onion, chopped
1 garlic clove, minced
3 oz carrots, chopped
3 cups crumbled tofu
2 tbsp tomato paste
1 ½ cups crushed tomatoes
Salt and black pepper to taste
1 tbsp dried basil
2 lb zucchini, spiralized

**Directions** and Total Time: 45 minutes

Pour olive oil into a saucepan and heat over medium heat. Add onion, garlic, and carrots and sauté for 3 minutes or until the onions are soft and the carrots caramelized. Pour in tofu, tomato paste, tomatoes, salt, pepper, basil, and Worcestershire sauce. Stir and cook for 15 minutes. Mix in some water if the mixture is too thick and simmer further for 20 minutes. Melt butter in a skillet and toss in the zoodles quickly, about 1 minute. Season with salt and black pepper. Divide into serving plates and spoon the Bolognese on top. Serve immediately.

## Tofu Cordon Bleu

**Ingredients** for 4 servings

1 ¼ cup grated cheddar cheese
4 tbsp olive oil
2 cups grilled tofu
1 cup smoked seitan
1 cup cream cheese
1 tbsp mustard powder
1 tbsp plain vinegar
Salt and black pepper to taste
½ cup baby spinach

**Directions** and Total Time: 30 minutes

Preheat oven to 400°F. Place the tofu and seitan on a chopping board and chop both into small cubes. Mix cream cheese, mustard powder, vinegar, and cheddar cheese in a baking dish. Top with tofu, seitan, and season with salt and pepper. Bake until the casserole is golden brown on top, about 15 to 20 minutes. Serve with some baby spinach and a generous drizzle of olive oil.

## Creamy Broccoli Gratin

**Ingredients** for 4 servings

1 (10 oz) can cream mushroom soup
2 cups grated cheddar cheese
1 cup mayonnaise
1 tbsp olive oil
3 tbsp butter, melted
2 cups broccoli florets
3 tbsp heavy cream
1 medium red onion, chopped
¾ cup breadcrumbs

**Directions** and Total Time: 50 minutes

Preheat the oven to 350°F. Heat the olive oil in a medium skillet and sauté the broccoli florets until softened, 8 minutes. Turn the heat off and mix in the mushroom soup, mayonnaise, salt, black pepper, heavy cream, and onion. Spread the mixture into the baking sheet. In a small bowl, mix the breadcrumbs with the butter and distribute the mixture on top. Add the cheddar cheese. Place the casserole in the oven and bake until golden on top and the cheese melts. Remove the casserole from the oven, allow cooling for 5 minutes, dish, and serve warm.

## Grilled Zucchini & Kale Pizza

**Ingredients** for 4 servings

½ cup grated Parmesan cheese
3 ½ cups whole-wheat flour
1 tsp yeast
3 tbsp olive oil
¼ cup capers
1 tsp salt
1 pinch sugar
1 cup marinara sauce
2 large zucchinis, sliced
½ cup chopped kale
1 tsp oregano

**Directions** and Total Time: 30 minutes

Preheat the oven the 350°F and lightly grease a pizza pan with cooking spray. In a bowl, mix flour, nutritional yeast, salt, sugar, olive oil, and 1 cup of warm water until smooth dough forms. Allow rising for an hour or until the dough doubles in size. Spread the dough on the pizza pan and apply marinara sauce and oregano on top.

Heat a grill pan, season the zucchinis with salt, black pepper, and cook in the pan until slightly charred on both sides. Sit the zucchini on the pizza crust and top with kale, capers, and Parmesan cheese. Bake for 20 minutes. Cool for 5 minutes, slice, and serve.

## Spinach & Bean Casserole

**Ingredients** for 6 servings

1 (15.5-oz) can Great Northern beans
3 tbsp olive oil
1 onion, chopped
2 carrots, chopped
1 celery stalk, chopped
2 garlic cloves, minced
1 (15.5-oz) can Navy beans
1 cup baby spinach
3 tomatoes, chopped
1 cup vegetable broth
1 tbsp fresh parsley, chopped
1 tsp dried thyme
Salt and black pepper to taste
½ cup breadcrumbs

**Directions** and Total Time: 35 minutes

Preheat oven to 380°F. Heat the oil in a skillet over medium heat. Place in onion, carrots, celery, and garlic. Sauté for 5 minutes. Remove into a greased casserole. Add in beans, spinach, tomatoes, broth, parsley, thyme, salt, and pepper and stir to combine. Cover with foil and bake in the oven for 15 minutes. Next, take out the casserole from the oven, remove the foil, and spread the breadcrumbs all over. Bake for another 10 minutes until the top is crispy and golden. Serve warm.

## Asian Chickpea Wraps with Peaches

**Ingredients** for 4 servings

2 cups torn Iceberg lettuce
1 (14-oz) can chickpeas
3 tbsp tahini
Zest and juice of 1 lime
1 tbsp curry powder
Sea salt to taste
1 cup diced peaches
1 red bell pepper, diced small
½ cup fresh cilantro, chopped
4 large whole-grain wraps

**Directions** and Total Time: 15 minutes

In a bowl, beat tahini, lime zest, lime juice, curry powder, 3-4 tbsp of water, and salt until creamy. In another bowl, combine the chickpeas, peaches, bell pepper, cilantro, and tahini dressing. Divide the mixture between the wraps and top with lettuce. Roll up and serve. Enjoy!

# DESSERTS

## Smoothie Popsicles

**Ingredients** for 6 servings

2 cups chopped fresh raspberries
1 cup chopped mango
¾ cup milk
½ cup shredded coconut
½ tsp maple syrup

**Directions** and Total Time: 5 minutes + freezing time

In a food processor, blend everything until almost smooth. Transfer to ice pop molds, leaving a bit of space at the top. Freeze up until solid.

## Seedy Choco-Banana Muffins

**Ingredients** for 6 servings

3 bananas
1 cup milk
2 tbsp butter
1 tsp apple cider vinegar
1 tsp pure vanilla extract
1 ¼ cups whole-grain flour
½ cup rolled oats
¼ cup muscovado sugar
1 tsp baking powder
½ cup cocoa powder
¼ cup sesame seeds
A pinch of salt
¼ cup dark chocolate chips

**Directions** and Total Time: 45 minutes

Preheat the oven to 350°F. Lightly spray 12-cup muffin tin with cooking oil. Puree bananas, milk, butter, vinegar, and vanilla in a blender. In a large bowl, add the rest of the ingredients. Pour the wet ingredients with the dry ingredients and stir until combined. Scoop batter into the prepared muffin cups. Bake in the oven for 20-25 minutes. Let the muffins cool completely in the muffin tins. Serve and enjoy.

## Matcha Pudding

**Ingredients** for 4 servings

1 lime, zested and juiced
1 (14-oz) can coconut milk
1 tbsp coconut sugar
½ tsp vanilla extract
2 tbsp chia seeds
2 tsp matcha powder

**Directions** and Total Time: 5 minutes + chilling time

In a food processor, blend all the ingredients until smooth. Transfer to the fridge for 20 minutes to chill before serving. Enjoy!

## Peach-Coconut Tart

**Ingredients** for 6 servings

½ cup rolled oats
1 cup Brazil nuts
1 cup soft pitted dates
1 cup milk
2 peeled peaches, chopped
½ cup shredded coconut

**Directions** and Total Time: 10 minutes + freezing time

Put oats, nuts, and dates in a food processor. Blend until it holds together. Transfer the mixture into a pie pan. Press firmly. In a blender, add the milk, ½ cup of water, peaches, and shredded coconut. Purée until smooth, 1 minute. Pour the filling into the crust, and level with a spatula. Freeze the pie for 30 minutes. Once frozen, remove from the freezer for 15 minutes to soften.

## Almond Cookies with Chocolate Chips

**Ingredients** for 6 servings

¼ cup chocolate chips
2 eggs, beaten
1 banana, mashed
½ cup demerara sugar
½ cup butter
2 cups cooked quinoa
3 tbsp lemon juice
1 tsp lemon zest
1 tsp pure vanilla extract
1 tsp baking powder
1 ¼ cups ground almonds
½ cup chopped pistachios

**Directions** and Total Time: 45 minutes

Preheat the oven to 360°F. Prep a baking sheet by lining it with parchment paper. In a large bowl, combine banana, sugar, and butter until smooth. Stir in quinoa, eggs, lemon juice, lemon zest, and vanilla until well mixed. Carefully stir in baking powder and almonds until just mixed. Fold in pistachios and chocolate chips. Scoop and shape into 12-16 balls. Arrange the balls on the baking sheet and flatten them with your hand. Bake for 20 minutes. Cool for a few minutes on the baking sheet before cooling them completely on the cooling rack. Serve and enjoy.

## Coconut Fat Bomb

**Ingredients** for 6 servings

½ cup pecans
¼ cup pecan butter
¼ cup coconut oil
¼ cup butter
½ tsp vanilla extract
1 tsp pumpkin pie spice
½ tbsp shredded coconut
1/3 cup date sugar
A pinch of salt

**Directions** and Total Time: 15 minutes + freezing time

Place a skillet on the stove and turn the burner on medium. Toss the pecans in and roast them. Stir often to keep them from burning. Put the pecans on a cutting board and chop them up. Lower the heat to low and put the skillet on the burner. Toss in the pecan butter, coconut oil, and butter. Allow this mix to melt, then pour in the vanilla, pumpkin pie spice, date sugar, shredded coconut, and salt. Put the pecans in equal amounts in ice cube trays. Ladle the coconut mix into the ice cube holes over the pecans. Put in the freezer for 30 minutes. Once frozen, put on the counter for a few minutes, then crack them out of the ice cube tray gently. Store in the fridge.

## Sweet Quinoa Balls

**Ingredients** for 6 servings

2 tbsp butter
2 tbsp rice syrup
¾ cup cooked quinoa
¼ cup sesame seeds, toasted
1 tbsp chia seeds
½ tsp vanilla extract
1 orange, zested
1 tbsp raisins
¼ cup ground almonds

**Directions** and Total Time: 25 minutes

Mix butter and syrup in a medium bowl until smooth. Mix well with the remaining ingredients until they can hold their shape together. Shape into 12 balls and arrange on a parchment-lined baking sheet. Refrigerate for at least 15 minutes. Serve and enjoy.

## Avocado-Berry Cake

**Ingredients** for 6 servings

1 cup rolled oats
1 cup walnuts
1 cup soft pitted dates
1 tsp lemon zest
2 avocados, peeled and pitted
1 cup raspberries
2 tbsp rice syrup
4 tbsp lemon juice
2 tbsp mint, minced

**Directions** and Total Time: 10 minutes + freezing time

Add oats, walnuts, dates, and lemon zest in a food processor. Blend until the mixture holds together. Transfer the mixture into a pie pan. Press firmly. Pour avocados, raspberries, rice syrup, lemon juice, and mint in a blender and blend until smooth. Pour the filling into the crust, and level with a spatula. Freeze for 2 hours.

## Festive Apple & Pear Crumble

**Ingredients** for 6 servings

3 peeled apples, chopped
2 peeled pears, chopped
½ cup applesauce
3 tbsp maple syrup
1 tsp ground cinnamon
A pinch of salt
2 tbsp butter
2 tbsp rice syrup
1 ½ cups rolled oats
½ cup walnuts, chopped
½ tsp ground cinnamon
3 tbsp date sugar

**Directions** and Total Time: 40 minutes

Preheat the oven to 350°F. Combine apples, pears, applesauce, maple syrup, cinnamon and salt in a baking dish. Blend the butter and rice syrup in a medium bowl. When it is smooth, stir in oats, walnuts, cinnamon, and date sugar. Top the apples with the oat mixture and bake for 20-25 minutes. The fruit will be soft and the topping will be golden. Serve warm and enjoy.

## No-Bake Energy Bites

**Ingredients** for 6 servings

¾ cup ground macadamia nuts
1 cup dates, pitted
1 cup shredded coconut
¼ cup chia seeds
¼ tsp protein powder
¼ cup cocoa nibs

**Directions** and Total Time: 25 minutes

Add all the ingredients to a food processor and puree until crumbly and just coming together. Scoop out 24 portions and shape into balls. Arrange on a parchment-lined baking sheet. Refrigerate for at least 15 minutes to set. Serve.

## Vanilla-Lemon No-Bake Cookies

**Ingredients** for 6 servings

3 tbsp butter
1 ¼ cups flour
2 tbsp date sugar
1 tsp lemon zest
1 tsp vanilla extract
A pinch of salt

**Directions** and Total Time: 15 minutes + chilling time

Put the butter in a pan and melt it on low. Mix the butter, flour, date sugar, lemon zest, vanilla, and salt in a bowl and stir well. This mix will have the consistency of cookie dough. Make 1-2 inch balls out of the mix and put them on a plate. Put in the refrigerator for an hour, then serve.

## Chocolate-Almond Fudge Loaf

**Ingredients** for 6 servings

¾ cup creamy butter
½ cup corn syrup
1/3 cup coconut oil, melted
6 tbsp cocoa powder
1 tbsp chopped almonds
1 tsp flaked sea salt

**Directions** and Total Time: 15 minutes + cooling time

Line the bottom and sides of a loaf pan with two layers of plastic wrap. One layer goes in horizontally with many overhangs, and one layer goes in vertically, also with a lot of overhangs. Gently combine butter, corn syrup, and coconut oil in a medium bowl until smooth. Stir in cocoa powder and almonds until creamy. Transfer the mixture to the loaf pan. Top with sea salt. Wrap the fudge mixture with the excess plastic wrap. Freeze for at least 1 hour. When the fudge is firm, lift the fudge from the loaf pan and unwrap. Cut into 1-inch pieces. Serve and enjoy.

## Avocado Chocolate Mousse

**Ingredients** for 2 servings

1 (15-oz) can coconut milk
1 avocado, pitted and peeled
3 tbsp cacao powder
2 tsp vanilla extract
½ tsp lemon zest
1 tsp ground cinnamon
2 tbsp pure date sugar
1 cup fresh spinach
A pinch of salt

**Directions** and Total Time: 10 minutes

Open the can of coconut milk without shaking it. Dip out the solid cream and put it in a food processor or blender. Add the avocado, cacao powder, vanilla, lemon zest, cinnamon, date sugar, spinach, and salt. Blend until creamy. Serve and enjoy!

## Birthday Vanilla Cupcakes

**Ingredients** for 8 servings

½ cup vegetable shortening, softened
3 ½ cups organic confectioners' sugar
1¾ cups all-purpose flour
1 cup organic cane sugar
1 tsp baking powder
1 tsp baking soda
½ tsp sea salt
1 cup milk
½ cup canola oil
1 tbsp lemon juice
2 tsp vanilla extract
½ cup butter, softened
½ tsp orange extract
1 tbsp edible glitter flakes

**Directions** and Total Time: 25 minutes

Preheat the oven to 350°F. Place cupcake liners in 16 muffin cups. Whisk flour, cane sugar, baking powder, baking soda, and salt in a large bowl. Combine milk, oil, lemon juice, and vanilla in a medium bowl. Pour the wet ingredients into the bowl with the dry ingredients and stir until just combined. Scoop the batter into each cupcake liner to about 2/3 full. Bake for 16 to 18 minutes. A toothpick in the middle of the cupcake comes out clean. Cool. While the cupcakes cool, cream the butter, shortening, and orange extract in a mixing bowl. Add confectioners' sugar one cup at a time. Beat until the frosting is fluffy. Frost the cooled cupcakes with a butter knife and top with edible glitter flakes.

## Exotic Mango Granita

**Ingredients** for 6 servings

2 peeled mangoes, chopped
3 cups cubed watermelon
2 limes, juiced and zested
2 cups apple juice

**Directions** and Total Time: 10 minutes + freezing time

Combine all of the ingredients in a food processor and blend until smooth. Pour into a 1-quart freezer-proof container with a cover. Freeze for 4 to 5 hours. Before serving, let the granita thaw for 10 minutes. Use a strong spoon to scrape the amount of granita desired. It will resemble shaved ice. Transfer to a dish. Serve cold.

## Apple-Carrot Cupcakes

**Ingredients** for 6 servings

1 cup grated carrot
1/3 cup chopped apple
¼ cup raisins
2 tbsp maple syrup
1/3 cup milk
1 cup oat flour
1 tsp ground cinnamon
½ tsp ground ginger
1 tsp baking powder
½ tsp baking soda
1/3 cup chopped walnuts

**Directions** and Total Time: 25 minutes

Preheat the oven to 350°F. Combine carrot, apple, raisins, maple syrup, and milk in a bowl. Stir in oat flour, cinnamon, ginger, baking powder, and baking soda until combined. Divide the batter between 6 cupcake molds. Top with chopped walnuts each and press down a little. Bake for 15 minutes until golden brown and a toothpick comes out clean. Let cool completely before serving.

## Date Oat Cookies

**Ingredients** for 6 servings

¼ cup butter, softened
2 ½ tbsp milk
½ cup sugar
½ tsp vanilla extract
½ tsp lemon zest
½ tsp ground cinnamon
3/4 cup flour
¼ tsp salt
¾ cup rolled oats
¼ tsp baking soda
¼ tsp baking powder
2 tbsp dates, chopped

**Directions** and Total Time: 20 minutes

Use an electric beater to whip the butter until fluffy. Add the milk, sugar, lemon zest, and vanilla. Stir until well combined.Add the cinnamon, flour, salt, oats, baking soda, and baking powder in a separate bowl and stir. Add the dry mix to the wet mix and stir with a wooden spoon. Pour in the dates. Preheat oven to 350°F. Drop tablespoonfuls of the batter onto a greased baking pan, leaving room in between each. Bake for 6 minutes or until light brown. Make all the cookies at once, or save the batter in the fridge for later. Let them cool and enjoy!

## Healthy Chickpea Cookies

**Ingredients** for 6 servings

1 cup canned chickpeas
2 tsp vanilla extract
1 tsp lemon juice
1/3 cup date paste
2 tbsp butter, melted
1/3 cup flour
½ tsp baking powder
¼ cup dark chocolate chips

**Directions** and Total Time: 25 minutes

Preheat oven to 320°F. In a blender, blitz chickpeas, vanilla extract, and lemon juice until smooth. Remove it to a bowl. Stir in date paste and butter until well combined. Then mix in flour, baking powder, chocolate chips. Make 2-tablespoon balls out of the mixture.

Place the balls onto a parchment-lined cake pan, flatten them into a cookie shape, and bake for 13 minutes until golden brown. Let cool slightly before serving.

## Fall Caramelized Apples

**Ingredients** for 2 servings

2 apples, sliced
1 ½ tsp brown sugar
¼ tsp cinnamon
¼ tsp nutmeg
¼ tsp salt
1 tsp lemon zest

**Directions** and Total Time: 25 minutes

Preheat the oven to 390°F. Set the apples upright in a baking pan. Add 2 tbsp of water to the bottom to keep the apples moist. Sprinkle the tops with sugar, lemon zest, cinnamon, and nutmeg. Lightly sprinkle the halves with salt and the tops with oil. Bake for 20 minutes or until the apples are tender and golden on top. Serve.

## Cheddar Stuffed Apples

**Ingredients** for 4 servings

½ cup cheddar cheese
¼ cup raisins
2 apples
½ tsp ground cinnamon

**Directions** and Total Time: 25 minutes

Preheat oven to 350°F. Combine cheddar cheese and raisins in a bowl. Chop apples lengthwise and discard the core and stem. Sprinkle each half with cinnamon and stuff each half with ¼ of the cheddar mixture. Bake for 7 minutes, turn, and bake for 13 minutes more until the apples are soft. Serve immediately and enjoy.

## Banana-Lemon Bars

**Ingredients** for 6 servings

¾ cup flour
2 tbsp powdered sugar
¼ cup coconut oil, melted
½ cup brown sugar
1 tbsp lemon zest
¼ cup lemon juice
⅛ tsp salt
¼ cup mashed bananas
1¾ tsp cornstarch
¾ tsp baking powder

**Directions** and Total Time: 40 minutes

Combine the flour, powdered sugar, and coconut oil in a mixing bowl. Place in the refrigerator. Mix the brown sugar, lemon zest and juice, salt, bananas, cornstarch, and baking powder in another mixing bowl. Stir well.

Preheat the oven to 350°F. Spray a baking pan with oil. Remove the crust from the fridge and press it into the bottom of the pan to form a crust. Place in the oven and bake for 5 minutes or until firm. Remove and spread the lemon filling over the crust. Bake for 18-20 minutes or until the top is golden. Cool for an hour in the fridge. Once firm and cooled, cut into pieces and serve.

## Mexican Hot Chocolate Fat Bomb

**Ingredients** for 5 servings

¼ cup coconut butter
¼ cup coconut oil
¼ cup butter
2 tbsp cacao powder
½ tsp vanilla extract
¼ tsp cayenne pepper
½ tsp ground cinnamon
2 tbsp pure date sugar
A pinch of salt

**Directions** and Total Time: 10 minutes + freezing time

Put the coconut butter, coconut oil, and butter in a skillet and melt on low. After the mix is completely melted, toss in the cacao powder, vanilla, cayenne, cinnamon, date sugar, and salt. Put the mix in ice cube trays and put in the freezer for 30 minutes. Set them on the counter for a few minutes, then crack them gently out of the ice cube tray. Store in the fridge.

## Pistachio Clusters

**Ingredients** for 6 servings

3 tbsp butter
¼ cup heavy cream
1 tsp vanilla extract
1 tbsp maple sugar
1 cup chopped pistachios
¼ cup chocolate chips

**Directions** and Total Time: 15 minutes + chilling time

Put butter in a pan and melt it on medium. Stir throughout to make sure it doesn't burn. When gold, take off the heat. Lower the heat to low, return the pan to the burner, and add the heavy cream, vanilla, and maple sugar. Cook for 5 minutes on low, stirring throughout. The mix should be thick and dark; take off the burner and add the pistachios. Lay parchment paper or a silicone mat on a cookie sheet, then place 2 or 3-inch piles of the mix on it. Place the cookie sheet in the fridge for 10 minutes. Put the chocolate in a bowl that can go in the microwave and melt it, which takes about 30 seconds. Drizzle the chocolate on top of the pistachio clusters.

## Caramel Popcorn

**Ingredients** for 6 servings

½ cup popcorn kernels
¼ cup vegetable oil
1/3 cup muscovado sugar
1 tsp sea salt

**Directions** and Total Time: 10 minutes

In a medium saucepan, stir in all of the ingredients to coat the kernels. Cover and cook over medium heat. When you hear popping, shake the pot back and forth over the heat until the kernels pop more frequently. Remove the pot from the heat after 30 seconds on rapid popping. Continue shaking until the popping happens about every 1 to 3 seconds. Pour the popcorn into a large bowl and let cool for 10 minutes. Gently break apart the popcorn with a spatula. Serve and enjoy.

## Agave-Peanut Butter Chia Pudding

**Ingredients** for 4 servings

1 (15-oz) can coconut milk
2 tbsp peanut butter
1 tbsp agave syrup
1 cup mixed berries
1 tsp vanilla extract
¼ cup chia seeds
1 tbsp cacao nibs
1 mango, sliced

**Directions** and Total Time: 10 minutes + chilling time

Open the can of coconut milk without shaking it. Dip out the solid cream and put it in a food processor or blender. Add the peanut butter, agave syrup, and vanilla. Blend until the mix gets thick, then add the chia seeds and fold them in. In 4 glasses, add ½ the coconut/chia seed mix, then pour in the mixed berries, then the other ½ of the coconut/chia seed mix. Put lids on the glasses or bowls and put them in the fridge overnight or for up to 3 days. Add some cacao nibs and mango slices when ready to serve. Enjoy!

## Easy Rum Brownies

**Ingredients** for 6 servings

½ cup cocoa powder
¾ cup all-purpose flour
¾ cup organic cane sugar
½ cup olive oil
1 tsp vanilla extract
1 tbsp corn starch
1 tsp baking powder
½ tsp sea salt
½ cup milk
1 tsp dark rum

**Directions** and Total Time: 35 minutes

Preheat oven to 360°F. Whisk flour, sugar, cocoa powder, corn starch, baking powder, and salt in a large bowl. Stir milk, oil, rum, and vanilla in a medium bowl. Pour the wet ingredients into the large bowl with the dry ingredients. Stir until well combined without overmixing. Pour the batter into a greased baking pan and bake for 30 minutes. A toothpick in the middle with come out clean. Cool completely. Serve and enjoy!

## Salted Chocolate Chip Cookies

**Ingredients** for 6 servings

1 ½ cups chocolate chips
2 ½ cups all-purpose flour
1 cup dark-brown sugar
½ cup organic cane sugar
2 tbsp corn starch
1 tsp baking soda
1 tsp sea salt flakes
1 cup sunflower oil
½ cup pumpkin puree
2 tsp vanilla extract

**Directions** and Total Time: 30 minutes

Preheat the oven to 360°F. Line 2 baking sheets with parchment paper. Whisk flour, brown sugar, cane sugar, corn starch, and baking soda in a large bowl. Stir in sunflower oil, pumpkin puree, and vanilla until it comes together in a thick dough. Fold in chocolate chips. Scoop 1 heaping tablespoon of the cookie dough and roll into a ball. Place the cookie dough balls on the baking sheet with at least 2 inches of space in between. Bake for 10 to 12 minutes until the edges start to brown and the center is set. You may have to bake in batches. Top with salt and cool on a rack for at least 10 minutes. Serve and enjoy.

## Fresh Banana Pudding

**Ingredients** for 4 servings

3 bananas
1 cup milk
¼ cup maple syrup
1 tbsp corn starch

1 tsp vanilla extract
1 tsp lemon zest
1 tsp ground cinnamon

**Directions** and Total Time: 10 minutes + freezing time

Add 1 banana, milk, maple syrup, corn starch, and vanilla to a blender jar. Blend until the mixture is smooth. Pour the banana mixture into a saucepan and let it come to a boil over medium heat. When it starts to boil, reduce the heat and whisk for 3 minutes while it simmers. When the mixture has thickened and sticks to the spoon, remove it from the pan and let it sit in a container to cool for an hour. Cover and refrigerate for at least 4 hours. To serve, slice the rest of the bananas. Layer each dessert dish with a layer of pudding and a layer of bananas. Repeat the layers until all of the ingredients are used. Top with lemon zest and cinnamon. Serve.

## Homemade Chips Ahoy

**Ingredients** for 4 servings

1 tbsp coconut oil, melted
1 tbsp maple syrup
1 tbsp milk
½ tsp vanilla extract
¼ cup oat flour
2 tbsp coconut sugar
¼ tsp salt
¼ tsp baking powder
2 tbsp chocolate chips

**Directions** and Total Time: 20 minutes

Combine the coconut oil, maple syrup, milk, and vanilla in a bowl. Add the oat flour, coconut sugar, salt, and baking powder. Stir until combined. Add the chocolate chips and stir. Preheat oven to 350°F. Pour the batter into a greased baking pan, leaving a little room in between. Bake for 7 minutes or until golden. Do not overcook. Move to a cooling rack and serve chilled.

## Lemon Pie Bars

**Ingredients** for 6 servings

½ cup confectioners' sugar
1 cup all-purpose flour
1/3 cup coconut oil
½ cup lemon juice
½ cup milk
1 cup organic cane sugar
1 tsp peppermint extract
3 tbsp corn starch

**Directions** and Total Time: 20 minutes +chilling time

Preheat the oven to 350°F. Lightly spray a baking pan with cooking oil. Mix flour, oil, and confectioners' sugar in a medium bowl until it comes together in a dough. Press the dough into the baking pan with about ¼-inch thickness. Bake for 8 minutes. The crust will still be white and soft. While the crust is in the oven, add lemon juice, milk, cane sugar, and peppermint in a small saucepan. Stir over medium heat. In a small bowl, whisk corn starch and ½ cup of water. When the lemon juice starts to boil, reduce to slow and stir in the slurry slowly. Simmer for 3 to 5 minutes, stirring occasionally. The lemon mixture will thicken and stick to the spoon. Pour the lemon mixture evenly over the crust. Cover and refrigerator overnight. Before serving, take the lemon bars out of the refrigerator, cut, and dust with confectioners' sugar. Served chilled and enjoy.

## Cinnamon Tortilla Crisps

**Ingredients** for 4 servings

1 (8-inch) tortilla
Cooking oil
2 tsp muscovado sugar
½ tsp cinnamon

**Directions** and Total Time: 10 minutes

Preheat oven to 350°F. Slice the tortilla into 8 triangles like a pizza. Put the slices on a plate and spray both sides with oil. Sprinkle muscovado sugar and cinnamon on top, then lightly spray the tops with oil. Place in a baking sheet in a single layer. Bake for 5-6 minutes or until they are light brown. Serve warm and enjoy.

## Mango Cobbler with Raspberries

**Ingredients** for 4 servings

1 ½ cups chopped mango
1 cup raspberries
1 tbsp brown sugar
2 tsp cornstarch
1 tsp lemon juice
2 tbsp sunflower oil
1 tbsp maple syrup
1 tsp vanilla
½ cup rolled oats
1/3 cup flour
3 tbsp coconut sugar
1 tsp cinnamon
¼ tsp nutmeg
⅛ tsp salt

**Directions** and Total Time: 30 minutes

Preheat the oven to 320°F. Place the mango, raspberries, brown sugar, cornstarch, and lemon juice in a baking pan. Stir with a rubber spatula until combined. In a separate bowl, add the oil, maple syrup, and vanilla and stir well. Toss in the oats, flour, coconut sugar, cinnamon, nutmeg, and salt. Stir until combined. Sprinkle evenly over the mango-raspberry filling. Bake for 20 minutes or until the topping is crispy and golden.

## Orange-Chocolate Cake

**Ingredients** for 6 servings

¾ cup flour
½ cup sugar
7 tbsp cocoa powder
½ tsp baking soda
½ cup milk
2 ½ tbsp sunflower oil
½ tbsp orange juice
2 tsp vanilla
2 tsp orange zest
3 tbsp butter, softened
1 ¼ cups powdered sugar
A pinch of salt

**Directions** and Total Time: 35 minutes

Use a whisk to combine the flour, sugar, 2 tbsp cocoa powder, baking soda, and a pinch of salt in a bowl. Once combined, add milk, sunflower oil, orange juice, and orange zest. Stir until combined. Preheat oven to 350°F. Pour the batter into a greased cake pan and bake for 25 minutes or until a knife inserted in the center comes out clean. Use an electric beater to beat the butter and powdered sugar together in a bowl. Add the remaining cocoa powder and vanilla and whip until fluffy. Scrape the sides occasionally. Refrigerate until ready to use. Allow the cake to cool completely, then run a knife around the edges of the baking pan. Turn it upside-down on a plate so it can be frosted on the sides and top. When the frosting is no longer cold, use a butter knife or small spatula to frost the sides and top. Cut into slices.

## Berry Streusel Cake

**Ingredients** for 6 servings

2 tbsp demerara sugar
2 tbsp sunflower oil
¼ cup almond flour
1 cup pastry flour
½ cup brown sugar
1 tsp baking powder
1 tbsp lemon zest
¾ cup milk
2 tbsp olive oil
1 tsp vanilla
1 cup blueberries
½ cup powdered sugar
1 tbsp lemon juice
⅛ tsp salt

**Directions** and Total Time: 60 minutes

Mix the demerara sugar, sunflower oil, and almond flour in a bowl and put it in the refrigerator. Whisk the pastry flour, brown sugar, baking powder, lemon zest, and salt in another bowl. Add the milk, olive oil, and vanilla and stir with a rubber spatula until combined. Add the blueberries and stir slowly. Coat the inside of a baking pan with oil and pour the batter into the pan.

Preheat the oven to 310°F. Remove the almond mix from the fridge and spread it over the cake batter. Put the cake in the oven and bake for 45 minutes or until a knife inserted in the center comes out clean and the top is golden. Combine the powdered sugar and lemon juice in a bowl. Once the cake has cooled, slice it into 4 pieces and drizzle each with icing. Serve and enjoy.

## Banana-Almond Delights

**Ingredients** for 4 servings

1 ripe banana, mashed
1 tbsp almond liqueur
½ tsp ground cinnamon
2 tbsp coconut sugar
1 cup almond flour
¼ tsp baking soda
8 raw almonds

**Directions** and Total Time: 30 minutes

Preheat oven to 300°F. Add the banana to a bowl and stir in almond liqueur, cinnamon, and coconut sugar until well combined. Toss in almond flour and baking soda until smooth. Make 8 balls out of the mixture.

Place the balls onto the parchment-lined baking pan, flatten each into ½-inch thick, and press 1 almond into the center. Bake for 12 minutes, turn and bake for 6 more minutes. Let cool slightly before serving.

## Holiday Pear Crumble

**Ingredients** for 4 servings

2 tbsp coconut oil
¼ cup flour
¼ cup demerara sugar
⅛ tsp salt
2 cups finely chopped pears
½ tbsp lemon juice
¾ tsp cinnamon

**Directions** and Total Time: 40 minutes

Preheat oven to 320°F. Combine the coconut oil, flour, sugar, and salt in a bowl and mix well. Stir the pears with 3 tbsp of water, lemon juice, and cinnamon into a baking pan until combined. Sprinkle the chilled topping over the pears. Bake for 30 minutes or until they are softened and the topping is crispy and golden. Serve.

## Nutty Banana Bread

**Ingredients** for 6 servings

2 bananas, mashed
2 eggs, beaten
¼ cup milk
1 tbsp apple cider vinegar
1 tbsp vanilla extract
½ tsp ground cinnamon
2 tbsp maple syrup
½ cup oat flour
½ tsp baking soda
2 tsp butter

**Directions** and Total Time: 30 minutes

Preheat the oven to 320°F. Mix the bananas, eggs, milk, apple vinegar, vanilla extract, cinnamon, and maple syrup in a bowl. Toss in oat flour and baking soda until smooth but still chunky. Divide the batter between 6 cupcake molds. Top with butter each and swirl it a little. Bake for 18 minutes until golden brown and puffy. Let cool completely before serving. Enjoy!

## Peanut Butter-Banana Roll-Ups

**Ingredients** for 4 servings

4 spring roll wrappers
¼ cup molasses
¼ cup butter
2 bananas, halved crosswise
1 tsp ground cinnamon
1 tsp lemon zest

**Directions** and Total Time: 20 minutes

Preheat the oven to 375°F. Place the roll wrappers on a flat surface with one corner facing up. Spread 1 tbsp of molasses on each, then 1 tbsp of butter, and finally top with lemon zest and 1 banana half. Sprinkle with cinnamon all over. For the wontons, fold the bottom over the banana, then fold the sides, and roll-up. Place them seam-side down in a baking dish. Roast for 10 minutes until golden brown and crispy. Serve warm.

## Raisin & Apple Puffs

**Ingredients** for 6 servings

1 tsp raisins
2 apples, finely diced
2 tsp cinnamon
½ cup sugar
⅛ tsp salt
6 phyllo dough sheets
½ tsp vanilla
½ cup maple syrup
¼ cup coconut oil
½ tsp salt

**Directions** and Total Time: 30 minutes

In a bowl, combine raisins, apples, cinnamon, 2 tbsp sugar, and salt; set aside. Unwrap the phyllo dough carefully. Put a large piece of phyllo on a clean, dry surface. Fold it into thirds and spray each portion with oil.

Preheat oven to 320°F. Spoon 1/3 cup of the apple mix at the base of the rectangle. Fold the bottom of the phyllo over the mix. Continue to fold up, forming a triangle. Put the apple-filled triangle in a greased baking dish. Repeat for all the remaining phyllo and apple mix.

Bake the triangles for 10 minutes or until browned. Add the vanilla, maple syrup, coconut oil, remaining sugar, and salt to a small pot. Boil over medium heat, stirring constantly, until it simmers and eventually thickens. Plate the apple puffs and add the caramel sauce. Serve warm.